Coming
Through the

Coming
Through the
Whirlwind

Case Studies in Psychotherapy

Michael Eigen

Chiron Publications • Wilmette, Illinois

Library of Congress Catalog Card Number: 91-623

Printed in the United States of America.
Editing and book design by Siobhan
Drummond.
Cover design by Michael Barron.
Original cover art by Sally Strange.

Library of Congress Cataloging-in-Publication Data:
Eigen, Michael.
    Coming through the whirlwind : case studies in psychotherapy /
Michael Eigen.
      p.   cm.
    Includes bibliographical references and index.
    ISBN 0-933029-53-5 : $16.95
    1. Psychotherapy—Case studies. 2. Interpersonal relations—Case
studies. I. Title.
RC465.E34 1992
616.89'14—dc20

91-623
CIP

ISBN 0-933029-53-5

To My Patients
In Common Struggle

Scarce are they planted,
Scarce are they sown,
Scarce hath their stock taken root in the earth;
When He bloweth upon them, they wither,
And the whirlwind taketh them away as stubble.

Isaiah 40:24

True, most things can be corrected, but few,
if any, cracks or ruptures can be put together
so well that there will be no impression or scar.
This scar on the flesh of man influences the
whole structure of human life.

Adin Steinsaltz, *The Long Shorter Way*

CONTENTS

PREFACE

The work in this book is based on the premise that a sense of self and other go together. There is no such thing as self without other, or other without self. A distinction-union structure pervades experience. We may place more emphasis on distinction or union, but both are present.

I quickly add that the distinction-union structure covers many dimensions of experiencing. For example, sensations of materiality and immateriality blend and separate many ways. We may be more mental or spiritual or physical at any given moment.

Therapy is concerned with tearing down and building up our sense of self–other and mind–body. It provides a milieu in which reshaping processes can evolve in more satisfactory ways. Reshaping of self–other and mind–body is not only mediated by cognition and mental representations but is connected with the elusive play of attitudes, affects, and sensations.

By sensations I do not simply mean the senses: touch, hearing, vision, smell, etc. I mean also sensations of the psychical and perhaps something more. Touch and hearing and vision do not simply give us information. They give us themselves: the amazing experience of seeing, touching, hearing—what touching or feeling or seeing is like. One may also experience an I-sensation or God-sensation, a foreboding, a premonition, a faith. There are also self-sensations, a sense of self and various forms of lack of self. Too often such sensations are viewed as derivative from other mental structures, but they constitute our psychic life, they are elemental builders of the texture of our world.

It is often unnecessary to analyze explicitly what is going on between patient and therapist. Much work goes on in the covert interplay of affective attitudes without being expressed in words. Often the expression is in new dream images, perhaps new ways that parents appear in dreams, or new figures altogether, or new possibilities in living. Many of my interventions are not directed to the details of transference or to the "real relationship" in therapy, but to emergence of new capacities and to the tone or spirit of communications. Sensitivity to tone or spirit or affective attitude is akin to what used to be called "discrimination of spirits," although the form of discrimination evoked here involves sensing more than judgment and is anything but judgmental.

Therapists must school themselves in the dimensions that constitute the self. Like the ball player who takes batting and fielding practice, the therapist learns his or her way around nuances of self–other and mind–body relations. Nevertheless, when the moment for work comes, the work itself takes over. One drops into the realm of sensing, a kind of mute immersion.

It is not that one forgets what one learns. Learning contributes to the ways in which a present experience can be structured and creativeness builds on learning. One moves from inspiration to inspiration and spends much time working over raw inspiration, not always right, not always wrong. At the same time, a lot of therapy runs itself off in a rote way and marks time. Standing still is important. Nevertheless, something naked or original occurs that makes a difference.

The Impact of Affective Attitudes: Growing a Psyche

Self–other and mind–body form the personal arena for the interplay of attitudes. We exist distinct from, yet united with, the Other. We are distinct from, yet united with, ourselves. In therapy, we work with highly charged affective attitudes which play a role in how we unite with and distinguish ourselves from others, and how we relate to ourselves. Attitudes mold affects and are permeated by affects. When we work with attitudes, we work with the ways in which affects are structured. Affects arise within attitudinal contexts, and attitudes contain implicit references to self and other.

Therapists train themselves to be open to the interplay of attitudes. This training is elusive because much of the interplay may be unconscious. Nevertheless, the therapist learns to stay open to the affective-attitudinal impact at hand and allows it to grow into useful actions, images, and ideas. One does this as well as one can, with variable success, depending on many factors including sensibility, fatigue, intelligence, quality of interest, caring, mood, and raw ability.

Perhaps the most important qualifying factor is a general one: how much and what sort of psyche one has. The truth is that we are all deficient in processing affective-attitudinal impacts. Some of us are a bit better at it some of the time. But we are all in the business of growing a psyche capable of meeting the tasks that having a psyche generates.

Therapeutic prejudices inevitably bias growth processes. One works with attitudes through attitudes. We cannot escape funneling one another into categories. To be attitude-free is impossible; what is important is that which is mediated through our attitudes. We *can* become more sensitive to our impact on one another and the way we process these impacts.

Any human interaction may have catastrophic elements. A wrong attitude wrecks the self for a time. To build a tolerance for ourselves is hard enough, but personal growth also demands fine tuning. Psychotherapy nurtures sensitivity rather than "spoils" it. It opens channels for new qualities of experience. As we work, we learn to become sensitive to moment-to-moment catastrophes without succumbing to them or, more accurately, we learn to come through our succumbing.

We poison *and* elevate the psychic atmosphere by our tone, our attitudes, our spirit and actions. We come through all this. We come through our sensitivity and ourselves—repeatedly. Therapy helps release the capacity to come through ourselves and circumstances. How we come through our sensitivity and ourselves is crucial.

To come through oneself is to be reborn. Achievement of rebirth is always fragmentary. The problem of building resources capable of sustaining psychic life does not go away. The sense of rebirth, far from being a solution, creates its own problems. Therapy is filled with problems, like all human activities.

One of therapy's impossible tasks is to help build resources that make it possible to tolerate therapy. Insofar as therapy itself remains something of an unknown, it becomes a venture in discovering what the *x* of therapy is or, at least, in continuing to learn what one can do with it. A "good" slant on a "good" impossible goal (like a "good" mistake) can make a better life a bit more possible.

A Note on Body Self and Mental Self

A crucial aspect of the union-distinction structure relates to mind–body. Either mental or physical aspects of life may be more or less prominent in experience at any time. They may interweave and blur, but they are never identical. The "I" may distinguish itself from or identify with either mind or body at a given time. In illness "I" may detach from enemy body and in health spread through yummy body. "I" may forget body while engrossed in thought, or lose body and thought in mystical bliss.

Almost any permutation of mind–body distinction-union that can be imagined has made an appearance in therapy at some time or other. Aspects of mental and physical experience assume a variety of roles in relation to each other. Either mental or physical self may be more self or other at a given time. Together they may mirror or caricature aspects of the parent–child relationships in which they play a structural role. Their relationships are typically subtle and complex, since each is apt to be experienced as both self and other in a variety of ways. The boundaries between them shift, so that there is latitude in what may be considered mind or body as conditions change.

I have not found it satisfactory to adopt Freud's position that the ego is first and foremost a bodily ego, but it is not useful to ignore his position either. We simply do not know enough to declare either mental self or body self primary. Data can be marshaled for either viewpoint. We can see both as part of a larger reality, whether unknowable or not, but this does not add much except to profess our conviction or intimation that the divisible is ultimately indivisible. A sense of the divisible indivisible helps keep our framework open.

Either mental or physical self can be used defensively against one another and each can be used defensively against itself. Mental and physical self enrich and amplify one another in myriad ways. Their antagonism or alliance may be over- or underplayed. My clinical work emphasizes the radical contribution of both and seeks to release their evolution and interplay.

Although many analysts acknowledge different contributions of mental and body self in a general way, this distinction is not usually used in systematic clinical work. The evolution of body self, the evolution of mental self, and the evolution of their interplay is rarely charted. In my experience, tuning into what body self and mental self are doing is an indispensable part of useful clinical encounter. In a sense, my work is a kind of biography of body self/mental self in heart-to-heart, mind-to-mind encounter.

My previous book, *The Psychotic Core* (1986), and many of my papers (see Eigen 1991d) emphasized variations of a core mental self/body self structure: a detached, covertly transcendent, steellike mental ego vis-à-vis an explosive-fusional body ego. I took this to be the basic pathological psychic structure of our day. The present book is able to explore this and other mental self/body self relationships in more detail, since the work concentrates on two cases.

Cynthia and Ben

Cynthia and Ben were not as apparently "ill" as many cases I wrote about previously. Neither was clinically psychotic or had to be hospitalized. They were professional persons trying to live normal and productive lives. They were not withdrawn or isolated or cut off from everyday richness of living, but very much in the thick of things, trying to maximize their potential and do their very best.

Yet something was wrong. Their lives did not work. Each was

unconsciously mired in patterns that destroyed possibilities of living and tore down and defeated what they built. Each pitted one dimension of life against another.

Cynthia's loyalty to spiritual commitments stopped her from taking up significant psychological problems. She felt that spirit encompassed psyche and that spiritual work would necessarily lead to psychic reordering. As time wore on, Cynthia had to face the fact that she was in trouble. She sought help and began the work of relinking spirit and psyche in ways that did justice to both.

In contrast with Cynthia, Ben spent his life working with psychological processes. He was a psychotherapist and used psychological truth as a weapon. He felt he should control life with psychological knowledge. For him, psyche was the gateway to power and pleasure. Yet life slipped through his net and became increasingly uncontrollable. He could not use psyche to stay on top of things. He crumbled and desperately began the process of reordering priorities. In his case, psyche had to reach out to spirit. For Ben, there could be no reordering of psyche without a reordering of values.

Cynthia and Ben each began their work with catastrophic dread attached to growing a psyche and promoting enlivening circulation between spirit, psyche, and everyday life. Mental and body self structures evolved in relation to each other and as conduits for the multidimensionality that adds mystery, possibility, and richness to living.

The course of each therapy followed gradients that led to important deficits, choice points, battles never fought, secret madness, and the struggle for integrity. When a person with a good "official personality" opens up, we find many of the factors which inform apparently less fortunate souls. We are all cut from the same fabric, although the clothes we wear may be very different.

Nevertheless, the fact that we are united by commonalities ought not blur significant differences (and vice versa, the fact that we are uniquely different ought not blur commonalities). Cynthia and Ben both gravitated to core impasse points, the x that felt wrong, and entered the whirlwind that manufactured the wrong existence or unsuitable products. Each therapy led to very specific creative actions and psychological discoveries, the crystallization of specific psychological jewels. Cynthia and Ben used therapy to create and communicate experiences that enabled them to take the next step in their lives, to reset themselves and better move along their paths.

A Community of Voices

Consciousness oscillates between a sense of catastrophe and joyous faith. Disaster has always been a part of existence. Part of striving is based on fear: we worry about our lot and how we will make a go of it. Beneath daily worry is our awareness of the banana-peel aspect of existence. The comedian slips and falls and gets up again. But in real life, we cannot take getting back on our feet for granted.

Our real sense of possible disaster is complicated by the fact that psychic life is shaky. We can fall apart and come together many different ways throughout a day. Some aspects of body or mental self may be more shaky (or rigid) than others. Rigidity partly compensates for shakiness. We may use some aspects of experience to organize others and hold on to these handles for dear life.

The very birth and growth of personality may be experienced as catastrophic. If we grow enough of a psyche so that we can work decently with ourselves, we may be able to become more or less creative catastrophes. We need to admit the unevenness of personality development. We remain embryonic throughout our lives. In some ways, we are born too quickly, in others not quickly enough. We never get to some psychological births while in others we are born somewhat.

We are far from assimilating the discovery that we are conscious–unconscious beings with a sense of self. Aspects of religion, philosophy, art, and depth psychologies grope for ways to fashion tools to approach this momentous discovery. What we mean by self–other and mind–body is not a settled issue. We do not know what we mean by mind, nor what we mean by body; the meanings we discover keep growing. The clinical explorations in this book are pointers to the ongoing process of discovery of which we are all part.

The centrality of the distinction-union structure places paradox and ambiguity at the heart of experiencing. The Hindu may say, "I am but am not my body; I am but am not my mind; I am but am not my I." The Christian may say, "I yet not I but Christ in me." The Jewish heart bursts with divine love in an earthly frame: "Holy, Holy, Holy—the whole earth is filled with His glory."

The cases in this book bear witness to the primacy of joy or bliss at the center of our heart's journey, but it is not a primacy to be taken for granted. The sense of self is variable. Self is a family, a community of voices. Sensitivity sours, rigidifies, or becomes sticky without proper exercise. A baby's smile is as spontaneous as a cry. Joy and faith are as basic as fear, suspicion, and outrage. Our basic sensitivity takes many forms, draws on diverse sources, takes many turns. It is subject to shattering, recovery, and reshaping processes, for better and worse. The chapters ahead depict structures and vicissitudes of our basic sensitivity.

Psychotherapy turns impasse points into crossroads. The major work of therapy may lie in growing a personality capable of supporting the transformation of one kind of crossroad into another. Many crossroads race by. The trajectory of one's path depends upon the angle of departure. Forks ahead become footprints behind. Some forks turn into fruitful plants that intertwine as they grow. One tries to dwell with twists that grow out of the navel of one's being, so that life bears fruit.

This book is a celebration of subjectivity. What a miraculous gift subjective life is, a gift that makes demands on us. Like the patients in this book, we must learn to become partners with the processes that make us up and discover/create our own psychological gems. The work of psychotherapy presents opportunities to learn more about the intricacies of partnership, sensitivity, and the art of coming through ourselves, each other, our circumstances—everything.

EIGEN

ACKNOWLEDGMENTS

This book has undergone an important journey. It was begun before the death of my father and my major analyst, Henry Elkin. Prior to this time, my mystical sensibilities were partly organized by oriental, Catholic, and depth-psychological writings. At my father's funeral I said *kaddish*, which initiated a deepening of my relationship to Judaism, including Chasidic treasures. This book has had to absorb this movement, and it may sound odd to thank a book, but I am glad that it did not give up, but dared to grow with me.

I am thankful for the support and advice of my publisher, Chiron Publications, and its staff, who not only tolerated, but encouraged the book's evolution. Here is a group interested not only in marketing, but the living psyche. Dr. Nathan Schwartz-Salant's suggestions were imaginative and practical in a way that grasped and aided the spirit of the book. I am indebted to his thoughtful reading in both substantive and structural issues. Dr. Murray Stein's comments contributed to the final trimming and reshaping process. I am grateful for the caring discernment of both men as the book reworked itself into its present form. Ms. Siobhan Drummond provided mechanical know-how to try to drum a measure of respectability through a surging text.

All my writings are celebrations of psychic life, an avowal and bearing witness. What a precious, complex gift we have been given! I am thankful to be able to reach out to a larger community to share the unshareable. Psychoanalytic writing is not a recitation of preorganized findings, but an act of discovery, a communication from silence to silence. That this is done through words, concepts, and images makes the mystery more intense, rather than dampening it.

If I had to situate my writings, I think I see myself as part of a budding subculture of psychoanalytic mystics, more of whom may be coming out of the closet. I wish to express thanks to one of them, and her publisher, Marion Milner and Tavistock Publications, for use of an extended quotation in Chapter 2. Marion Milner, like Wilfred Bion, has not been afraid of the mystical dimension in depth psychology, where no contradiction exists between the holy spark and the most practical and physical realities.

I am also grateful to the various institutions which provide supportive outlets for my probings: the National Psychological Association for Psychoanalysis, the New York University Postdoctoral Program in Psychoanalysis, the Institute for Expressive Analysis, and New Hope Guild. In addition, for many years I have been conducting private seminars on Bion, Lacan, and selected topics, and the work of these seminars contributes to my writing. I am grateful to the group members who not only enrich discussions, but open evolution of our beings.

My wife and family have endured the stress that writing generates. I can only hope they reap some of the benefit, at least indirectly. My debt to them is great. I could not have completed this, or any of my books, without them.

Most of all, I wish to thank my patients, especially "Cynthia" and "Ben." By a quirk of fate, Ben is in therapy with me, rather than me with him. I pray I do as well with him as he might have done with me.

ONE

The Thing That Does Not Change

Life and Death of the Self: Dramas of Quality

Momentous dramas concerning the life and death of self characterize the dullest of therapies. People seek therapy because something is wrong, stagnant, painful, or, in luckier cases, because something is not right enough, something more or different is wanted. In every case, the quality of life and sense of self is of ultimate importance.

In the most severe cases, whether one lives or dies may be an issue. In all cases, how one lives or fails to live is crucial. Whether one lives and how one lives are parts of the same basic question. An individual may suffer a living death in which self is ossified, collapsed, or mutilated. Or one may be alive and intact yet feel that things ought to be different. When a healthier person reaches an impasse point, issues and states that would radically overwhelm a severely afflicted individual may emerge.

In the consulting room, there is a pull to speak about what is wrong or not right enough. Often one escapes what is wrong with protestations about what is right, and sometimes talking about good things promotes them. Nevertheless, therapy has an eye on what needs work. This is one reason why therapy can go on forever. There is always a deficiency or conflict or flaw that is bothersome. There is always the hope that something more can happen.

Many people who enter therapy have bad feelings about themselves. They see everything that is wrong and little that is good. In such cases, awareness of defects does not help. These people do not work with what they see constructively. They need help not merely in learning to appreciate themselves, but learning to work better with what they see or imagine.

It is difficult to say who has the harder time in therapy—the person who believes he is terrible, or the one who champions his goodness. Both are overconfident. In the present age, it is hard to say which is more dangerous. People who are overconfident push ahead in spite of intimations of weakness. If they gain significant political or economic power, their confidence can help or destroy multitudes. The more inhibited individual may display intermittent explosiveness, but often feels pangs about the exercise of power. The attitude of either extreme can be tyrannical.

Therapy tries to help people find better ways of seeing themselves and others. Patients learn to work with a variety of elements in their personalities and build up psychological binocular vision. One who sees mainly good or mainly bad is thrown off balance by therapy. Still, a certain privilege is given to what is wrong with oneself and one's life in therapeutic processes. If one cannot address one's flaws properly, one's virtues may prove destructive.

One of therapy's blessings is to promote the freedom to allow all sorts of psychic productions to swim into view, so that we become a little less afraid of ourselves. Not only does therapy let us see more of ourselves, but it does so from many different angles. In time, we begin to transcend any given vision. We are more than the sum of the thoughts, images, feelings, and actions that we produce. We do not possess immunity from our attitudes, beliefs, and frailties. But we discover that home is not identical with anything we can pin down. We come through ourselves. We come through our own personalities. To come through one's personality is to be reborn.

EIGEN

The Sense of Rebirth

The theme of rebirth is inexhaustible. It comes alive anew not only in each generation, but repeatedly throughout a lifetime. Some people live close to the sense of rebirth, while others seem to know of it only by hearsay. Nevertheless, if one examines closely the experience of persons who appear to be marking time, a rebirth pattern is often discerned.

The relationship between the sense of rebirth and real growth can be very complicated. In therapy, a patient may not seem to be getting anywhere while a silent growth process is incubating. On the other hand, an individual may feel he is making progress yet be fooling himself. The other two possibilities exist as well. One feels he is growing and is; one feels he is not growing and is not. Since mixtures of these states are likely, we often are at a loss to know precisely what is happening at a given time.

Therapy goes on in a kind of darkness. Its method requires faith. Therapist or patient may cut a fruitful project off because short-term results are lacking, or go on and on after reaching the point of diminishing returns. In the former, one needs faith to continue; in the latter, one needs faith to stop. Such quandaries highlight the fact that uncertainty is an important part of therapeutic experience. How one grows in relationship to uncertainty is a key index of therapeutic outcome.

Part of the uncertainty that clings to therapy is the inherent variability of rebirth processes. There are many ways to be reborn or fail to be reborn. Rarely is rebirth total. Progress in therapy, like growth in general, is uneven. A person may experience a new sense of aliveness which permeates some aspects of life more than others. One is usually not stuck in a uniform way. In therapy, one learns to "jiggle" or "shake" the psyche and pull on loose ends. Often the loose ends of experience save us.

Rebirth as Heartfelt Ideal and the Idealization of Rebirth: Cynthia and Ben

Cynthia and Ben, the two persons focused on in this book, based their lives on the importance of rebirth. To be reborn again and again, as more whole and full and better persons, was of momentous significance to each of them—as an ideal and living reality. They were good people trying to live the best lives they could. They felt life should be lived from rebirth to rebirth and tried to help others share this vision.

Yet their lives exploded and, in excruciating ways, worked against them. The sense of rebirth mocked them and egged them on. Their lives did not go the way they wished, yet they kept trying. They were not capable of giving up. Rebirth was too real to betray. It took ill fate and the passage of time before they could begin to distinguish between the sense of rebirth and the growth that failed to come of it.

Rebirth as a heartfelt ideal and lived experience inspired them. Yet their idealization of rebirth blurred the details of what they were up against.

When the Dust Settles: Cynthia

Cynthia began adult life trying to be a minister. She wanted to "turn others on" to the joy and freedom of rebirth through the living God. Her mission had a strong ethical component. She wanted to help those less fortunate than herself, especially the poor. For many years, she found it difficult to seek help herself.

We will see how Cynthia destroyed her attempt to be a minister and took a detour that worked better for her. For many years, Cynthia remained stagnant in a hidden way. Her life went around the same circles with different faces. Spiritual and erotic "highs" kept the sense of rebirth alive, but when the dust settled, *she* was nowhere to be found. She gained from her experiences, yet did not seem to get anywhere. She wanted to do work that was meaningful and also raise a family, but her life did not build on itself. As she moved into her thirties, things did not come together. She feared her life would be a series of scattered experiences that did not have weight.

Cynthia's capacity for enjoyment, love of God, and passionate commitment to the human spirit, made it difficult to admit that she was stuck. She lived close to the sense of rebirth: the sense of rebirth pervaded her life. It was the core of her existence, the heart of her values. How was it possible that she could be so close to the rebirth feeling, yet not be getting anywhere? How could she feel so deeply, yet live such a surface existence? Cynthia could not make sense of her life. She was stymied by diverse pulls that cancelled each other out.

Her depression confused her. How was it possible to feel such joy and wonder, to have such faith, such love of life, yet also be despondent, at odds with herself, at wits end? She sensed that she moved from dead end to dead end. Her wonderful sense of rebirth did not lead to personality change or to the kind of life she wanted. It was a humiliation that spirit alone did not save her and that she needed psychological help.

Cynthia's dreams produced images of death, wreckage, disease, and massacre, as well as creative possibilities. For her sense of rebirth to serve her well, it would have to expand to include painful elements she scarcely imagined. She would have to develop the psychological tools her problems required. Once in therapy, Cynthia gravitated to the wounds, deficits, conflicts, perceptions, and attitudes that held her back. In spite of herself, she sunk to what was wrong with her or wrong with her life—her impasse points. So much of the imagery in her dreams had a downward movement. She had to go down, let down. Her sense of rebirth was wonderful but puffed up. It would take much work for her to begin to grow into it.

Fooled by Truth: Ben

Ben was a psychotherapist dedicated to discovering psychological truth. He was warm and sensitive and often helped people contact themselves in new ways. Ben had an eye for seeing how others defended against experience and stopped themselves from living. He worked hard at getting others to start anew by telling the truth about themselves.

His success fed his egoism and personality weakness. In personal relationships, he used "truth" to bludgeon others and stay above anything inconvenient. He used "truth" to get what he wanted. He could be hostile and controlling under the guise of helping. The fact that he frequently did help others compounded the difficulty. He was fooled by his own great sincerity. He was a rebirth hound who could not abide hiding in others, yet was unaware of how his zeal masked a standstill in his own life.

If Ben's personal life was to be as successful as his professional life, he would have to approach himself in new ways. He would have to learn to listen to the claims of those dearest to him and to voices in his own being other than his egoistic use of truth. Being a therapist was a temptation to play God. When this worked well, it felt wonderful, but hidden megalomania wreaked havoc in his daily existence.

Ben expected to enlist me on the side of his great sincerity in his fight to dominate loved ones. We two therapists knew the truth. We knew about defenses, lies, evasion. Together we would find ways of getting through to others and making them see the light. We would get those closest to him to see things our way. He would get me to side with him against his symptoms and support his ego through thick and thin.

What Ben did not realize was that *he* needed support against his own ego. His ego had turned into a kind of fiendish rebirth/ truth machine, a "therapeutic" Pac Man that fed on the blood of life and that ultimately could devour itself. It would not be possible, nor desirable, to leave truth behind. Once bitten by the lust for psychological truth, one cannot wish this dimension away. Ben's struggle was to disengage truth from ego. His underlying sense of truth was greater than his egoistic use of it. He would have to fight his ego's monopolistic claim on truth. Ben's very sense of truth, so important to him, would have to undergo a rebirth process.

In his manic relationship to truth, Ben expected rebirth to be once and for all. He found it difficult to relate to the fragmentary nature of growth processes. Like Cynthia, he found it difficult to understand how the "high" of a rebirth experience was so often followed by a "hangover," a sense of emptiness or depression.

Why was it that after each breakthrough, he had to go back to the drawing board, as if starting from square one? Why should advances act like setbacks?

In therapy, Ben would be called upon to deepen rather than give up his love of truth. He would be forced to revisualize how rebirth works for him. Little by little, he engaged processes that overturned his simplistic exploitation of truth and rebirth. The rebirth he longed for was a fantasy. The rebirth he actually would undergo took time and work. Part of the work involved building the sort of psyche capable of participating in the evolution of growth processes. He would have to learn to chip away at problems a bit at a time. The rebirth that counted grew from work in the trenches subject to unending correction over years.

A Warning about Rebirth: Structural Processes with Values

While therapy may be said to be about rebirth, the idea of rebirth tells us very little about what kinds of structural processes rebirth is made up of or depends on. We learn from Cynthia and Ben that rebirth can mean many things. Neither Cynthia nor Ben was reborn once and for all or in a "total" way. Rebirth shares the unevenness and variability of all processes.

Although this book focuses on ways individuals are reborn through therapy, the term *rebirth* does not appear often in moment-to-moment work in chapters ahead. My emphasis is on the detailed movement of subtle structural processes. What is at stake is how individuals grow or fail to grow. Therapy is nothing if it does not heighten lived experience. At the same time, lived experience collapses and undoes itself without a sense of inherent structure. In therapy, we study the raw impact of events and the attitudes, images, and ideas that grow out of a felt impact. We try to explore and interact with ways raw affective impacts are transformed into meaningful personal movement.

We usually say good things about rebirth. How good it is to feel fresh, to start again, to move past a barrier. We trust that rebirth (and therapy) moves in a decent direction: one becomes a better and fuller person.

Rebirth is not always so kindly. Hitler used rebirth imagery. Decapitation rituals were part of the French Revolution. Fanatic cults often are inspired by a sense of rebirth. One can feel fresh, alive, or whole for many reasons. Do we know the limits to self-deception and the psychopathic manipulation of human capacities?

One cannot count on rebirth to save oneself. What makes rebirth work for good or ill is something beyond it. Rebirth occurs in a context which includes values that shape it. One's basic attitudes, temperament, and character, together with the external conditions one faces, help give a rebirth process its particular direction and tone.

We have reached a bind. Our attitudes, temperament, and character often block processes or renewal, yet rebirth, above all, is a change in attitude. Therapy works with attitudes and character traits that block personal evolution. Therapeutic values inevitably play a role in shaping the quality and direction of the sort of rebirth an individual may undergo.

This is a circle we cannot avoid. Rebirth involves a change of heart, a change of attitude, yet depends upon a system of attitudes for its valence and direction. The best we can do is to study specific processes in a given context. We try to see what kinds of processes hinder or aid a particular individual's evolution, while we ourselves are part of the processes that we explore. To say that we should not have such a problem is to wish we were a different sort of being.

We rely on perception, imaginative reflection, and an elusive quality of will, good or bad will. Circumstances stimulate our capacities. Providence or luck plays a role. Therapy, like fiction, deals with issues of character vis-à-vis sources of turbulence beyond one's control. The story that is told in therapy or a novel is meaningful because it is a story about a human subject told by a human subject. The story is about renewal or the failure of renewal and is directed by a sense of values. The tragic dimension is rooted in tensions between values or between values and the hard facts of life.

A child dreamed that he helped rabbits build houses to sell in stores. The dream is about building places in which to live and implies making babies and thoughts and feelings. This child was proud of helping and selling. The dream marked an achievement. Previously this boy told me, "Sometimes I stay up all night because I'm afraid I'll have a bad dream." Such a fear is habitual when the building process fails. Fertility is aborted as unspoken dangers menace and overwhelm the life drive.

As time went on, this child taught himself to go back to sleep after a bad dream and wait for a good dream. In sleep, he learned to tolerate anxieties that are part of living during the day. Little by little, he worked with more sides of himself and others. In this context, selling does not mean selling oneself short. Selling becomes part of creativeness, linking inside with outside, a making public.

In such an outcome, it is unlikely that one's night terrors will be unleashed as a daytime reality for an entire civilization. The boy's values and my own coincided. The destructive element was worked within a larger creative and caring context. It is unlikely that people will have to pay with their lives for what this child may or may not achieve. Rebirth and renewal became part of his everyday-everynight life. Building useful thoughts and feelings for himself and others to live and play with became the context for destructive elements, which also had their say.

This dream is significant for what it achieves, but also for what it leaves out. The child now exercises capacities that were paralyzed or blocked. He reached an impasse point and moved on. Now he builds and sleeps and dreams. Night and day work together. There was a time, not long past, when night and day worked against each other, adding to each other's terror. No successful building process could be sustained in dreaming. Dreaming could not spill into daytime activity without horror. Raw material now used for building was once unworkable stuff that acted as an impasse.

We will see, in the chapters to come, many ways that growth feeds on impasse points. Living processes thrive on limits appropriate to them. Rebirth does not do away with limits so much as relates to them as starting points for new experiences. The cutting edge of personality lives through limits. Sometimes a limit shifts, gives way, reforms, disappears, or gains meaning. One may achieve a more intimate, humorous, wise, fierce, and appreciative relationship to limitations. Banging one's head against walls enough times and mere cessation of banging *can* open new dimensions, vistas, or perceptions of direction.

Transcendence of all limitations once and for all is not possible for anyone. Creative use of limits is an ideal. For many, life may be too horrible to taste such a process. Others may be in a position to appreciate this work but need help in building a tolerance for it. For others, creating personality or self becomes a full-time job. We may try to do away with limits. The saint, madman, or killer may succeed in various ways. All of us may shed limitations momentarily and be uplifted by a sense of the Infinite, with more or less enduring consequences. But in day-to-day life, we work with the materials at hand. We build ourselves and others with what we have available.

Working at the cutting edge of personality means, by definition, working with or against limiting factors. Rebirth in psychotherapy moves from impasse to impasse. Part of the grinding slowness of rebirth processes in therapy has to do with the amount of attention given to barriers or deficits in human personality which impede growth. A major part of the work often involves building the personality so that it can support growth processes.

Our attention will now turn to what depth psychologists have said about barriers, deficits, or complexities in personality that make growth difficult.[1] Rebirth moves through impasse points. Religious disciplines often advise ignoring ingredients of impasse. I have heard practitioners of yoga, Chassidus, and various forms of Christianity advise protégés to bypass or simply not to advert to disturbances of the lower self. Psychoanalysis does not have this luxury. People enter therapy because such disturbances can *not* be ignored or whisked away by moments of transcendence. We *must* focus on what others may get away with by ignoring. People seek therapy because their various bypass techniques have failed.

---

[1]Winnicott, Bion, and Elkin are among the writers who have influenced my clinical work most in the past twenty years. One also can see the silent influence of C. G. Jung, whom I read earlier. My temperament was such that as a young man I read Jung before Freud and continue to share Jungian concerns with a deeper self vis-à-vis everyday reality. This theme is the central point of Chapter 2.

The contempt heaped upon psychoanalysis for being attracted to the garbage of the psyche, a fly attracted to manure, is unwarranted. Psychoanalysis pays respect to the fact that change is difficult. Attitudes are tenacious. Recalcitrance and inertia are built into our human equipment. We must pay more than lip service to the ways we are blocked and fail to change. In order to grow, we must in some way deal with and take up what I call "the thing that does not change." After this is done, we can begin the story of two extended clinical encounters and get into the nitty-gritty of therapeutic processes.

The Thing That Does Not Change

In the study of therapeutic processes, many schools of thought have arisen. A close look suggests that most schools grew out of the same dissatisfaction, a sense that therapy does not work in some way, that something in clients does not change.

Freud

Freud (1920, 1940) asked why people repeat self-destructive patterns. Why do they remain stuck in ways that make their lives worse than they might be? Freud approached this question from a number of perspectives and felt less than fully satisfied with the results. His work is a testimony to how difficult growth can be.

Freud's concepts of regression and fixation portray a tendency to go back to or remain stuck at earlier developmental positions. He spoke of the stickiness of libido and noted the individual's reluctance to abandon forms of gratification he has enjoyed. We grow in spite of our reluctance to grow. Our forward movement pushes past resistances. We are aware of an undertow, a countertendency.

Freud also noted a need to repeat sources of pain as well as pleasure. Traumatic events obsess us. We repeat them in hope of mastering them. Attachment to sources of trauma takes precedence over gratification. The ability to resist growth because of attachment to infantile pleasures is an achievement. One must become free enough from traumatic injury before one can suffer the luxury of fighting maturation because of primitive desires.

Freud's postulation of a death instinct summarizes the clinical concern here. For Freud, the death instinct represented the conservative principle of instincts *par excellence*. The tendency to stay fixated or go back to earlier positions was extended to include returning to an inorganic state. It was as if the psychobiological organism did not have the resources to support its own life: psychic aliveness was too much for it. The psyche could not tolerate its own sensitive consciousness and sought the respite that death could provide.

In practical terms, this meant that a tendency to dull or numb oneself conflicted with the desire to experience life fully. One becomes corpselike at the same time one wishes to maximize the intensity of existence. A pull to absolute zero threatens to undo attempts to build a meaningful life.

The criticism that Freud's death instinct is a pseudo-biological concept may be true, yet such criticism often diverts attention away from the urgent problems Freud addressed. Freud was vexed at the persistence of a "negative therapeutic reaction" in psychoanalysis. The individual tended to undo advances made, so much so that the analytic struggle or an individual's life might be in jeopardy.

Freud also noted that no matter how much an individual gained from therapy, something that did not change persisted. The individual clung to a smaller version of himself than he needed to. It was as if an area of death stained the personality and the best therapy could hope for was to help an individual take up a better attitude toward it. The individual had to build up a tolerance for his tendency to diminish himself or die out or kill himself off.

Freud's case presentations use the language of conflict, fragmentation, and splitting. One aspect of personality pits itself against another. The self fragments under the stress of its own internal conflicts and realistic difficulties. A sense of unreality may grow as conflicts prove insuperable and internal splitting proliferates.

EIGEN

The sense of unreality may increase as the need to die in the face of one's sensitivity mounts. One of the greatest weapons of the death drive is to make life appear to be unreal. From the point of view of death, life may seem unreal. A patient may say, "Why bother? I'm going to die anyway." A variation of this attitude is characteristic of teenage suicides today.

Waves of psychoanalytic and other psychological theories arose to deal with a growing sense of unreality and something sick in the personality that did not change. Freud's belief, that depersonalization (the self as unreal) and derealization (the outside world as unreal) were offshoots of internal–external conflicts, did not seem to do justice to the ways in which people turned off in the face of their own sensitivity or never allowed their sensitivity to develop. Nevertheless, his notion of a death wish was expressive of the kinds of phenomena that clinicians must face.

Federn

Federn (1953) observed that a sense of unreality regularly preceded psychotic breakdowns. This does not mean that depersonalization or derealization is necessarily followed by a breakdown, but that if breakdown occurs, a sense of unreality is part of it. Federn's work is mainly concerned with psychosis but his vision of ego development implies that a sense of unreality is part of human life and may be widespread.

Federn suggests that the primordial ego has no boundaries. The I is at first a cosmic I. I-feeling is infinite and everywhere. As time goes on, the infant learns that being infinite does not work. The boundless I comes up against the facts of life. If spatial limits are disregarded, life becomes more painful. The infant learns to contract his I-feeling to fit the contours of his body, as he builds a map of physical and social reality.

At first, the infant does not know he has a body or has to be where his body is. It takes time to realize that I-feeling is limited to a particular locale, the area inhabited by one's body. Diverse reactions are possible to the discovery of body as envelope or container. One is happy to have a body when it adds to one's sense of aliveness. But at times the body is a liability or even a torture chamber. Even in benign situations, the baby screams furiously at his own helplessness, trying to do things that he cannot get his body to do.

Federn uses the term *mental or psychic ego feeling* to describe the primary, larger ego, and *body ego feeling* for the later, smaller ego. For Federn, mental ego feeling precedes body ego feeling. I-feeling may be so expansive that it exceeds corporeal limits. Under adverse circumstances, such as severe physical illness, I-feeling may contract so that it excludes the body. I-feeling expands or contracts so as to include more or less of the body as conditions change.

Federn's portrayal of ego development implies that the sense of unreality is rooted in the I's inherent capacity to expand and contract. If one accepts and is firmly rooted in body ego feeling, aspects of mental ego functioning may seem unreal. If one is absorbed in thought, corporeal reality slips away. One tolerates a sense of mind or body seeming more real or unreal at any moment and develops a flexible attitude to shifting states of being.

However, a sense of something missing or having gone wrong may persist. Perhaps too much cosmic I-feeling was sacrificed to the demands of adaptation. Or perhaps one failed to develop sufficient realistic skills out of loyalty to the early sense of boundlessness. It is likely that everyone suffers various kinds of failures in coordinating primordial, cosmic I-feeling and the everyday, practical I.

Freud believed that a certain malaise or normal unhappiness was an inevitable byproduct of being civilized. The individual reined in and redirected aspects of his instinctual life as he became schooled in reality. The developing ego suffered many traumas centered around birth, weaning, toilet training, and the Oedipus complex. Everyday events taught him that he was not an omnipotent god and that he had to tolerate many injuries to his pride and self-esteem. Running through Freud's account is the idea that one repeatedly discovered limits and had to learn to act accordingly.

Federn emphasizes the limits discovered by a boundless I-feeling. One has to squeeze the I into a limited spatial framework. Not everyone is willing or able to make such an adjustment. It is not always obvious that the benefits from suffering this restriction will outweigh a loss or diminution of the sense of one's boundlessness.

Like Freud, Federn advocates learning to live with a certain amount of depression and depersonalization as the price for becoming more fully human. If one cannot contract in order to fit into the world, one will forfeit the ability to expand within realistic limits. One will be much too big or small for any situation that arises. For Federn, the therapist acts as a kind of bait for the patient's longings. The big I gets attached to the therapist, so that the therapist can begin to convince it to accept the limits necessary for real living.

The problem is more complicated for most people who seek help. Many suffer from too little imagination rather than too much. They have contracted to fit a materialistic lifestyle too well. The larger I has been left out of the scheme of things and the subject must grapple with loss of meaning.

For many individuals, spiritual or materialistic grandiosity oscillates with depletion and loss of self-worth. Materialistic realism can act as a saving limit to unbridled narcissism, but it also tempts one cynically to manipulate larger capacities. The task of the therapist is to mediate between the larger and smaller I and allow both to find a viable place in the greater scheme of things.

Depression and depersonalization often acts as signals that something is amiss in the individual's mediating function. Perhaps the smaller or larger I has been shortchanged. Imbalances in one direction or another are inevitable. However, it makes a difference, in the long run, whether or not an individual tries to determine what demands his double self is making. The quality of one's life is often enhanced by listening to the interplay of voices one did know one had. The thing that does not change shifts in meaning. One sees new things at the impasse point. One becomes a little more accustomed to seeking one's frontier, the point where boundlessness and limits meet.

Winnicott

Winnicott's (1958, 1965, 1971; Eigen 1981a, 1986, 1989, 1991a) core clinical concern was the unreality that pervades a human life. He tried to find ways of being that would enable his patients to develop what he called the true self. He contrasted true and false self living. The latter was given over to adaptations for the sake of imaginary safety. One lived more in terms of what one thought would please others, rather than from one's own authentic roots.[2]

Each of the developmental scenes Winnicott depicted showed ways the true self evolved to encompass more of life's possibilities. He portrayed an early self enjoying its sense of omnipotence with the mother functioning as the milieu supporting the infant's vital spark or ongoing being. In time, the baby's sense of aliveness is deepened by a growing capacity to symbolize aliveness. The baby symbolizes himself in transition, i.e., creates symbols of growingness. In this transitional area, in which growth symbolizes itself, self and other are intertwined. Separation or the not-I is experienced within a greater context of connection or continuity, so that it becomes impossible and superfluous to ask where I leave off and you begin.

The infant's fury stimulates his growing sense of otherness. There is no way to avoid fury. What is crucial for Winnicott is how the infant's fury is met. If the caretaker responds in a retaliatory manner or caves in, the infant is left with the sense that his fantasy of omnipotence is final. His fury can diminish the other, take the other away from himself, break the other's center. The possibility of otherness collapses and the infant is left in a fantasy world in which omnipotence has the first and last word.

If, however, the other responds to the self-affirmation in the infant's fury without compromising oneself or the infant, a fresh sense of self and other evolves. The baby experiences appreciation and love for the reality of an other who survives onslaughts and who supports vital being. The infant's destructiveness finds

---

[2]I learned about A. Phillips's *Winnicott* (1988) too late to incorporate it in my present discussion, but I am impressed by the ways our views amplify one another (see Eigen 1991a).

itself within a creative context in which mutual injury is transcended.

It is of paramount importance to note that for Winnicott even the infant's sense of omnipotence takes place within an intersubjective milieu. Eventually, the infant discovers the intersubjective basis of human life and spontaneously begins to symbolize his realization. Infantile omnipotence and fury, if met properly, have a developmental direction. They call for a response from an other. The quality of the responsive context contributes to what one learns about life.

Omnipotence can turn into realistic self-confidence, if it is met with loving and judicious care. The infant cannot at first perceive how dependent it is, yet no individual outgrows dependency. One of the great tasks in life is to allow the sense of interdependency to deepen. If things go well, our relationship to the intersubjective basis of our psychic lives evolves. We learn how to use the fact of dependency for growth purposes. A foundation is laid for a sense of vital aliveness and true self feeling to develop in social living and the broader cultural world.

It is difficult to imagine a clinician more accepting or respectful of actual persons than Winnicott. I never spent time with a therapist who was less judgmental. Yet Winnicott was a purist. In his work, a quiet battle raged between true and false selves. His clinical attitude was aimed at supporting the unfolding of the true self. He was on the side of integrity of personality and exercised extreme care to avoid seduction, manipulation, and control.

His purist inclination led Winnicott to deepen what Freud meant by the analyst's free-floating attention and the patient's free associations. For Winnicott, the session became a time of free play. This meant the cultivation of the art of doing nothing so that there might be space enough for something real to happen. He could tolerate hours of seemingly meaningless activity in the hope that an authentic moment might emerge.

The drop into meaninglessness or chaos is not easy. Patient and analyst persist in busywork which runs along well-rehearsed channels. Yet Winnicott's patience and perceptiveness encouraged individuals to let rigidities go, at least long enough for moments of unintegration or creative chaos to occur. Not only did Winnicott not want to intrude upon the patient, he taught people not to intrude upon themselves.

COMING THROUGH THE WHIRLWIND

Winnicott believed there is something precious and inviolable about human personality. He expressed this precious something in various ways: a vital spark, a sense of ongoing being, true self, psychosomatic unity. Although this precious something requires an intersubjective milieu and is itself thoroughly intersubjective, Winnicott also depicted it as private and incognito. To seek to know it in order to possess it is to trespass elemental grace and courtesy.

For Winnicott, the worst violation is tantalization. To tantalize is to tie personality in knots, or turn it into a yo-yo, or send it into a steady spin leading nowhere. Tantalization keeps the personality on the edge of disintegration. One suffers a terror of disintegration or, worse, is treated to increasing doses of a disintegration process which never ends. Since the personality becomes obsessed with its own disintegration, it does not have the chance to believe in or experience renewal through unintegration or chaos. Tantalization offers a macrabre version of play which makes one cynical. It forecloses the kind of faith that enables a healing letting go.

There are many ways to trespass the sanctity of the self besides tantalization. During a visit with Winnicott in 1967, he told me the following, in order to evoke a sense of the hairbreadth reality involved. A patient tried to place Winnicott's image in the center of a mirror which she held in front of her while he sat behind her. He saw that if he moved a little, he could help her do it. The instant he moved his head to help, he realized his mistake. The next session, his patient told him that had he done that months before, she would have had to return to the hospital. He had respected her style and pace as little as her mother, whose helpfulness robbed her of the chance to do things in her own way and time. Through their work together, his patient was able to tolerate the upheaval following his error. She was able to tolerate a gap or rupture in her sense of being because she finally did have a growing sense of being. Winnicott had a keen sense of the importance of the analyst's failures as opportunities for growth. With practice, the patient learns to develop through the interplay of limitations.

An almost biblical sense of drama emerges from Winnicott's work. Living a lie poisons our lives. We need the help of others to spot and correct or outgrow our lies. Nevertheless, something very private remains. We remain subject to disruptions and compromises which falsify ourselves. We must be watchful. At the same time, we must let ourselves go so that our built-up personality dissolves and comes back together in fresh ways.

We are thoroughly intersubjective yet alone together. We are extremely sensitive to influence, yet are most truly alive in the discovery of our capacity to experience. A genuine appreciation of others grows upon finding that our need to be ourselves can be tolerated. The rage in our souls is a necessary part of life. If met properly, it opens possibilities of real living. However, there is always the danger of something going wrong. Through experience, we learn to look beyond and make use of our partial breakdowns.

Our capacity for concern is not rooted simply in guilt over destructiveness. It grows out of what we go through together. If things go well enough, our concern for ourselves and others as sensitive subjects deepens. Joy comes through our pain as we survive each other. There is an integrity that comes from a source deeper than our built-up personality and our fantasies about ourselves. We grow by coming through what we make up about each other over and over again.

For Winnicott, the inviolability of the self is a psychological and ethical imperative which must not be compromised. The principle of inviolability is so important precisely because of how prone to violation we are. We do not seem to be able to live without violating each other, whether in gross or subtle ways, and Winnicott does not expect us to live without violating ourselves and others.

It is as if Winnicott tunes in to a pure slide of self-feeling, or how we would feel if violation were not a part of life, or how we can and do feel when we are not being violated by ourselves or others. He envisions the self that creatively transcends the sense of violation as serious and playful. There appear to be no limits to how new this self can become. Newness permeates sophistication. If one tires of life as one ages, one's appreciation of fresh moments may shine all the more.

The prophet's vision that we may always start fresh is the backbone of Winnicott's work. Will we be born into or find conditions through which we can recreate and rediscover ourselves in ways that do not perversely mock existence? People become unreal to themselves and die because of lack of intersubjective nourishment. Opportunities for fresh living are given daily. Will we discover how to stop trying to tie existence up, so that our basic aliveness has a chance?

The tone of Winnicott's work is optimistic, the voice of someone who cares. Often his words are sunlight and butter. They melt in our mouth and light up our heart. Not that Winnicott is unaware of horrific dangers; he is keenly aware of what can and does go wrong. But a seeing, loving heart comes through all difficulties.

Bion

Bion (1970; Eigen 1985, 1991d) emphasizes how dangerous we are and how catastrophic psychic life is. The very fact of consciousness or self-awareness is troublesome. Psychic aliveness is akin to a big bang, an explosive shock or succession of shocks. We must gradually build a tolerance for the stream of experience. Whatever tolerance of turbulence we manage to achieve is minuscule compared with the awesome psychic universe that confronts us.

We numb or deaden ourselves to avoid overload and vulnerability. We hate the aliveness that threatens to overthrow us at any moment. If lucky, we mute of filter it in workable ways. Our sensitivity develops a signal system which operates in a premonitory manner, preventing total upheaval. A permeable contact barrier between psychic systems arises.

Difficulties are compounded by our growing sense of emotional truth and falsehood. A mind that grew up to handle survival may be ill equipped to deal with issues of integrity. A conflict arises between the need to survive and the way one survives: one poisons oneself by the lies one lives. Our ability to work with the discovery of emotional truth is embryonic. However, unless we catch on to ourselves, bare survival may be in jeopardy. The drive to discover the truth about ourselves is part of our lives, and we must enter partnership with the capacity that produced such a momentous passion.

The discovery of emotional truth is one example of our tendency to produce ideas and objects faster than our ability to assimilate them. It is not clear what we have to do in order to learn how to work with what we produce. We need to grow the psychic apparatus and mental tools to work with our discoveries.

The discovery of a truth about the way we live can be shattering. Truth is destructive as well as nourishing. Nevertheless, to ignore inklings about who we are leads to corrosion and erosion of self. We are trapped between compromise and a purist sense of truth and refine ourselves by working with this duality.

Falling apart is as much a part of life as coming together. We dis- and reintegrate many ways on a daily basis and throughout our lifetimes. The terror of turbulence and intensity oscillates with self-dampening and insulation processes. Openness to our sense of inner–outer reality requires faith. Depression and paranoia adhere to our piecemeal lot, but so does the quiet ecstasy of being undone and redone by a still, small, explosive voice.

Elkin

Elkin (1972) distinguishes subpersonal, transpersonal, and personal dimensions of rebirth. He depicts the infant as first immersed in a collective-erotic fusion with its affective milieu. At this very early stage, the infant possesses a kind of animal consciousness capable of vital sensing and subject to emotional contagion.

By two or three months of age, a more *personal* consciousness emerges. The infant smiles at a face or eye-nose configuration in a coherent, radiant way, suggesting a delightful awareness of self and other. The early awareness of self and other undergoes a momentous drama.

The drama opens with the other as a background or support for the emergence of the infant's sense of aliveness. The infant lives in his own fullness, unaware of the importance of the other. This blissful state cannot last. The infant experiences pain (hunger, temperature changes, shifting somatic sensations) as other, as something that happens to him. The sense of otherness is now tinged with insensitivity and malevolence. The other is a devil who inflicts hellish torments. The baby screams in panicky fury. The baby may stop screaming and drop into a stuporous state if the caretaker does not come soon enough.

When the other comes and rights the wrong and well-being is restored, a new sense of self and other emerges. Emotional recognition is given to the importance of the other in maintaining and restoring aliveness. The other functions as a merciful God in whom the self can trust when agony threatens to obliterate one's being.

Elkin points out that such a drama occurs before the infant realizes he has a body. By five or six months, the infant is building a body image, as expressed in growing eye-hand-mouth coordination. However, the drama of the rise and fall and rise again of self–other awareness occurs as early as the smiling response. The infant is immersed in an intersubjective milieu, alive with the interplay of emotions and intentions, before a realization of the spatial and material nature of bodily life dawns.

Before the infant is aware of physical death, he has undergone many psychological deaths and rebirths. By the time awareness of physicality as such arises, the experience of the loss and return of consciousness has been well established as a governing, underlying pattern. It remains as the unconscious background upon which future threats and dramas are played out.

The rebirth archetype becomes the mold for further experience. No matter how bad things get, the unconscious can produce an image of a saving other, which protects one's integrity. If this is an illusion, it can be a salutary one.

The early sense of self and other undergoes further dramas as awareness of embodiment proceeds. Perception of size becomes important, particularly the infant's realization that he is little and his parents are big. The infant dreads that love and trust are less important than physical power. Does love rule the world or does might make right? The infant's personal integrity is threatened, not simply by sensations that lack a frame of reference, or by a global, encompassing, immaterial other, but by the implications of embodiment as such.

Insofar as fear wins out, the infant relies on seduction, manipulation, and control to defuse the giant's power. Since this requires a compromise of integrity, fury turns into hatred. One accepts a certain amount of self-poisoning as the price for entry into the social-material matrix.

If the mothering person can admit fault, yet possess confidence and empathic joy in parenting, she becomes the kind of person the infant can forgive. Mother and child often hurt and misunderstand each other. For mutuality to prosper, mother and child have to be able to forgive each other. If, however, the mother is perceived as not only a bully, but a know-it-all who always has to be right, no room for forgiveness is possible and fear and hate harden. The pretension to omniscience makes the other unforgiveable. One needs appropriate humility for forgiveness to occur.

Mutual forgiveness makes give-and-take possible. Through forgiveness, a thread of psychic integrity is preserved in work and personal relationships, and one learns to make the best of realistic limits. The primacy of love provides a context for the use of power. The faith at the foundation of personal being is lived out in the dramas of everyday life.

The Quest for Personal Being

None of the above depth psychologists underestimates what we are up against. Freud wonders whether we can survive our own makeup. The struggle is not simply between ego and drives but what sort of drive will win out. Will loving creativeness be greater than destructiveness?

Federn's work underlines the importance of the tension between everyday limits and a primordial sense of boundlessness. The sense of boundlessness may become attached to positive or negative objects and intentions. One dreads that one's own or another's malevolent intentions are limitless. One's deficits and faults may seem insuperable. One may be paralyzed by the demand that self and other be infinitely better, yet only the hope of something infinitely better may lure one on.

For Winnicott, the quality of the intersubjective milieu provides nutrients for personal maturation. In a good-enough environment, one discovers that self and other survive destructiveness because there is a primacy of love. The love Winnicott has in mind is characterized by a respectful and accurate response to one's own or the other's essential qualities and actions. It is also characterized by a willingness to respond in ways that show one's limitations. The growing child feels at ease with an other who wants to know him but lovingly accepts a partial inability to do so.

Not knowing is an important part of Winnicott's clinical work. What one believes one knows often turns out to be a composite of opinions and judgments made by others. Often an individual invents a unidimensional story about his life to explain his faults. He pins his failures on one or two elements at the expense of others, so that his view of himself becomes stereotypical. Therapy is a place for people to let go of their ordinary view of themselves so that regrowing is possible. The true self surprises the habitual self.

Bion emphasizes the immaturity of mental apparatus in light of what it must cope with. Our productions far outstrip our ability to handle them. We are taxed by inner and outer worlds and must grow capacities to handle our creations. We often react to our embryonic status with a frustration that can become intolerable. At moments, we become so enraged at our helplessness that we try to stop our creativeness.

Individuals may develop a malevolent attitude which seeks to destroy awareness of frustration and deficit. A kind of global "sour grapes" attitude poisons psychic life. The individual who is unable to tolerate his partly embryonic status may try to undo mind and experience entirely. This seems easier and even more logical than the struggle to grow. At least annihilation promises a total outcome, whereas growth is always partial.

We must learn to tolerate our deficits and growth processes and catch on to the falling apart/coming together rhythm of the latter. To become partners with our capacities includes learning to work with the ways we undo and redo ourselves, so that we stay fresh. We incessantly write and rewrite our lives. We give up and start again, sometimes with worse, sometimes better results. The striving to be more truly ourselves resurfaces through our false-hoods. We never fully lose our pristine nakedness or the problem it sets: how to let "our original face before we were born" grow into real, adult living.

Elkin's work focuses on the profound intermingling of personal and transpersonal (or better, superpersonal) dimensions in everyday life. At one moment, the infant undergoes hellish agonies at the hands of insensitive and malevolent devils. In another moment, the infant's sense of personal being is uplifted by a merciful God. In time, personal relationships to multifaceted individuals develop, but a sense of numinous drama remains as the background and horizon of consciousness.

In daily life, we unconsciously identify with various aspects of God and devil images (see Eigen 1984). When things are well, we may become benevolent, magnanimous gods. When we are thwarted, we can become devils fighting devils. A chronic attitude of fear/hate poisons psychic life. When we are fearful/ hateful, we are self-righteous and rationalize the seductive, manipulative, and brutal maneuvers we employ. In psychotherapy, we are hopeful that a primacy of love/truth will win out, as it did when God triumphed over the devil in the infant's primordial consciousness.

Adult truth is not identical with infantile truth. The quality of one's relationship to truth and falsehood changes as one grows. We discover that we are not always or even often right or that we were right in ways we played down or glossed over. Our own and other people's feelings are ambivalent. The meaning of events is obscure. Multiple viewpoints clash within and outside ourselves. A growing respect for experience makes us treasure complexity in spite of frustration. We mull over possibilities and wonder what the next surprise or hardship will be.

We learn to come through events as we did as infants, but with an awareness that our job is to keep trying to learn how to come through better. It would be nice to think that we correct or compensate for what went wrong in our upbringing, that we learn to distribute our sense of God and devil better, that we become better persons. Therapy helps us appreciate the materials of struggle. It intensifies awareness of what our quest for personal being is up against—in ourselves, others, and in the world around us. It provides a testing ground where personal being can surface and try its rhythm of dying out and returning. It gives us a chance to learn that personal being is necessary and that it is possible to forge links between private and public affairs.

TWO

Plasticity and Persistence: The Divisible Indivisible

Directionality and Unknowing: Jung and Bion

Jung's Wholeness

All depth psychologists are one in embracing some notion of personality development. Jung's work is unique in its richness of rebirth imagery. His work, in part, may be seen as an extended meditation on symbols of rebirth which humanity has accumulated through the ages. For Jung, therapy "is not a kind of psychological water-cure, but a renewal of personality, working in every direction and penetrating every sphere of life" (1958, par. 184).

Central to renewal is a change of attitude (Jung 1958, par. 142–146). In therapeutic struggle, the individual learns to give various sides of his personality their due. The "trick" is to let conflict transform into the self-corrective play of opposites. An attitude develops which permits more fruitful interplay and evolution of diverse psychic spheres.

Jung described this new attitude as the "transcendent function"—an attitude that transcends the claims of various conscious or unconscious systems and facilitates the creative interaction of warring parties. In practice, such a process makes one more open to *the "other" voice*: insofar as one "does not admit the validity of the other person, he denies the 'other' within himself the right to exist—and vice versa. The capacity for inner dialogue is a touchstone for outer objectivity" (Jung 1958, par. 187).

For Jung, the unconscious is "the other" *par excellence*. One receives its messages as though from outer space. It may seem alien and strange, yet nothing is more intimate. Inner space is as transcendent a reality as outer space (both may be aspects of the *same* transcendent reality). What we have are its bleeps in consciousness—thoughts, images, convictions, affects, intimations, actions, perceived patterns and loss of patterns, our interpretations or understanding and lack of understanding. We can read and sense in the tea leaves of consciousness workings of a deeper self. For Jung, this self is the center of centers, an other which is the subject of the psychic totality. The center of centers or subject of subjects is also other, and this other of others is also subject.

For Jung, one progresses along the path of opposites to become more whole. The self unfolds and lives out its destiny in a lifelong process of individuation. Wholeness may be symbolized by mandala imagery, in which components of life, spirit, and personality are dynamically balanced around a center (the centered circle/square).

Bion's Radical Openness

How strange a geometric image of completion seems next to Bion's (1970; Eigen 1984, 1985, 1986) descriptions of radical openness. He sees in the analyst's attitude (Freud's "free-floating attention") a suspension of memory, understanding, expectation, and desire. Over and over one starts at zero. Bits and pieces of psychic life come and go like foam or dust. If one bears the waiting, sooner or later something coheres. Images and ideas grow out of raw affective impacts. Radioactive psychic particles leave traces which form paths. Psychic paths cut their way through dreams and mythic images. They may evolve into narrative networks and be used as models for dimly sensed processes.

Bion also writes of helping the patient achieve a certain "at-onement" with his psychic evolution (which Jung referred to as "the basic pattern" or "ground theme") (Bion 1970, p. 104; Jung 1958, par. 190; 1954, par. 417). However, Bion did not use geometric images to portray psychic totality but to show how an individual opens and/or closes possibilities (Eigen 1991b). For Bion, "wholeness" is one term of a larger movement. Wholeness achieved may block movement toward wholeness yet to come. The tendency to totalize personality is alien to Bion even as an ideal. An individual may use the sense of wholeness to defend against fragmentation or may fragment wholeness because of an inability to sustain development. In either case, incompletion is part of openness.

Whatever wholeness may be achieved is balanced by deficiency. Bion envisions the psyche as embryonic in important ways. For example, there is a gap between psychic products (e.g., the sense of emotional truth, or geometric images of dynamic unity and complementariness of opposites) and our ability to use them.

Our experience of the sense of wholeness is fragmentary, although immersion in a fragmentary experience can evoke a sense of wholeness. To compromise either term of this paradox is to miss an aspect of experience. To mock wholeness may be cynical, but to ignore fragmentariness makes one a liar.

If Jung maximized the rhetoric of wholeness, Bion maximized the rhetoric of unknowing. Bion remarked that if you think you are seeing the same patient twice, you are seeing the wrong patient. Such radical openness is an ideal, of course, as much an ideal as the completion or wholeness expressed by the mandala. Nevertheless, such ideals have practical consequences.

Through repeated attempts to wipe the slate clean and start fresh, one gains experience in observing how one's personality reforms with a particular patient over time. The same hang-ups may persist, yet one also becomes sensitive to subtle differences. The therapeutic attitude communicates a respect for limitations, while exploring what the nature of these limitations may be. The patient grows, in part, by coming up against the therapist's refusal to be tied to any one version of himself or the patient—a rigorous commitment to experiencing what the next turn of self might be. In time, the therapy partners build the ability to sift through noise and nonsense and achieve moments that count.

Jung intersects with Bion when he calls attention to the ambiguity inherent in images of centered wholeness. He writes of the mandala, "although it looks like the structure of a center, it still is uncertain whether within that structure the center or the periphery, division or non-division, is the more accentuated" (Jung 1954, par. 417). This view reverberates with his description of symbols as "tendencies whose goal is as yet unknown" (Jung, par. 668). This aspect of Jung's work joins the radical openness so central to Bion's explorations.

Plasticity and Persistence

We are encouraged by depth psychologists to let directionality grow out of unknowing. Freud's "free-floating attention," Bion's bracketing of memory, expectation, understanding, and desire, Jung's sense of symbol as a vehicle for psychic movement not yet grasped—all suggest receptivity to reverberations of an unknown transcendent reality, a reality of which we are a part and for which we speak. I think of Eddington's,"Something unknown is doing we know not what."

The thing that does not change, the permanence of a shifting impasse point or barrier in personality and psychotherapy, forces practitioner and patient to be still. One may object to sitting like Job while one's life is collapsing. But Job did more than ride out the storm. His complaints, recriminations, outrage, and agony shook inner and outer heavens. His sense of injustice tried to match with emotional violence the violence done to him. His curse of his birth bore witness to how unbearably alive he still was. He did not budge from his spot. The intensity mounted and the reversal came: a vision of the Creator's mysterious power— the awesome shock of the malleability of everything in His hands. A life can be given, crushed, reshaped, and restored: "Yea though He slay me, yet will I trust Him" (Job 13:15).

A whole people, Israel, is repeatedly crushed and renewed, like spices in a crucible. In each generation, the vision of God resurfaces, the call returns. Fragments reshape themselves and act like seeds. A whole people hears the still small voice of thunder that warns and inspires and works through upheavals. God is a magnet for a love that uplifts everything. "Holy, holy, holy — the whole earth is filled with His glory" (Isaiah 6:3), a glory that comes through catastrophe.

The biblical slaughters, plagues, quakes, longings, sacrifices, prayers, obedience-rebellion, lusts, visions, laws: all can be used to portray, experience, and observe the plasticity and persistence of self. Personality deforms, undoes, and reforms itself in so many ways. We wipe ourselves out and start again on a daily or hourly basis. Our stubborn hang-ups persist. We try to throw them off or work with them. We fall through cracks in our personality and see the fault lines. We come back a little wiser, a little more appreciative.

The cross — symbol of agonizing standstill, the place where things come to a grotesque stop — disoriented even Jesus for moments that seemed to last forever. Then the pivotal reversal: resurrection. From hell to nothingness to joy. This sequence is emblematic of the amazing extremes of experience human personality can undergo.

In biblical terms, God is the reality that undoes and resets distinctions. He breaks things apart and puts them together again — trying to make it right. Creativity gets another chance. There is no end to rebirth possibilities. Like a giant baby, God tears and liquifies reality, trying to let the best that he can do shine.

Psychoanalysis joins biblical reality in emphasizing radical plasticity and persistence of personality. Perhaps Freud's greatest contributions are his descriptions of the malleability or plasticity of psychic processes and the problems faced in working with concepts of plasticity and structure. Freud gave voice to the amazing plasticity of psychic processes at the same time he noted how difficult growth can be. A being who moves from waking to dreaming consciousness and back again is a being for whom psychotic or psychoticlike states are reversible. Moving in and out of altered states of consciousness is part of daily life.

This multiplicity marks Freud's descriptions of libido itself. Libido can act like a liquid or electrical charge and take many forms. Yet it can be sticky and resist change. It flows yet is also characterized by inertia. It is active (the pure activity of the philosopher's God) yet can be sluggish and oscillate between active and passive positions.

EIGEN

Freud further distilled this doubleness in his vision of two great drives. We have an urge to create greater unities and complexities and evolve in a way more capable of supporting conflicts and friction. But we also are collapsible and follow an entropic gradient. Freud means something more than the natural oscillation between vigor and fatigue, although this primitive rhythm is part of the background of experience that feeds his observations. He also means something more than thinking being more tiring than walking, although his conception suggests how hard it is to support psychic life. His depiction of incessant building up and breaking down (loosely drawn from a biological model of metabolic processes) was rooted in observation and experience of the radical plasticity and rigidity of personality.

The Timeless-Spaceless Unconscious: Matte-Blanco

Perhaps nowhere is the radical plasticity of self more emphasized than in Freud's conception of a timeless-spaceless unconscious. In the Freudian unconscious, the laws of contradiction and negation vanish. Distinctions melt and are reworked by unconscious processes. Contraries are churned into butter which can be poured into many molds. This radical fluidity makes condensation and displacement possible. Freud was especially fond of noting the plasticity of words. As Lacan emphasized, language itself provides structure and slipperiness as signifiers slide like colors into each other. Elusiveness is part of the play of meaning.

For Matte-Blanco, the psyche is characterized by bivalent logic: the logic of indivisibility (the unconscious) and the logic of division (consciousness). Even as distinctions are necessarily generated and maintained,

> each stratum is present in a mysterious way in every one of the strata which are nearer to the surface. . . . the indivisible is mysteriously present in the profound depth of anybody, however covered and asymmetrical the surface may appear; present yet not directly or immediately grasped. The indivisible is there but it is invisible. (Matte-Blanco 1988, p. 55; italics Matte-Blanco's)

COMING THROUGH THE WHIRLWIND

With Matte-Blanco, the category of *mystery* enters psychoanalysis as a working principle. Matte-Blanco uses the term *mysterious* repeatedly. That a wafer can become God's body and also be a symbol is mysterious (Winnicott gives this as an example of transitional experiencing (1953, p. 6)). The myriad forms of self in what Freud called "identification" are also mysterious (Matte-Blanco 1988, pp. 121–123). The tendency to divide-and-unite is so pervasive a characteristic of cognitive operations that we take it for granted. Life may wear the sense of mystery down, but it is there at all times supporting us.

Matte-Blanco used modern logic to explore bimodal processes, but it is difficult to avoid thinking of Kabbalah when reading many of his passages. "Everything is connected with everything else . . . everything not only *is in* everything else but also *acts upon* everything else" (Scholem 1969, pp. 122–123). Infinite plasticity underlies division. *Ein Soph*, the Infinite of infinites or Unrepresentable One, is the foundation and horizon for the world of forms and the pull of polarities. Scratch time-space objects or forms or representations or polar tensions and *infinite indivisibility* shines through.[1]

Winnicott: "In the Beginning"

Winnicott (1971) has beautiful passages which suggest the critical importance of a clinical methodology that does not give in to premature form-making. He tries to create an atmosphere that permits the patient to let his or her official, built-up personality drop away. How good it is to let chronic poses go and get underneath rigidities that keep personality in place. Winnicott emphasizes the importance of building a tolerance for chaos. A real

---

[1]Bion (1977) told me how important Kabbalah was to him. Matte-Blanco and Bion read each other. Of course, Matte-Blanco did not have to leave his Catholic heritage to find mysticisms of indivisibility–divisibility, "negative" and "positive" theologies which, respectively, emphasize no-thing and plenitude.

sense of self grows out of "unintegration" rather than out of a false sense of control (Eigen 1986, Chapter 8; 1989, 1991a).

At such moments, the therapist is a sort of background other who holds things together by his presence and percipience. In time, the patient gains the courage to see this holding is a non-holding, for the analyst, too, is "held together" by the same objective reality that gives birth to the unconscious–conscious subject. We are all part of the same hand, with soft palm, sensitive fingertips, and hard but breakable bones. Winnicott's clinical method or attitude encourages us to use tips of self to feel around the psychic darkness.

The "form-ing" experience is more important for Winnicott than "formed" experience. He emphasizes the potential healing effect of timeless creative moments that tick over into time (Lacan speaks of "pulsations through a slit" and William Blake likens creative moments to pulsations of an artery).

No analyst has placed the sense of creativeness at the center of psychological development more than Winnicott (Eigen 1983a; 1991a). He amplifies the moment of aliveness expressed by the words, "In the beginning. . . ."

Winnicott might have enjoyed a rendering of the first words of Genesis by the *Bahir* (Kaplan 1979, p. 5) which can be read: "*In-the-Beginning* created God." When we go into God to be renewed, it surely is not the monolithic "God" created by a leaden Germanic term, but the living *In-the-Beginning* which we can feel is creating us now.

Milner: Emptiness, Orgasm, and Madness

Milner described a kind of intense or pregnant emptiness out of which the moment of vision or something new grows. One is struck by the importance of emptiness in some of the best English psychoanalysts, especially Milner, Winnicott, and Bion. Milner, like Bion, connects psychoanalytic emptiness with the emptiness of the mystics and describes different kinds of mystical psychoanalytic emptiness. In this, Milner and Bion cross paths with many Jungian workers (it seems that Milner read Jung before she read Freud and that Bion's interest in mysticism antedated his psychoanalytic training).

Milner (1957, 1987; Eigen 1983b), like Winnicott, relates letting go to fear of madness. We may, at times, seem mad to ourselves and each other, as we dip in and out of commonsensical reality. What images, feelings, impulses slip between the cracks of our habitual self! Will we be overthrown? Will we come back? What do we do with the discovery that altered states of being and consciousness give us psychic orgasms? We may fear our creativeness as we do madness. Our creativeness may seem mad. We move from orgasm to orgasm in creative madness. Symbols of psychic creativeness communicate our most valued states and create these states through perception of new relations. Yet what gaps may unfold between ourselves and our orgasms of illumination—what spiritual and psychic hangovers we may endure.

New dimensions of experiencing open by not rushing past polarities or forcing one side of self to fit another. Milner is especially interested in moving past an ideology of control. Her remarks help set the tone for the studies in this book:

> [C]hange of heart, growth of spirit, does not come about in the same way as that by which we alter our material surroundings, it does not come from purposeful activity, by having an ideal or plan and then working directly to achieve it. . . . For it seems that true change of heart, growth to maturity of feeling, only comes about through facing the psychic pain of the recognition of opposites in ourselves, the pain of the difference between how nice we would like to be and how nasty we often are. (1956, p. 186).
>
> [C]hange of character and growth in stature . . . seems to have as its starting-point those moments when the patient is able to look at his sins, defects, weakness, without either trying to whitewash them nor trying to alter them in order that they themselves may become more admirable people. They are in fact moments in which hopelessness about oneself is accepted; and it is this which seems to enable the redeeming force to come into play. In fact it seems that when one can just look at the gap between the ideal and the actuality in oneself, see both the ideal and the failure to live up to it in one moment of vision, without

either turning against the ideal and becoming cynical, nor trying to alter oneself to fit it, then the ideal and actuality seem to enter into relation with each other and produce something new. (1956, p. 187).

Such passages are typical in Milner's work. As a matter of course, she melds psychological and religious language: true change of heart, growth of spirit, growth to maturity of feeling, change of character, growth in stature, sins, defects, weakness, the redeeming force, a moment of vision, something new. To traverse realms, languages, dimensions seems natural to her. She takes us to the melting point, life at the boundaries. Something hard endures. Personality melts and is restored.

Ehrenzweig's "Undifferentiated Matrix"

In earlier works (Field 1934, 1937), Milner used "dying god" images to organize her sense of what happened when she gave up rationalistic control and experienced a kind of creative surrender. Ehrenzweig (1971) amplified this aspect of Milner's work by showing how aspects of the dying-god theme symbolized phases of creative processes. As the "ego" immerses itself more fully in its work, it moves from surface perception through projective fragmentation, to unconscious union, a phase in which distinctions meld, permitting rapid unconscious scanning and reshuffling of possibilities. This timeless, spaceless unconscious connects with Matte-Blanco's "symmetrical unconscious," the invisible indivisible, in which anything can be everything else.

Jung: Filters and Crystals

Jungian archetypes function as a kind of unconscious filter system which mediates the flow of timeless-spaceless numinosity into time-space. When archetypal structures are in good working order, they help keep us on target with regard to "eternal values," the centering background/horizon of a life well lived. They act like psychic DNA, orienting our unfolding so that we are more real and true to ourselves—today and *sub specie aeternitatis*.

Jung used alchemical images to show how personality can be pulverized and reworked. If St. Augustine's God was the Physician, Jung's God was the Alchemist. Jung combined mythic, religious, scientific, and alchemical imagery to portray the journey of self. The alchemists failed to transform lower into higher forms of physical reality. Nevertheless, Jung (1955, par. 446) sensed in their dogged persistence a premonition of as yet unheard-of discoveries, such as modern chemistry on the one hand and psychological exploration of symbols of individuation on the other. The alchemists could not let go of their work, in part, because of the satisfaction contact with images of unconscious depths yielded. Jung further crystallized their efforts by dwelling on the psychospiritual meaning of their images.

Religion, Art, Science

Jung noted that the saint enters God in order to be transformed, while the artist uses archetypal realities to enrich his work. The psychologist is in a more ambiguous position. He relates to archetypal realities as fuel for personality growth, which may or may not be linked with mystical union. In some instances, mystical union must be overcome for growth of character. In other instances, character must be outgrown for transformative union to make sense. One stands one's ground in face of archetypal pulls, yet is transformed as the ground shifts.

The saint is God's work and God is the saint's work. The saint will do anything to be close to God, to do God's will, including and especially nullifying his own will or ego. The saint's reworking of his own personality is a byproduct of his desire to be close to God. Shatter or loss of self may be part of this movement: "God may rise up in my soul and shatter me" (A. Silesius, quoted by Jung 1955, par. 444).

The saint also is aware of failure. He knows only too keenly how far he is from God. A numinous blast of light can irradiate all too clearly one's faults, deficits, and distortions. Even virtues may seem puny and act as barriers. An artist, too, is keenly aware of flaws and shortcomings in his work. He has learned to make use of limitations to open and explore possibilities. At times, he may be more struck by what his work fails to do, than pleased with what it achieves.

In one way or another, mystic and artist deal with plasticity and its limitations. The scientist, too, may explore his world as plastic material which can assume many forms depending on its treatment. Freud (1927, p. 31) noted that the possibility of changing metals to gold, closed to the alchemist, is open to the scientist. He called special attention to the gold inherent in dream "dreckology," made available through the plasticity of language (Masson 1985, pp. 290-1; 1905, p. 34).

The mystic experiences this plasticity most radically and directly. His communications are directed toward and from it. Even the dry bones of corpses can come alive, as Ezekiel saw. In mystical experience, death is reversible and heaven is within us now. The Bible is a compressed, multifaceted image of the Great Conscious–Unconscious Machine or Being or Person or One or Force or Process that incessantly grinds up, reworks, and resets possibilities. The terms we use are possible pointers, profiles within profiles.

Many Sparks

There are many sparks in depth psychology concerned with dissolving, reworking, and resetting personality. Balint (1968) describes an "interpenetrating harmonious mix-up" of self and other which leads to a "new beginning." Psychic transparency characterizes Elkin's (1972) depiction of dramas between an immaterial Self and Other, prior to mapping body boundaries. The sense of self and other arises in an intuitive (not merely instinctive) medium, ruled by mood or spirit, to which physical states contribute.[2]

Fragmentation, liquification, and reshaping processes are explored in different keys, perhaps with different scales. Major theorists are not reducible to one another. They live in different worlds of experience. Their ideas and images are more than ways of observing experience: they help create the tone and direction of experiences they express. To organize an experience is to select some shapes out of many, and each shape (or system of shapes) has its trajectory. Each theory has different filter systems (systems of signifiers) for human personality at the crossroads.

Milner's "emptiness," Winnicott's "unintegration," Ehrenzweig's "undifferentiated ego matrix," Matte-Blanco's "symmetrical unconscious"—all emphasize dropping out of time-space, unforming, returning reworked and renewed. In Matte-Blanco's words, "The Infinite is here to stay" (1975, p. 395). Freud's depiction of the id as a "cauldron of seething excitations" is one way of portraying the meltdown of distinctions in the psyche's nuclear core. But it is only one hand upon the elephant, one profile with its subinfinities.

---

[2]We could mention Rycroft (1968), Grotstein (1979, 1981), Green (1975, 1976), Noy (1968), Schwartz-Salant (1982, 1989), Ogden (1989), Stolorow and Lachman (1980), Ulman and Brothers (1988), Robbins (1989) in art therapy, and Lifschitz (in press) in psychoanalytic gestalt therapy. These and many other workers are concerned with issues of plasticity-persistence of self at levels that underlie and include "higher" order "ego" processes.

I Know All This

After many years of therapy, a "hard-core resistant" patient might say, "I know all this. How does it help? I'm just the same." In such a case, therapy did not manage to break out of the knowledge game. Knowing or insight is not enough. A change of *being* is necessary.

One has to get underneath knowing and make contact with *experiencing*. Knowledge is important as a scaffolding, a frame of reference. But it must function as a bridge or link or jump-off point for further experiencing. There is a subtle interplay between experiencing and knowledge. To an important extent, the quality of experiencing gets fine tuning from the breadth, depth, and subtlety of knowledge available. If one is in touch with experience, the more one knows the better. But if the link is broken, one goes round in circles.

More likely someone may say, "Many things I came for are still the same, yet I changed in ways I didn't anticipate." In such a case, the person's personality problems did not vanish. They became part of a larger field of experience.

Many people think that spiritual enlightenment cures personality problems. Nothing could be further from the truth. Suzuki (1970) tells us that enlightenment does not do away with problems, but opens a larger horizon which transcends or encompasses egoistic-erotic drives and attitudes. Thomas Merton noted that he talked to Buddhist monks who were unable to eradicate ego after a lifetime of work. The ego is experienced as the flaw in the ointment, the spoiler, the rigid sore spot of character.

Merton himself was overcome by eros after years of monastic discipline. Close physical contact with his nurse during an illness proved too much. I cannot avoid linking (pure speculation, of course) his "accidental" death in India (electrocution by a fan) with conflict over the lovely erotic upsurge. To the end, Merton remained a spokesman for the human spirit, although his war against ego and eros may have killed him.

There are important strands in depth psychological writings that join Suzuki's transcendent attitude of enlightenment. Jung's individuation process and transcendent function point to a dialogical process in which all aspects of personality contribute. Bion maintains a radically open attitude in which he says what he sees as experience evolves or dies or enters a psychotic warp. His open attitude allows the living moment to speak — or, if necessary, to give death its due. One of the best expressions of this open attitude that I know is William Blake's vision of heaven as war in which all voices of self speak maximally to the benefit of all (and one imagines this includes the voices of all schools of depth psychology as well).

Analysis is not simply a game of words and images. It may be that, but it is much more. It is a life-and-death matter. In therapy, people struggle for their lives. The quality and direction of self is at stake. The analyst's tone and attitude, vision and bearing, play a role in what may or may not happen. Yet no matter how good the therapist or sincere the patient, there are no guarantees.

Growth in transcendent attitude is not enough. Work in the cellar is necessary. The problem is not only lack of psychological education, although that is a major contributor. Too much emphasis has been placed on "control": ego over id, secondary process thinking binding primary process thinking, and so on. The problem goes deeper. In most cases, the primary process itself is not working right. No amount of successful control will undo or correct the matter.

The job of primary process is to process affects, especially catastrophic impacts. Global catastrophic impacts need to be broken up and metabolized, filtered through dream images, reveries, and eventually symbols which give rise to imaginative reflection. Unconscious fantasy that works right has a serpentine flow. It undulates through many positions and reversals.

All too often fantasy flow gets broken or stifled and hardens in narrow molds (e.g., the strict scripts of perversions). The primary process serpent becomes knotted and stiff and suffocating. The subject's openness dies or becomes useless. Better secondary control may prove socially beneficial or personally expedient but is a poor substitute for an alive and healthy primary process flow. Only the latter keeps the subject open from his roots up. Psychotherapeutic work may fall short of this mark, but it must not be totally removed from it.

EIGEN

The Point of Meeting

The timeless-spaceless unconscious provides a privileged point of contact between *Ein Soph* and psychic life. It, so to speak, is one of the special places (like Mt. Moriah, Mt. Sinai, Mt. Zion) through which the psyche plugs into divinity with special intensity. The psyche works over the point of impact by producing dreams, myths, narratives, polarities, and generally dampens the intensity by distributing it throughout temporal-spatial life. The latter becomes the filter or mediate system through which we maintain distance yet contact the Unrepresentable One. In theory, any point on the time-space continuum can become Mt. Moriah or The Place of Meeting—and *is* so. But, in fact, the characteristics of some places lend themselves to numinosity more than others. Matte-Blanco's timeless-spaceless unconscious is one such "place." The analyst's office (because of the "call" of the situation) is presumably another.

The analytic office or situation and the presence of the analyst stand for the unconscious or unknown that comes to the rescue (see Eigen 1986, Chapter 8; Bollas 1987; Emery, unpublished paper; Kurtz 1989). At times, the patient's expectations are confirmed. Often enough the wound brought by the patient meets the wound of analysis. How can faith in the healing unknown persevere when wound meets wound?

Yet to say wound meets wound is to say life meets life. Life, like the Divine Presence, is everywhere. While we are alive, there is really no other place for us but life. We cannot escape aliveness, whether joy or plague, blessing or curse. We can tune into the sense of raw aliveness (in which forms melt into sensations and feelings) or emphasize our awareness of the growth of forms.

Nevertheless, we *do* escape life and we can do this by using weapons of life. We can try to turn life off by turning up the volume of raw aliveness until forms are obliterated. We may also lose ourselves in forms at the expense of aliveness, using forms to mute or encapsulate aliveness.

There is also such a (no)thing as dead or horrifying formlessness (Eigen 1986, Chapter 3; 1991b; 1991c). Today more and more patients are pained by "dead spots" (Rosenfeld 1987, pp.

105–153). In certain instances, dead formlessness has replaced the Divine Presence and the alive formingness of life—and is indeed everywhere. Today dead formlessness, in part, seems to be an inner complement to the surfeit of artificial forms vomited up by greedy misuse of technology.

Between the Divine Presence and dead formlessness is the scream (Eigen 1984, pp. 94–99; Bion 1970, p. 13). There are many screams, even many primal screams. A scream may last forever. It becomes encoded in the musculature as mute tightness or self-holding. One almost hears it in one's throat or inner ear as whisper or cackle and imagines one is imagining it. It provides a link between goodness and destruction: one screams as goodness is being destroyed.

One may scream in protest or horror. Perhaps one screams to frighten the bad thing way, scream as a kind of weapon. In screaming, one clings to goodness or its remnant. One sides with God against devil. Yet devils scream, too; a devil may be an extended scream. One screams to hold oneself together as one falls apart and disappears. A scream may be all that is left as one drops away, and the scream dies out as well.

Therapy, too, may be a drawn-out scream. In therapy, the scream gets broken down and psychically metabolized. Frozen screams of horror can thaw out and turn to weeping. Through one's scream, one cries one's heart out. A broken heart is precious. It is a gateway to caring. From frozen scream to the wholeness of a broken heart, a healing brokenness, may take years of passing through the bitter coating.

A supervisee spoke about her patient's scream. Her patient is a fragile, sensitive woman. Her pent-up life welled up in her and burst out as a scream. She frightened herself. She was afraid to return to the room in which she screamed. She was in terror that the scream was still there, waiting for her.

Perhaps her scream is rage, passion, strength. Its blast may unite many currents which in time will have a say. For the moment, it was a sort of honking horn, an announcement: "Look! I'm here, whatever I am. You can't get past me anymore." The patient tried to isolate it, to keep it in a room. She did not yet realize that the scream was everywhere, more accessible in some places than others. She did not leave it in a room—she found it there. One must credit this room as a place of meeting, at least in some preliminary form linked to foreboding. Her therapist might expect the scream to seek further avenues of communication.

The scream, like the Divine Presence, cannot be tied down to the places it favors. The Place of Meeting moved from transportable tent to immovable temple, but then the temple was destroyed. The experience that remains is greater than the sum of the rocks into which it is hammered.

The Fragmentary Nature of Psychotherapy

In psychotherapy rebirth is modest, if far-reaching. Rebirth is always partial—never total. No matter how great one's epiphany, sooner or later one's ordinary personality resurfaces. One goes through what one has to, then says, "Hey, it's me again—just plain me!" But with what change of resonance and appreciation! Psychotherapy works with details of one's ordinary personality in painstaking ways. Tiny bits of real rebirth can be of infinite value.

By its nature psychotherapy is extraordinary. Two individuals meet alone together to discover the truth about a life. The idea of truth orients the direction of discourse, although attempts to be truthful are flawed. At least one of the two individuals knows how elusive personal truth is, yet tries to stay open to the truth beyond reach. By the time therapy ends, two people are more dedicated to this searing yet uplifting openness.

Psychotherapy is a passion. It involves a love for subjectivity, a drive to drink oneself in and marvel at all personality can be. In psychotherapy, one tastes oneself slowly and begins to satisfy the hunger for contact with depths of life in more wholesome ways. I do not believe that one becomes solipsistic by focusing on self. The depths of human subjectivity are intersubjective (Lacan 1977, 1978; Leavy 1980, 1988; Eigen 1986, Chapter 4; Elkin 1972; Schwartz-Salant 1989, pp. 37–50; Grotstein 1981; Atwood and Stolorow 1984). The personality of patient and therapist incessantly pass through each other in fragmentary rebirth processes.

Every individual has his own style of evasion or subterfuge. In psychotherapy, we learn to pay homage to our foibles, inasmuch as they enable us to become more humorous and wise. Wisdom would be nothing without vanities to practice on. Work on ourselves is never at a loss for material.

Most people gain from psychotherapy. If all cases are partial failures, most are also partial successes. In my several decades doing therapy, I can count on one hand those for whom therapy might have been more loss than gain. Even those who hated me, and with whom I made bad errors, rarely went away without something useful. It is my impression that not only is this so with the hundreds of people with whom I worked, but with the great majority of people seen by students and colleagues. In this respect, the term *helping profession* is not a misnomer.

Psychotherapy can be dangerous. A certain portion of people who come to therapy commit suicide, go mad, or break up families. Perhaps they would have done so anyway, but psychotherapy did not help them to do otherwise. Clearly, psychotherapy is limited in its ability to help people. Its limitations make it human. But it tries and often tries its best. More and more impossible cases become feasible. More and more previously inaccessible areas of the self become accessible.

The two individual cases in the following chapters were not my most ill patients. On the contrary, they were verbal, highly motivated, highly skilled professionals. They were not withdrawn and isolated but very much in contact with life. Nevertheless, something in their lives was not working or did not feel right.

There were enough obvious complaints. In their very different ways, Cynthia and Ben destroyed or undid their love relationships. Cynthia's destructiveness and sense of deficiency marred the workplace as well. Ben achieved vocational continuity but undermined his financial stability. He squandered resources of every sort—material and emotional. Both Cynthia and Ben seemed bent on throwing their lives away in important respects. Yet both were honest searchers. They wanted more than mere survival. They were determined to live the best life they could, the life that was most true and right for them.

In spite of (or precisely because of) their high motivation and relative sophistication, Cynthia and Ben were blind to themselves in important respects. They were dumbfounded by the invisible worm that ate their lives. They used their virtues against themselves and could neither discover nor correct what was wrong. Often what was wrong kept shifting. They were both committed to maximum aliveness. Their cutting edge would change—yet intractability persisted.

In time, each person went more deeply into the *x* that did not change. The challenge was to find ways of going further with areas about which one felt hopeless. Invisible tools had to be created for invisible woes.

I have written about more severely disturbed people in previous works (1977, 1980a, 1980b, 1984, 1986). The present work emphasizes how serious disturbances in less "ill" people can be. So many personalities are marked by hidden despair. One learns to make do with what cannot be changed. Yet the residue of despair that accompanies giving up on or prematurely making peace with oneself can be poisonous. One may not be able to change the unchangeable, but one can learn to work with psychic poisons, especially self-poisoning processes. Cynthia and Ben learned to go deeper than their hidden despair.

One builds a certain strength by working with barriers. Faults and impasses never go away. But by keeping one's cutting edge close to the impasse point, one discovers a joy deeper than despair. One smells out psychic truth like a bloodhound and finds ways to work with this capacity so as not to destroy oneself or others.

The discovery of our psychic universe is breathtaking. One marvels as galaxy after galaxy comes into view. In therapy, one cannot go in all directions at once. Patient and therapist must split off parts of bodies from inner space and explore selected bits at a time. One has faith that the various explorations are connected, although discontinuities remain. In conceptual work, we try to verbalize networks of possible connections, but in practical experience we rely on the hidden order of unconscious processes.

Cynthia and Ben:
An Overview

Cynthia

Cynthia floundered in life throughout her twenties but was not an unhappy person. She had a sense of mission. She was dedicated to helping others and doing some good in this world. Yet many of her attempts to be useful proved destructive to herself.

She had an ill-defined sense that her life was not working right. Nothing quite went as she hoped it would. She seemed to go from trouble to trouble, although many of her experiences were caring and ecstatic. Each incident was meaningful but her life as a whole seemed to lack continuity. She wondered if she would ever find the right path for herself and kept trying.

Cynthia was a beautiful and vibrant woman who often felt like an "awkward giraffe." She felt badly that her sense of values put her at a disadvantage and added to her awkwardness. She was not as glib as many of the professional people she met. She acted well but was not as quick, smooth, and strong as others.

She seemed to be caught between going more deeply into herself and becoming more adept at surface interplay. She could not do both at once. As a result, she felt discontented with her ability to contact herself, as well as her ability to do better with others. Her life was meaningful, but neither deep enough nor capable enough.

Cynthia wanted to marry and raise children and was beginning to fear that hidden problems prevented her from doing so. Her relationships with men became dead ends. She was afraid that psychoanalysis would not understand her spiritual needs and would work against her. Cynthia felt that family and vocation should be manifestations of a deeper spiritual reality and dreaded not finding an analyst who respected her vision.

Her fear that her thirties would race by as her twenties had done propelled her to seek professional help. Her own efforts and the counsel of friends and spiritual advisors left the knots of her personality as tight as ever. She was caught between surface and depth. Her personal relationships went around in circles. Cynthia was aghast that help did not come naturally, that it did not grow out of the depths of her being, as God meant it to. Therapy seemed so unnatural, mechanical, ungodly. Was it a trick of the devil that she had to give therapy a chance? The point came when she could not do otherwise.

Ben

Ben was a successful psychotherapist who began to fall apart after the breakup of his marriage. He imagined that he was the center of his wife's universe and was appalled to find out that she was the center of his. His difficulties gradually initiated a deeper commitment to life and made a successful marriage possible with another partner.

When he began therapy, his new relationship was in danger of breaking up for many of the reasons that his marriage did. Ben was blind to how his narcissistic demands affected his partner. Although he was a good therapist with others, he was naive when it came to himself. Much of our work cultivated a psychological sophistication that rounded out his view of himself.

Ben was stunned to realize how much of his life was spent in search of immediate gratification. He rarely took a long-range view of personal matters. Consequently, his most precious relationships were unwittingly on the edge of being destroyed. He was so absorbed in becoming the imaginary center of the other's attention that he nearly destroyed the possibility of becoming a father. Had he succeeded in his blind egomania, he would have thwarted his deepest longings.

A love of truth stamped Ben's life. He even justified his egomania by his love of truth. Although he often used his sense of truth against others, in the end it became an ally in therapy. As long as Ben suspected that he was lying to himself, he was moved to go farther. He could not rest as long as he detected falsehood in his personality, and this led to a very long and productive therapy.

48

Spirit and Psyche:
Defense and Opening

Cynthia used spirituality as a defense against psychology. She feared that psychology reduced the scope of life, that it would kill what she most valued. Perhaps there are people whose psychic foundations are reworked by going into God; Cynthia certainly had many peak experiences related to the God feeling. Her connection with God kept her heart open. Yet she could not gather herself together into something that she could say counted. She blew up whatever she built. She went from explosion to explosion and watched in growing horror as her life remained dispersed.

For Ben, spirituality had never been an active issue. He was mired in a semihedonistic psychology in which psychological truth of some sort was extremely important to him. In therapy, his sense of truth spread and deepened. It became far more than a form of engineering to ensure the success of egoistic strivings. His ego gradually connected with deeper wishes and values. To his surprise, Ben found himself facing a psychospiritual universe he dared not believe existed. His psyche underwent transformation partly as a result of its contact with spirit. The psyche is surrounded by spiritual reality: it lives in a medium larger than itself.

There had been no God in Ben's life because his ego occupied God's position. As Ben wrestled with therapy angels, he suffered the saving, humiliating realization that God was not limited to ego, that ego was not God's principal residence. In Ben's case, God was linked with social relationships, community, and a growing sense of "something more."

For Cynthia, spiritual experience was her home base, but she remained psychically stagnant. Cynthia was high on God yet her psychological wheels kept spinning. In time, her spiritual life was in danger of aimlessly spinning as well. For Ben, psychological experience was his home base, but he went around circles as well. Years of dedication to his version of psychological reality jeopardized everything. Neither Ben nor Cynthia made the sort of spirit-psyche connection that could take life forward across dimensions.

Each had a vision or perspective that sought to maximize life

EIGEN

(and succeeded in some specialized way)—yet sold life short. The spirit-psyche interplay was short-circuited. Cynthia and Ben could not move past a certain point. Each saw nothing but disintegration at the point where movement ends.

Personal Integrity and One's Everyday Personality

Psychotherapy takes place in an ivory tower divorced from everyday life. The patient has the luxury of talking himself out to a good listener—not once but many times, as long as therapy lasts. Therapy is like a cocoon in which the patient can shed his protective coating and let what is inside him shine. The butterfly that emerges in the therapy office is often shot down in real life.

As time goes on, one's everyday personality makes more claims in the therapy office. The everyday self is resentful that the butterfly self gets so much time in therapy. An argument something like the following begins.

EVERYDAY SELF "Why should you get so much attention here? You rarely show up in real life. *I* carry the burden. I'm the one who sees things through. You don't survive outside your special little hothouse."

BUTTERFLY SELF "Don't I give you inspiration? Don't I make life more beautiful?"

EVERYDAY SELF "Your inspiration is a tease, a promise that never comes true. If I listened to you, we'd have both been dead long ago."

BUTTERFLY SELF "It's true I don't always have my feet on the ground. My ideas can be pretty flighty. But if I left, life would be drab. If I didn't bother you, you'd think that you were all there was to life."

EVERYDAY SELF "There's plenty to occupy my time without you. I'm not empty, you know. I'm interested in lots of things. I have loves. Life is colorful without you. I'm not just a survival machine."

BUTTERFLY SELF   "As the day goes on, you get worn out. You fade away. The best in you dies out. You sense how suffocating things are without me. You miss me. You wish you had taken better care of me—of us both. You shine more brightly and last much longer when I'm there."

EVERYDAY SELF   "There you go again. You're so arrogant. You take credit for my struggles. It's infuriating. Why don't you stay away and see what happens."

BUTTERFLY SELF   "You won't blow us all to pieces? You won't miscalculate what you're up against? You won't be naive?"

The argument has no end. The everyday self resents the butterfly self. It feels that it does the work while the other gets the credit. The butterfly self transcends common sense and opens more subtle realms of experience. The soul flies ahead of experience and tastes hints of feelings that leave it breathless. Emotions without names uplift it. In a moment, it thrills to a matrix of possibilities that may provide common sense with material to work on for hundreds of years.

Yet common sense is right to insist that it contributes color and originality, too. Eros permeates everyday life. Everyday life is not all business. What a pleasure it is to put subtleties aside and enjoy a fine walk or talk. What a relief to be in a familiar world, solidly grounded amidst solid things, the earth below, the sky above. How good not always to be at the cutting edge beyond which the soul flies.

In optimal circumstances, common sense and the vision of the ideal feed and balance each other. Either alone may be destructive. A fertile tension exists between them. Our ability to tolerate this tension is variable. We try to simplify our situation by becoming too prosaic or poetic. We need to realize that it is natural to zigzag between polarities.

Therapy provides a place where we can let the various sides of our nature have their say as fully as possible. Our job is to begin to hear the voices within and let them stake their claims. We are torn apart by conflicting desires and possibilities. Psychoanalysis asks us to do nothing except say what we must. The tension that arises by the injunction to do nothing but speak and listen can become unbearable. Psychoanalysis provides practice in building up a tolerance for unbearable dialogical tensions.

It is natural to act. Action does more than discharge tension. It leads to discovery. Psychoanalysis focuses on that aspect of action which evades tension and discovery. Often we live in a state of partial collapse. We do not let the natural arc between tension-action-discovery develop. We are unable to support the growth of our capacities and short-circuit our movement. Psychoanalysis seeks to stimulate growth of a psychic apparatus more able to sustain the tension-action-discovery movement. It brings action within the circumference of dialogue.

At its best, action is a form of dialogue. However, much action depletes dialogue. Talking, too, can be an action which gets rid of self and other. Idle gossip may be fun and even necessary for sanity, if one humorously acknowledges the pleasures of mindlessness. Psychoanalysis has been called a delicious form of gossip. Nevertheless, there is a danger that gossip can become a way of life. The clown's mask may extend to the depths of one's being. One becomes a caricature of oneself and cannot break out of one's mask even in one's depths.

In time, the fight between everyday and butterfly selves becomes caricature. Claims become exaggerated. A sense of ideal truth attacks the compromises of the everyday self and bemoans the personality's loss of integrity. The everyday self accuses ideal truth of being unrealistic, an illusion, the greatest lie of all. Each resents, envies, and distorts the other. Therapy magnifies their distortions. Therapy is a kind of magnet that draws the worst of each position out. Therapy thrives on exaggeration.

In therapy, the best in each position also becomes magnified. Therapy acts as an amplifier for the voices in personality. The goodness of each position comes through distortions. There is real danger that basic goodness gets swamped in mutual accusations and the fight for survival. An aim of therapy is to distill what is precious in each viewpoint. To do this, it is necessary to build a tolerance for caricature and the capacity to explore exaggerations. It is this combination of subtlety and grossness that creates part of therapy's tension.

The essential battle in the chapters ahead is the fight of each individual for integrity in everyday life. I have chosen two individuals who could not easily bear compromising either personal integrity or the pleasures and achievements of everyday living. Immersed in daily living, Cynthia and Ben loved the concrete and took their commitment to life for granted, speaking about their relationships, their work, their daily disturbances. Neither were satisfied with the status quo. Each battled with the suffocating and distorting qualities of their circumstances and personalities. Ties which nourished them held them back. Their convictions and connections acted as barriers to further movement. They felt twisted out of shape by the loves and work that supported their survival.

The antidote was going deeper into personality, into love, into work. The tension between integrity and survival had to evolve. The ability to let attitudes reshape themselves needed to grow. A mental framework or inner horizon developed which encompassed a more complex and open relationship to personality. Decisions that felt right grew out of these evolving horizons. Each came through distortions and estrangement to reconnect with an underlying sense of truth and love in life.

Dreams as Stepping Stones

As therapy progresses, the "what," "how," and "why" of one's words become less important than "who" is speaking. The same linguistic "I" runs through sentences beginning with I: I am tired, I am angry, I am sad, I love. Yet the I who tries to seduce and coerce the other does not feel exactly like the I that sees through these maneuvers and is repentant. The I that follows envious desire and ambition is not the same as the I that seeks to return to its connection with God.

A sense of doubleness or multiplicity characterizes accounts of the human subject since antiquity. In psychotherapy, the sense of multiplicity becomes highly significant. One moves through I after I, who after who. One sheds profiles of I like a snake sheds skins. One can tune into this process at high speeds and see through a multiplicity of I's at a glance, as one races through the repertoire of personality.

Seeing the dance of I's does not, in itself, lead to the kind of personal growth that is helpful. Transcendent vision does not always reflect a change of heart or the ability to make a change of heart effective. Bit by bit, work in the trenches often takes place in dreams. A multiplicity of I's struggle in dreams. The personality breaks up into various facets which menace or complement each other. Although dreams may be repetitive, the repetitions have their differences. One reexperiences traumatic situations in the hope of overcoming them. One undergoes maddening agonies and anxieties in the hope of leaving them behind.

Eventually what becomes important is not mastery, since trauma and anxiety are never simply overcome. The important thing is the kind of person one becomes as a result of grappling with the concerns of dreams. One feels more thoroughly the pain of trying to reset oneself, the agony of something gone wrong trying to right itself. One feels more intensely and sympathetically the struggle of the self trying to find its way amidst shatter.

The timelessness of dreams does not mean that dreams are outside of time. A single dream may depict aspects of early shattering, current disturbances, and catastrophic intimations of the future. Past, present, and future are condensed in dreams. Similarly, significant themes and affects may be radically condensed and juxtaposed in dreams. In dreams, one may move from catastrophe to bliss and back again in short intervals. Bliss often succeeds work on catastrophic dread, if one is not too embittered.

Many dream sequences move toward and away from a healthy element. They produce a moment of freedom and integrity, a sense of the best that is in us, but they cannot support such moments for long. The personality produces a healthy figure, then falls away from it. The personality as a whole needs practice in supporting the best that it can do. It tends to collapse after a good birth. One tries to reset oneself but bad attitudes, inertia, and catastrophic anxieties overwhelm the moment of health or good will. With practice, one learns that the best in us does not die out when it disappears for a time. Healthy elements grow

COMING THROUGH THE WHIRLWIND

with weeds and bugs. A sense of new life comes through madness after madness.

Therapy helps one to recognize healthy elements in dreams that one might otherwise dismiss. Dreams transform raw affective impacts into feelings and attitudes that can be experienced and worked with. No matter how catastrophic a dream seems, it probably has broken off bits of a larger catastrophe to work with. Dreams are prisms that break up global impacts into discernible colors. Healthy elements emerge in the refractions. An explosion may produce a universe, as cataclysm produced a Moses in the bulrushes. In one's rush to run away from catastrophe, one may run away from healthy life as well.

An aim of therapy is to help people develop sensitivity with appropriate insulation. Dreams act as filters for raw experience. In therapy, one stays close to the work dreams do. By speaking about dream experience, one exercises sensitivity in relatively tolerable doses. One learns the art of modulating sensitivity, to remain true to experience without fatally being done in by it.

By speaking, one loses aspects of dream experience. This is a necessary loss. If experience is left totally mute, it collapses. One aims to speak truly, to let dream experience speak, to let each element of the dream have a say. Yet one cannot go deep without bias. One commits oneself to an angle of vision, even if one may be unable to know what limitation is practiced at a given moment. One can be sure that one is moving along some unconscious gradient. As one follows one trail after another, one trusts that the movement is fruitful.

In the sessions ahead, dreams are stepping stones. Not only do they chart progress and impasse, they are bits of work enabling movement from one place to another, bits of reorganizing processes in progress. Dreams show what is wrong with the self and what the self is doing about it. But they are more than mirrors. They are arenas of longing and struggle in which the self seeks to come through its frustrations and flaws. They are crossing points of larger currents that result in moments of growth or failure to grow.

A partnership between the waking and dreaming self is necessary if growth processes that occur in dreams are to be effective in everyday life. Therapy provides an atmosphere where linking work can occur. The struggle between the best and worst within us spills into therapy. The therapy relationship gathers isolated and warring aspects of self into its movement. A crucial link is gradually made between the momentum of the therapy relationship and the movement of dreams. The therapy relationship is a kind of dream, but a dream between two people, which can be talked about.

The corrective work between the therapy partners must find its way into dream experience, and the corrective work of dreaming must be embodied in daily life. As one goes deeper into therapy, life often comes to the rescue. Events in everyday life check the imbalances of therapy and become part of workable dreams.

chapter
THREE

Cynthia

Radiance and the Failed Ministry

Cynthia was a tall and beautiful woman who felt awkward and dull. She made my heart smile when she entered the room. She was one of those lucky people who possessed a cheering radiance without seeming to know it. Yet she knew about this inner light and felt it a curse as well as a blessing.

Cynthia began her adult vocational life with the idea of becoming a minister. She was active in church and entered a seminary program. Cynthia was far more interested in personal relationships than in studies and found the politics of church life tedious. In time, she became deeply attached to the pastors she assisted, and she lightened the load of those with whom she came in contact. But trouble followed her.

Her naivete about the politics of church life became a credo, provoking a veiled contempt for everyday necessities. Cynthia clung to her innocence with a vengeance. She was more interested in helping people than in the mechanics of helping. Her superiors saw her as raw but potentially useful, if possibly troublesome. Her beauty as well as her stubborn blindness also aroused suspicion and not without reason. She left one position when her personal involvement with the minister in charge became threatening.

Finally, her honest flirtation with the ministry ended when an affair she was having with the head of her church became known. In defiance of authorities and her congregants, she moved in with

56

the minister and lived in church quarters. She had support from some colleagues and parishioners. Many wanted to see her succeed. But many more were appalled by her actions and pressured her to leave.

When I asked why the ire of the fold was not directed against the minister as well as herself, she shrugged. It seemed obvious to her that she should be the one to take the blame. She even welcomed it. She was relieved she hadn't damaged the man she liked. As far as she knew, neither he nor she meant harm. She followed her passion, her life feeling. She felt her desire was linked with her love of God. Everything was justified because it seemed so right, so good. She followed what was best and most real in herself. She understood society's verdict. People were hemmed in by falsity and fear. They were not ready for the big leap life invited them to take. If the man she was with was cowardly, it was not his fault. It was better that she lost her position than caused his downfall. But she was glad she tried and she would keep on trying. I sensed a trace of bitterness in her voice but she denied it. It was only a trace, for, by and large, her voice was crystal clear.

Wes

Cynthia's adult life was marked by a natural boldness and provocativeness, or so it seemed to her. She described herself as a farm girl who began an affair with a black man as soon as she went to college. She never expected the affair to last, but last it did. It was the biggest trick life played on her, or that she played on herself.

She felt safe with Wes. He was warm and comforting. Their sex life was good but her sex life was good with many men. He became a kind of ballast or home port. She could always count on Wes. He balanced her promiscuity. Yet she repeatedly tried to get rid of him. She was not really happy with him. She felt suffocated and stuck. She wanted someone she could talk to and who would talk back. Wes was quiet. Their relationship took place in silence. Whatever conversation they had was mundane. She did not feel

Wes knew or could know her. She did not even feel he wished to.

Cynthia gave Wes as the reason she sought my help. She was torn up and needed someone to talk to. She felt I listened and tried to understand. It was not long before she hinted that I was the kind of man who could save her—intelligent, sensitive, and white. She had come to New York to get away from Wes and find someone like me. She was a bit ashamed of Wes at certain kinds of parties and with certain kinds of people. He was extremely handsome and that made her proud. But he was not interested in anything outside the trivia of everyday life and had nothing significant to talk about. She was ashamed that she was ashamed. Her attitude toward him was not Christian but it was truthful. In many ways, Wes forced her to face the kind of person she was or was not.

The Farm

Every history has its mythology. Cynthia's included her image of herself as a prototypical midwestern farm girl. Whenever she asked herself why she did something, she could always say, "I'm a farm girl." Because she was a farm girl, she felt inferior in cities. She also felt the excitement of being off the farm. The campus and city represented the larger world, and she broke loose after years of being penned up.

Cynthia felt a mixture of pride and shame at being a farm girl. She was proud of her health and vigor and love of life. Yet she felt stained by something that ran deeper than shame. She possessed a sense of secrecy, as if everything important to her was beyond the pale and she had something to hide. Her sense of secrecy made her feel awkward. She wanted to get rid of it but could not pin it down. In part, she attributed it to her isolation as a farm girl. More than anything, it was this secrecy she wanted to throw off in the city.

Such feelings are a familiar part of therapy with many persons: feeling blocked, pent-up, proud, ashamed, hidden, longing to be free. A farm girl has no monopoly on universals. Yet living on a farm gives a specific texture to basic structures. Many girls are caught in sexual business with an older brother. But only on a farm can a stern and loving father catch his children doing something forbidden in a barn. The smell of hay and animals adds something direct, immediate, and irreplaceable to the breaking of a taboo. Her father did not say a word to Cynthia. He simply nodded and motioned to her brother, who followed him into the house. The incident was never mentioned again. A quiet strain was forever added to her conduct with her brother, in shocking contrast to the life and death of the animals in the barnyard.

As a child, she spoke more with her mother than her father. Both parents were quiet people. Her mother's quietness was more nervous, taut and sensitive, like a bird or deer. The afternoons Cynthia spent with her were filled with quiet understanding. She thought they talked more than they did. It felt like a lot went on between them. Cynthia felt at ease and peaceful.

Her mother often gardened or took care of the house. Cynthia liked gardening time best. Her mother was never more calm or masterful. Her movements were easy and sure. Cynthia loved to see her mother's hands at work in the garden. They knew just what to do. In the little world of the backyard, no problem seemed too big. All emotions found their right place.

Most of the time, her father was the calm one, the peacemaker. He defused daily tensions with his deep, measured voice. It was his arm around her or his spanking that kept things going. She liked being close to him. His animal warmth gave her faith. He was deep and steady and wordless as the animals and crops he tended. For Cynthia, he *was* the farm.

Her mother's nervousness was a signal of discontent, even imprisonment, a pointer to the outside world. Cynthia could picture her mother living in a town or suburbs of a middle-sized city. For her father, there could only be the farm. Cynthia never believed that her mother ever quite *lived* on the farm. She was always somewhere else. Her restlessness saved her from being anywhere. She was never totally taken in by anything. A reserve marked her personality. Cynthia came to feel marred and saved by a deeply withholding quality about her mother.

In one respect, her father also represented the outside world, although very differently from her mother. He stood for culture. He loved music and was something of a musician. He taught his daughters violin and piano. Perhaps he once pictured himself and his daughters as virtuosos in the real world. However, Cynthia never played as well as her sister and it was on her sister that her father's hopes and expectations fell. Cynthia never enjoyed the attention her sister did and came to feel something of a Cinderella in the family, an outsider, like her mother. In a way this was freeing, since she did not work as hard as her sister to make her father happy.

Her father's love of music rubbed off on Cynthia indirectly. She liked to draw. It was something she could do that no one in her family could take away from her. No one in her family knew anything about drawing. She was on her own, although her mother sometimes supported her. As she grew up, her drawings met with incomprehension by her mother as well as her father. But her own pleasure in her productions remained. Drawing came to be a profound aid, guide, and comfort in the years ahead. It stayed with her through godless times.

Puzzles Without an Outside and the Sermon on the Mount

Cynthia became aware of the twists and turns of thinking very early. She was aware that her mind worked paradoxically long before she knew that word. She called the in's and out's of revery *puzzles*. Her home life provided the basic raw materials. Her thoughts about her predicament led her round and round, like the inside of a seashell.

Her moments of deepest peace came from her restless and unhappy mother. Her mother also contributed a sense of distance that would never leave her. Cynthia associated her self-consciousness, watching what she was thinking and doing, with her mother. Like her mother, she could never be totally taken in by anything. She would always have herself. But this left her at sea, at odds with everything, especially herself.

The mute warmth of her father provided a modicum of safety and peace. On a dumb animal level, she could trust like he did, like a dog or horse or bull. She also identified with the grain in the fields: she grew like wheat and corn. If cut down, she would grow again. Cynthia often felt cut down by her father's way of caring. She could not find the Cynthia he loved, as if his Cynthia were another person, not the Cynthia she knew. He was like Wes in his quiet obliviousness to what it was like to be her.

The very things that gave her strength were the things that tore her apart and made her feel less than herself. The farm seemed to have no outside at all. Everything took place inside it. It seemed to be a secret from the larger world, an invagination invisible to the outside, yet all-encompassing. At the same time, Cynthia's was a family of outsiders. Father and mother, sisters and brother: whatever their harmony and however they belonged to one another, they did not really fit together. If Cynthia was Cinderella, it did not take her long to realize that her brother had a tougher time than she, and that her sister's suffering at being Daddy's favorite was at least as great as her own. There was no great advantage to being number one or two or three.

A decisive surprise came in church when Cynthia was sixteen years old. After years of hearing the Bible read and preached weekly, the Sermon on the Mount struck home. The last shall be first, the weak strong: it was miraculous. The words mirrored her mind and life, puzzle after puzzle. Paradox was freeing. Jesus was the center of all this complexity, the hub of the wheel. He *was* this complexity. He made it shine.

The Sermon on the Mount validated her family and supported her sensibility. It provided a frame of reference outside her situation which showed that everything in her situation was the way the Lord worked. Jesus worked paradoxically, with love and through discord, with peace and the sword. Her family's secret turmoil and failure participated in His mystery. Jesus moved in the depths of the unsolveable. He lived in hidden, unyielding puzzles.

By the time Cynthia finished high school, she wanted to become a minister. Her turmoil made sense. A deeper radiance shined through it. She had gotten enough to get started and now it was up to her to reach out to the Source of all and give others what she had been given.

Pandemonium

Pandemonium broke loose when Cynthia left for college. One man followed another, sometimes several at a time. Yet she did not feel as if she were promiscuous. A sameness ran through her experiences. The men she slept with all had their unique taste and quality. Sex was different with each one, but the basic urge that moved her toward each was constant. She felt her passion as holy. The unity she experienced through the Sermon on the Mount was embodied in her desire for men.

Still doubts came. Surely being with so many men could not be right. Her passion may be holy, but her use of it might not. Light was everywhere in sex. Surely it could not be wrong. She was determined not to give in to superficial pressures. She would ally herself with her deepest feelings and live from the inside, not the outside. But why did outside objects change so quickly? So many men? Would she ever be able to keep up with herself?

A very muffled voice, one she could hardly hear, told her that the unity she experienced in the Sermon on the Mount was deeper and different from the unity she knew in sex, even if the two also were linked. It took a long time for her to take this voice seriously, and once she did, she was more confused. If she stopped sex, she would betray herself. If she continued as she was, she would evade the voice. No matter what she did, something would be left out, a demand would not be met. The voice provided a potentially powerful insight, but no guidelines for specific actions.

For a time, Cynthia was saved by Wes. She felt contained within a safe and satisfying relationship and her promiscuity died out. She was able to study. She would have liked this easy time to last forever but eventually her need for diversity resurfaced and she felt compelled to act on it.

She fell into her familiar state of being torn apart. Her ability to study was erratic but produced ecstatic moments, like her passing sexual encounters. Orgiastic moments of mind or body helped her feel a sense of unity. However, these moments of unity were chopped-up instants which did not truly build on one another. Peaks of passion and pain oscillated with a sense of unity. If there was any learning from this period, it was that both connection and disconnection were necessary. But whether or how they were to work together remained a mystery.

After college, Cynthia went across the country to divinity school. She achieved periods of temporary peace by organizing herself around the pastors she helped. Her swings between peace and pandemonium were deeply rooted and it was only a matter of time before all hell broke loose. A series of minor cataclysms culminated in the major one, when she finally was forced to resign her position in order to save the man she worked with. She never finished divinity school. She felt horrified at being caught up by forces she could not control but recognized the strength in having followed her nature. If she was brash and arrogant, she was also sincere. If desire made her weak and vulnerable, she was also accessible, alive and real.

She was shipwrecked but not defeated. She drifted. It was a relief to do nothing. Cynthia did not want to see Wes during this period, but in the end she had to, in order to endure. She had been relieved to be away from Wes and wondered to what extent she had gone to divinity school to escape him. Her pattern was to go back to him when things reached an unbearable point. He took the edge off the pain and made it possible for her just to be. She would have preferred the purity of going it alone. She knew her sense of adventure would spin her away from Wes. He would simply be one ingredient, if a special one, in the kaleidoscopic confusion that was her life. But only with him in the background could she risk her aloneness.

The Law

As Cynthia drifted, fantasy and reality *felt* indistinguishable or reversible. She never lost her boundaries as a psychotic individual might. She remained oriented in time and space and was not delusional in any clinical sense. What shifted was her ability to tell what was real and what was fantasy in a profound sense. Was the farm a fantasy and life outside it real, or the reverse? What was real, what fantasy: her impulsive sex life, the constancy of Wes, the demands of the community, a mystical sense of unity? Everything seemed dreamlike.

In the midst of her quandary, Cynthia conceived the idea of becoming a lawyer. Law might be the ideal compromise. It was concrete enough to sink her teeth into, yet principles were involved. Law meant fairness. As a lawyer, she could help people, especially those in need. Maybe she was a dreamer, but law would keep her tied to reality. It was something she could use and give herself to, something she could learn.

She felt unfit for the ministry, but her vices would not be out of place as a lawyer. A lawyer who had many love affairs would not be living a lie. She knew pastors slept around, too, but she had to deal with her own conscience. As a lawyer, she could pursue whatever life-style worked or was necessary for her, without feeling two-faced.

In law, there was less danger of hypocrisy and evasiveness. Either she mobilized herself to meet specific challenges or failed as a person. As a lawyer, she could not be a wolf in sheep's clothing. Everyone knew what lawyers did and were supposed to do. She would not have to suffer the humiliation of using the Word as a political machination. She would have her tasks and employ what means seemed best. She would not stand in the pulpit and use God's Word as a means of ingratiating or advancing herself. If she were a whore, she would not have to use her religious life whorishly. Law seemed a way of keeping herself in the world and maintaining integrity.

The issue of what was real or fantasy would be settled. It would be irrelevant. Whether law was real or fantasy, she could help others with it in very tangible ways. Whether she was real or fantasy, she would have to be effective with other people in order to do any good. Law might be ambiguous, but she would not have to be deceptive. Surely there were unscrupulous lawyers and ways of misusing the law. But one can try to be humanitarian and do the best one can. Law would be her ministry.

Our First Meeting

Our first meeting was really several months of once-a-week meetings. A cluster of impressions and questions that arose in those first months belonged together. Our last session, three years later, was like a first meeting also, but with a different tempo, tone, and direction. It was enriched by what we passed through and Cynthia seemed more rooted in her choices.

There were many questions. Who was this new person who made me feel so happy to see her? I was afraid she would not like me, that I was too awkward or crude for her. She was taller than I and more graceful. How delicate the bones in her face and hands seemed, but her handshake was firm, tender, and inquisitive. Did she notice my anxiousness, my fear of losing her before we started?

How odd and strained therapy must seem to her. Two individuals meet together for the first time and one is expected to undress her personality in front of the other. Surely it is easier to undress one's body than to achieve the nakedness therapy exacts. One need not become totally naked in order for therapy to succeed. But an ideal of honesty remains the standard, and the art of self-deception provides raw materials for daily work.

Cynthia took to therapy like a duck to water. She worked with her dreams and drawings. She lay on the couch and talked herself out. She made use of silence and welcomed my remarks. It was as if she had been waiting for this for years.

I knew from experience what relief therapy could bring, but I knew its difficulties, too. Her initial rush of relief would not last. Discontents would surface soon enough. She would be annoyed that I spoke too much or not enough or at the wrong times or in the wrong way. She would find my therapeutic viewpoint irksome or burdensome and my language intrusive. She would be furious that I was trying to take her over or that I was not directive enough. She would not be able to get past what was wrong with me. She would stare at my weak spots and become unbudgeable or leave.

It took me awhile to realize that Cynthia would stay for whatever needed to happen. I would have to do an extremely bad job in order to drive her away. Security on the therapist's part is a luxury, even a liability. Too much comfort blunts sensitivity to shifts in mood and meaning. Changes in the therapist's well-being often are his most important tool for understanding what is happening. Nevertheless, as time went on, I was grateful to feel more at ease. Cynthia would wait for therapy to help her.

I was grateful that Cynthia was seeing me. I fancied she was someone I might fall in love with and pictured getting together when our work was over. Would my professional ethics have been strong enough if I were not a family man?

The Giraffe Shakes Hands

For some time, Cynthia's discontent pivoted around the fact that we were seeing each other for therapy and were not mates. At first I had to ask myself if I did not create this state of affairs. Did I seduce her into wanting me because I wanted her? Was I invested in her wanting and needing me? My answer was, "Yes, of course. But it would be grandiose to take all the credit."

Cynthia's agony with Wes became centered on me. For so many years, she had not been able to "solve" her relationship with Wes. He remained her on-and-off partner, her security blanket, someone she could not give herself to nor break away from. One reason she started therapy was to get help in marrying Wes or breaking up. She was thirty-one and wanted children and a family. She wanted to work but did not want work to be her whole life or even the most basic part of her life.

Cynthia had almost finished law school when she sought help. She was a clerk in a well-known law firm which she stayed with after graduation. Cynthia was outgoing and liked many of the people she met but felt she was not aggressive enough as a lawyer, especially in court. She was amazed at how nasty and crude lawyers and judges could be in the courtroom and made a concentrated effort to be louder and more assertive so that she could do justice to her clients' cases. She was ill at ease with her new persona and started to doubt her decision to be a lawyer, but there was no going back.

The people she met stimulated her ambition. She imagined

going into politics, winning great cases, and building a reputation as someone formidable and compassionate. At fashionable parties, she met men who seemed right for her: quick-witted, handsome, estimable. Conversation never lagged. They danced from one topic to another and she felt bright and effective, a professional in a world of professionals.

Wes paled by comparison. She felt held back by him. He followed her from city to city and moved in with her. She never lived alone or spent much time with herself. To be alone was unnatural, although she inwardly felt isolated since childhood. It became important for her to get her own apartment and withstand the upheaval such a move would cause. Once she made the move, she was surprised to discover how proud and relieved she was to have her own space for a time.

Her affairs with brilliant men she met were satisfying yet irritating. For a time, she felt affirmed by her new friends. She proved that she could be on a par with them. They liked talking and doing things with her and wanted to sleep with her. She was attractive and able. But there seemed to be a tension as to who was going to be in control, a battle to keep a competitive edge. This was as true in sex as in rhetoric. Winning or calling the shots seemed to be the most important driving force in the lives of those she admired.

The witty banter of her new partners no more fulfilled her than Wes's silence. They spoke about world affairs, law, government, politics, real estate, and the stock market. Some were idealists and worked for good causes, but mostly their own egos were at stake. Cynthia had to tune into their wavelengths or their words washed over her. They seemed dedicated to their monologues rather than seeing and responding to her as a person.

The gap between Cynthia's inner being and persona was painful. She could force herself to do well with work and friends if she made herself sharp and narrow. She grew in strength and ability at the price of something in herself she felt was precious. At times, she expressed the gap between herself and her life by describing herself as an awkward giraffe. As she walked down the street her head felt far above her body and gangling legs. Men turned and looked at her and she knew why but wondered, "Don't you see? Can't you see—I'm just a giraffe?"

At the outset of our work, she wished the giraffe would vanish.

COMING THROUGH THE WHIRLWIND

It did not fit her image of a successful person and ruined the way she hoped to look and feel. She loved the moments when the giraffe vanished and she was free and graceful. Yet she judged people by whether or not they valued the giraffe when it appeared. Cynthia began to feel that the giraffe was the key to her personality, and if no one really took *it* seriously, no one took *her* seriously.

She could let the giraffe out as much as she liked with Wes. She could be any way she wished with Wes and he did not seem to mind. He just wanted Cynthia to be with him and the form she took did not matter. He waited her out in confidence that the happy Cynthia would come back again. Wes's motherly obliviousness infuriated her. She was bound to him by the comfort he provided but infuriated by his easy-going tolerance. Cynthia wanted to be seen, not tolerated. She counted on but could not bear Wes's even-handedness. Cynthia needed to goad him into a more biting and significant awareness of her. She wanted to feel the realness of meaning something to someone.

Cynthia's professional friends and colleagues knew about the giraffe but did not care. For them, feelings of awkwardness or inferiority were background states to be taken for granted and ignored or mastered. They did not carry any important message. One treated what was cumbersome about oneself as noise or a barrier to be bypassed or overcome. The idea that an inner giraffe might be valuable in its own right and have a contribution to make was alien. Awkwardness was charming in children and a painful nuisance in adolescence. Adulthood was a time of power.

In the wake of Cynthia's realization that she was even more alone than she had realized, she turned to me. I was always there in the background, like Wes, but I was a successful professional. I was sensitive, stimulating, and comforting. I combined the best of both her worlds and seemed to lack the evils. Moreover, she sensed my appreciation of the religious dimension of life. More than once, she remarked that this, above all, made it possible for her to work with me.

She made it clear that she knew I was not perfect and outlined some of my faults. She knew I thought of other things when I was with her—my mind drifted. She caught me dozing. Sometimes I sounded crazy or mean or terribly wrong. I could be sharp and biting or boring. She suspected I might be asocial and awkward like herself. But she loved my giraffe and felt my love of God and the depths made up for everything.

Ends of sessions became more difficult. Cynthia did not want to leave, nor did I want her to go. I looked forward to seeing her but our time together became a problem. The delight I felt was painful. Each meeting we wondered—would this be the one, would it happen now? It became an achievement to get through each session.

We usually shook hands at the end of sessions, a custom Cynthia initiated at the outset. Now I looked forward to these handshakes. They said everything. Our palms were warm, moist sexual organs. They met across an abyss and returned to an abyss. They were shooting stars that exploded on contact and sent shivers through me. Sometimes our touch was lighter than anything imaginable.

I became attached to these handshakes and Cynthia could withhold them to punish me. We reached a point when I never knew whether or not she would extend her hand. I was at her mercy. When she touched my hand, I felt confirmed and when she left without a sign, I assumed the session failed. I *knew* this was not so but passion interprets events its own way.

Sometimes I extended by hand first and she responded with happiness and relief. When I did this, she could also make me feel that I breached a trust, that I had gone too far or not far enough. Her touch was forgiving and promising, yet also accusing, as if I had done something wrong, or not right enough, and my extended hand was a sign of it. At those moments, I felt that I might never do anything right and I was convinced that Cynthia was bitter.

The Containing Mind and Holding Heart

One of the dangers of therapy is that the patient's neediness can be preyed upon in subtle ways. The therapist is needy, too.

Patient and therapist can exploit each other. Often the exploitation is not directly sexual. Patients and therapists rarely sleep together. They prey upon each other's ego and exchange forms of self-worship or idolatry. The therapy partners, hungry for contact and understanding, can hide together as in a hothouse and grow in strange ways.

Was I preying upon Cynthia's need or she upon mine? Was I making myself the center of her universe and vice versa? Was she making herself important to me in a way she failed to do with others? Was our growing importance to each other the way therapy was supposed to work or another form of illness? I felt torn apart.

It dawned on me that I might be feeling precisely what Cynthia felt in her torn-apart states. To what extent was my pain a message about Cynthia as well as myself? My training taught me to question everything that happened during a therapeutic session. Was I colluding with Cynthia in setting up the kind of situation that she went through with others? Did she constellate an incestuous pull (with brother, father, mother) in order to repeat and work through early wounds and longings? Was I being Cynthia's double by feeling at her mercy and unable to do anything right? Did my helplessness enable her to experience an upsurge of power? She could enact the role of the sadistic authority and enjoy the victim's revenge. Through our relationship, she could taste strength and helplessness more purely. Cynthia's face and fingers touched my heart, but at the same time met a steel-trap mind.

The steel-trap mind is not simply an observing, evaluating ego. It also upholds the integrity of experience. It rescues joy and pain from oblivion and finds meaning in these twins. It certifies and enriches what is precious to us as well as what is horrible. It aims at truth and bursts illusions. Was Cynthia's radiance real enough to withstand the steel-trap mind? Would the steel-trap mind dissolve the magic?

For me, Cynthia's face was a joy forever. I did not want it destroyed. Yet the truth of feelings must be more, not less than analysis. Joy without risk remains infantile. At the same time, I almost hoped that our feelings for each other would not survive analysis. I was not about to destroy the family life I built. Cynthia tested my mind and heart. My love affair with therapy competed with my desire for Cynthia.

I allowed Cynthia's impact on me to build. I could not shut myself off from her if I wanted to and became more aware of the contrast between the ways her face and hand made me feel. I felt centered when I saw or imagined her face and thrown off balance by her handshake. Vision and touch threw me into different worlds. It was all right not to touch her face. Her face made me feel a spiritual radiance. It evoked an inner light. But the thrill of her touch made my hands want more of her in the most concrete way possible. When she withheld her hand, I was lost. When our hands touched, I also was in danger of losing myself. With touch I became a center of vacillation: will we or won't we?

The contrast between vision and touch need not be so great as they were in my experience with Cynthia. Often enough, seeing leads to touching and vice versa. Our senses work together. But with Cynthia, my senses were working on different planes. What an unbridgeable, if delicate, gap existed between spirit and flesh, and what a most delicate intermingling. Above and below tugged against and permeated one another. Was this an artifact of the therapy situation? Would sight and touch dovetail more perfectly if we were not therapist and patient?

If I could not tolerate my conflicting emotions, how would Cynthia build a tolerance for hers? Part of the therapist's job is to find a way of encompassing tensions inherent in therapy. This is an impossible task but one tries as well as one is able. Therapy touches the longings and weak spots of therapist and patient alike and often is in danger of breaking down.

I saw Cynthia's giraffe in my predicament. The long neck separates, as well as bridges, head and body. The long legs keep one high off the ground. How will head and body get together? How will both get grounded? I was Cynthia. My job was to bear being Cynthia as well as myself. To be torn apart between mind-body or spirit–flesh was the principal fact of our work.

The intensity of our attraction for one another diminished in time, although never ended. Through all our changing states, we kept on working. Sometimes a silent session expressed the violence of our longings but we did not die out for long. Psychic life is restless. One production follows another. Inner concerns have their rhythms. The need to grow presses against, interweaves with, and explodes barriers. We had more than we could do to keep up with ourselves. Cynthia's dreams were stepping stones. We moved from dream to dream and kept plunging in.

Eating Indians

Cynthia moved in and out with Wes three times in the three years I knew her. She never stayed separated for long. She enjoyed periods of being on her own but liked the solace she got from Wes. Her attempts to break away were unsuccessful. If she did not call him, he would call her, sounding pitiful. He tried his best. He went into therapy, and for a time Cynthia had joint sessions with Wes and his therapist. They tried seeing each other as friends. In the end, he moved in with her again and she loaned him money to start a business. However, she insisted that their arrangement was tentative. She needed to feel that she had the freedom to do otherwise if she wished.

Cynthia visited her parents several times a year and usually came back fragmented and depleted. After two years of work, a breakthrough occurred. She had a good time at home mainly because she was able to be more active with her mother. Following is an excerpt from her session after returning, which includes an important dream about eating Indians.

CYNTHIA "I would not let her get to me. I was determined not to be cowed. I don't know where it came from—it was a new feeling. I just said to myself, 'This is it. It's over. I will not let her get to me—no matter what.'

"When I got back from the farm, New York looked awful. I felt great about what I did with my mother, but I'm not sure if it was superficial or really came from a good feeling about myself. I feel stifled by my job and Wes. He's spending a lot of time at my place. We're going to live together again.

"What am I doing with my life? I sit on myself to go through the day. I do what I have to. I'm not too

wild about Wes. In fantasy, I tell him I can't take it
and must have another relationship. He says OK.
Just as I'm about to leave, I envision going through
the whole thing with someone else and I go after
Wes. I don't want to throw everything away. If I stay
around, New York will seem OK again. I'm glad I
didn't take my bad feelings out on Wes."

M.E. [Did struggling with and containing my feelings
toward Cynthia help her tolerate herself better? She
did not like a lot of her life but she worked with it.
Instead of leaving Wes and starting over for the ump-
teenth time, she had a fantasy about it. She valued
Wes and her relationship with him and did not want
to throw it out like garbage. She did not want to
spoil it or make it worse than it was. She felt less
spoiled herself. Perhaps being more herself with her
mother enabled her to be more inwardly active with
Wes.

Was I having a bad influence on Cynthia? Was
my attitude making her adapt to life instead of
changing it? Did my not going after her foster her
putting up with things as they were? Did my tolerance of our situation teach her to make do and get
along and not aim for the best? Was I teaching her to
give up or compromise? Were we both sitting on
ourselves?

I was happy that she did so well with her mother
and that she felt strong enough to handle her bad
feelings with Wes in fantasy. But at what price? Was
she catching my despair over not having her? Was
she building an inner world and becoming more centered? I felt trapped by guilt and self-doubt and said
nothing.]

CYNTHIA [Cynthia responded as if she heard my thoughts. She
said she valued her love for Wes and his for her and
did not want to attack it as she had for so many
years. Of course, she would have to go on attacking
it. But she was amazed it survived her poor treatment. She felt that at least her love for Wes was real,
if it was not all she hoped it would be.] "Wes *is* my

reality. Our relationship is not simply make-believe. We love each other. I wish Wes *knew* me, too. I get furious and want to make him *see* me. Sometimes I think he wants to but just doesn't know how. He can't help it. He's just who he is. I can't expect him to know me as I do. He's *not* me."

M.E. "He's as much not you as you're not him?"

CYNTHIA "We're each other, too, in ways but not in all the ways I'd like."

M.E. "You don't like it but you can live with it?"

CYNTHIA "I hope it's better than that."

M.E. "I hope so too." [I sided with what Cynthia said was *real* for her, but I could not suppress doubts. I knew patients dress to please (or frustrate) the therapist's desire. Perhaps Cynthia thought I wanted her to marry Wes, that I would feel successful in her life stabilized, that I would be relieved if she firmly planted herself with someone else. Yet my doubting consciousness reached only so far. Life carried her along. Cynthia's voice came from a deeper place than my doubts.]

CYNTHIA "I dreamt I was getting married. The gown wasn't ready. It was still at the dry cleaner. I went ahead with the wedding plans anyway.

"In another dream, I was underground with three white people and a bunch of Indians. I bought three dead Indians to eat but felt it unseemly to eat dead Indians in front of live ones.

"The first dream is easy. It shows my doubt but I go ahead anyway. I never dreamt of getting married before. Maybe I *am* getting closer.

"The second dream stops me. At home, I was alive with my mother. She was alive, too. We didn't kill each other. When I got back, I didn't kill Wes off either. I started dying. The Indians are something dead in me, something I killed off? I'm confused. It feels like a big dream but I'm lost."

M.E. [There was depression and deadness to face, but at the moment, she reached a dead end with this line. Inner deadness confused her. Here deadness was linked with eating, something active. The tension between eating and deadness might lead to something. I decided to support this tension and see what would happen.] "I'm wondering what stopped you from eating the dead Indians?"

CYNTHIA "It was so awkward—how can you eat dead Indians in front of live ones?"

M.E. "You inhibited yourself because of social reasons? You were afraid how you would look to others?"

CYNTHIA "Well, it *is* appalling to eat dead human beings. It's gruesome. I'm not a cannibal."

M.E. "What about the dream? Was it gruesome in the dream? Were you repelled in the dream itself?"

CYNTHIA "Well, no—not really. It was matter of fact, a thing you did. If the live Indians hadn't been there, I might have done it."

M.E. "Who sold the dead Indians to you—the lives ones or white men?"

CYNTHIA "I'm not sure now. Maybe they worked out a deal— they were in cahoots. One of the live Indians looked so sad. The others were matter of fact. They expected me to do it. But the sad one was so pitiful. I couldn't."

M.E. "You stopped out of pity?"

CYNTHIA "Yeah."

M.E. "I suppose it's good to have a conscience, but maybe you should have eaten them anyway."

CYNTHIA "The corpses looked tough and chewy. It sounds horrible.

"I don't know why—I've felt bad since coming back from vacation. I felt great about what I did with my mother but since then, it's been downhill. My office is awful. I'm a corpse. My mother spent a lot of time being dead when I was growing up. I'd pity her. We both held back. It was a kind of deadness, a deadening fear."

M.E. "You wouldn't eat her because of it."

CYNTHIA "No. I wouldn't dare. I couldn't disturb her. I was repulsed by her then. I sealed myself up and stayed away."

COMING THROUGH THE WHIRLWIND

M.E. "You pitied her?"

CYNTHIA "Pitied and hated her. She stuffed herself into me. I tried to spit out some of her and make her separate. But the pitiful Indian—his plaintive, alarmed look, like mother—stopped me cold. My pity was tied to death. If I showed strength, she went dead."

M.E. "Maybe you should say, 'Goddam it, if you're dead, I'll eat you anyway.' It sounds like you felt badly after you didn't eat the dead Indians."

CYNTHIA [Laughter] "I know what you mean. I like the idea. I always stopped myself with her. [More laughter] I feel better."

Session Afterthoughts: Strange Eucharist

I felt better, too. Cynthia was able to create an inner image of a wedding, although with qualifications. Her gown was still at the cleaner (therapy). Would our hand ritual have to dry out before she could marry? Her dream picture of a wedding lacked detail. It was undeveloped but it made her happy. It was now a possibility her unconscious could envision and work on.

Depression often involves rage against the self or poor self-esteem coupled with a sense of helplessness. Surely holding back rage at Wes contributed to Cynthia's depression. But Cynthia also raised her self-esteem by achieving this bit of inwardness. For years, she raged at Wes without effect. Why shouldn't she try to broaden herself by trying something different?

Cynthia had liberal, humanitarian values which acted as a barrier in the "eating Indians" dream. The dream image upset her everyday categories. Cynthia was on the side of the victims. She wanted to help Indians, who were wronged by white men. She associated Indians with nature and spirit in nature (linked with her mother in the garden). At the same time, an old stereotypical image of the silent Indian tied in with her sense of something mutely inaccessible in life (linked with the withholding quality of her mother). I imagined that eating Indians would help Cynthia dig deeper into her body and Mother Nature.

Was I giving Cynthia a false lead? Perhaps she was right to resist eating the dead Indians. Cynthia already may have swallowed too much deadness. Perhaps the dream was distinguishing between the living and the dead: hello to the living, goodbye to the dead. Was pity on the side of death or life? Was I wrong in feeling that the eater was the active, baby self? Perhaps she rightly refused to buy the dead ideas I stuffed into her, like her parents.

We eat the body of the dead and risen God—but dead Indians? In the eucharist, we eat a living body, not dead ones. The message of the god-man is that faith conquers death. However, the eucharist may take many forms. One cannot avoid deadness in life, nor ought one make it one's only food. If inner deadness is not faced and worked with, death spreads and is inflicted on others. Mothers feed infants death mixed with life. No mother is fully alive all the time, yet babies stay active and get what they want, even when mother is temporarily vacant. To an extent, the child learns to enjoy eating and copulating with corpses. It should not be his primary experience but it is an unavoidable one which he must make the best of.

Was Cynthia's god a dead Indian? Was eating dead Indians perverse or potentially freeing? Ought I trust my feeling that something good was happening? Was I white-washing myself? Did my self-doubt mirror Cynthia's need to attack good feelings or was it an appropriate response to my own self-indulgence?

The dream image itself was our only fact. It could not be seduced by interpretations. The possibility of eating dead Indians was not anything that Cynthia or I would have consciously devised, nor was it exhausted by our ideas about it. The dream scene was startling and intriguing, something to bounce off of, something for experience to gravitate around. It was freeing to think about it. What it might mean must, in part, remain a matter of vision, sensibility, and taste. Cynthia's laughter broke shells of doubt. But after laughter one starts again.

COMING THROUGH THE WHIRLWIND

Getting Ready

For several months after the preceding session, there were very few external changes in Cynthia's life and no momentous inner happenings. She spoke about the same old things: what to do about Wes and her job. She had misgivings about having given Wes money to start a business which was doing poorly. She did not like herself in her job, partly because of the sort of job it was. The law firm was a good one but not interested in anything other than making money. It expected high quality legal work, so Cynthia learned a lot. But she felt she was learning how to run a machine that did not make anything she wanted to use.

Cynthia spoke about herself, her parents, friends, Wes, and me in familiar terms. She went back and forth between things she did and did not like, without much intensity of feeling. Her chronic indecisiveness (should she get another job, marry Wes?) made her restless and uncomfortable but caused no great pain at this time. What struck me was the positive tone that ran through her obsessive thinking. It was almost as if she liked going around in circles for the pleasure of exercising her mind.

So much can happen when we mark time. Often hidden work goes on: consolidation, incubation, preparation. As the mind races around old tracks or goes blank, variations can occur and new directions emerge. If nothing else, marking time can be soothing and provide a respite. I also wondered if Cynthia was toning down in anticipation of our summer break, although it was still some months away. My overall sense was that she was enjoying a calm period in which she could test herself in a relatively unruffled way. I could feel a muted excitement and turbulence but, for the moment, there were few violent irruptions.

The sense of excitement and movement within safe confines was amplified in her dreams. In one dream during this relatively relaxed period, Cynthia was in a used clothing store, trying out wild, adventurous clothes. A man wanted her to make a comparison with other clothes and choose which to buy.

Cynthia doubted whether marriage would satisfy her need for adventure. She oscillated between her needs for stability and variety. She felt the wedding gown in her earlier dream and wild outfits in the present dream encompassed a polarity in her nature. In therapy she could link both urges for a time. She tried out wild impulses within the confines of a used clothing store (therapy). Nevertheless, she felt pressure to make a choice, presumably from me but also from her own developmental needs. Hopefully her choice would make room for safety and adventure. No solution was in sight.

In the same session Cynthia reported an image of men with the words, "Men are all curious." She spoke of her brother's and her own sexual curiosity, the freedom and intrusiveness of men, and her own swarming, inquiring mind.

She then related what she called a big dream, one that felt most important. In this dream Cynthia and her mother lived in the same apartment. They considered moving to a bigger, more costly place. A bigger place might be better if Wes joined them. Young men in the real-estate business wanted their decision. Cynthia and her mother were on the balcony watching teenagers jump and roll from a big tree to the riverhead. There was a secret place for enjoying love by the tree. Cynthia and her mother did not like being rushed by the real-estate men and decided to keep their apartment without a separate bedroom. For the time being, they felt comfortable, although Wes was not there yet.

In the dream Cynthia felt a closeness with her mother that was rare in real life. She could admit their sameness more deeply. Once her mother must have seemed like everything to her. The dream captured what was peaceful in their relationship long ago, when they loved and were comfortable with each other enough of the time to support Cynthia's good feelings about life. For the time being, the real-estate men's offer of a larger place with separate bedrooms was rejected. Cynthia watched the teenagers' healthy activity from a safe distance. Wes had not come yet. The individuating effect of men and her own active urges was postponed. It was a time to be with mother without disturbances.

She and mother had once been playful with each other. Perhaps she needed more time with mother in order to encompass the activity symbolized by males and teenagers from a safe base. Would she postpone the real-estate men's inviting intrusiveness, the teenagers' tree of life, and Wes's arrival forever? Or would the peaceful interlude with her mother enable her to extend herself less defensively than in the past?

COMING THROUGH THE WHIRLWIND

The ability to be together peacefully without ultimately sacrificing integrity was precious. Marking time with her mother, standing hand in hand, looking out the window of the world, was a blessing. Real strength might grow from it.

Our relationship created a mother she needed or gave the mother she needed back to her. Our ability to be together quietly without loss of integrity allowed Cynthia to feel that mutual closeness, empathy, and responsiveness were possible. Perhaps, too, sustaining an image of a warm relationship with a good mother foreshadowed the growth of Cynthia's ability to mother herself. Perhaps some "drying out" foreshadowed by the dry cleaner dream (p. 74) happened.

It would have been possible to emphasize Cynthia's envy of men and, particularly, myself. My intrusiveness, curiosity, erotic feelings, and demand for growth could be read in her dreams: therapist as clothes salesman, real estate salesman, teenage playmate, partner in hidden sexuality, co-seeker of the Tree of Life, and potential mate. We discussed such possibilities and much more. But in the end, the dreams and the experiences they expressed were hers. The need to decide, the bubbling activity (like laughter), the demand for more in life, the wish to simply be—were hers. My primary job was to let her have her own experience, just as I, too, had the right to mine. The main lines of development have to push through a good deal of psychic noise.

An important consequence of Cynthia's experience of her dream mother was that Wes was *not* mother. For once Wes was placed on the other side of mother. For the first time in any of Cynthia's productions, Wes appeared as a man allied with men. He did not have to play mother. He could be a man with the mothering function as part of manliness. Perhaps he had served his function as an *ersatz* mother and could emerge as a larger figure or collapse into oblivion.

In Cynthia's case, getting back to or recreating mother produced a greater psychic order. On the one hand, the males in her dreams symbolized the activity between mother and herself, but also represented the world beyond their dual unity. A chance for the constitution of otherness emerged because sameness was admitted or, better, a level had been reached in which sameness–otherness created each other.

EIGEN

Container and Hostage

Over the summer, I thought that Cynthia's determination to be herself with her mother marked a turning point. Her ability to sustain the fight and distance required was a growth in autonomy. This, paradoxically, led to an experience of greater closeness with mother and herself. When I thought of Cynthia, I thought of the movement, perhaps a rhythm, between self-affirming activity and communion.

When we met again, I learned that Cynthia had spent most of the summer building up the courage to leave her job. Her unhappiness at work was all she could think of. Perhaps it was the only area in her life she felt she could do something about. She could not control my vacation or solve her relationship with Wes. She felt tied to law and did not want to begin searching for her vocation all over again. But perhaps she could find a way of practicing law that was more in accord with her basic values.

In several months we would be completing our third year of therapy. If Cynthia left her job, she would lose the insurance that enabled her to pay my fee. I was anxious about this, especially because I did not want to lose *her*. She was torn between the benefits of her present position and the loss in status and income she might have to endure. I feared I might lose if I helped her but what a greater loss if I didn't. I enjoyed the fantasy that we might be friends if therapy were over, but my life would have had to be different for that to happen. The idea of what might be remained a pleasureable pain.

I was aware that Cynthia's wish to change jobs could be a way of expressing dissatisfaction with therapy. Often the two go together and we discussed this. But it felt more like her life was finding its own level, and it would be an error to stand in the way.

Our work went on with a momentum of its own. Image followed image in her dreams. It was as if her psyche were resetting itself. We *felt* something was happening and usually did not *know* what, although we expressed ideas and convictions. An objective thread of development pushed through parenthetical considerations.

Part of the work involved continued growth of a psychic containing function. Following is a brief conversation we had about one relevant dream image.

CYNTHIA   "I dreamt of a church on granite poles. Between the poles on the ground was a box. It was metal and looked like a Calder [sculpture]. I picked it up. It was light, empty, unconnected. I carried it out." [Cynthia mused about the box, then fell silent.]

M.E.   "It's always handy to have a container."

CYNTHIA   "It was sturdy, hard to open, no handle. I opened it. There wasn't anything in it."

M.E.   "It's ready for anything. You never know what wants to get contained."

CYNTHIA   "Not mother, not father. A whole, new possibility."

We might have filled the box with many contents: mother, father, sex, religion, therapy, work. We could have dwelled on the obvious reference to being opened or closed (vulnerable–invulnerable), empty, unconnected and depressed, her lack of marriage and baby, her lack of promiscuity. A container has many uses. For the time being, we let the box stay empty, as it was given to Cynthia, although she opened it. The ills of the world did not fly out of this box. Perhaps its emptiness was an ingredient Cynthia needed. Perhaps this little box was a place, a little blank screen, where unconscious fantasy and revery could grow, like Calder's firm, fluid pieces.

In the next session, the container theme was taken further and some of its contents were elaborated. To Cynthia's chagrin, a potential inhabitant of the box was her father. She dreamt that he had been taken hostage on a college campus, taken in tow by a big man who wrapped his arm around him. She could not see her father's face but he was silver haired and smaller than in real life. Cynthia felt protective of him, as if he were sweet and old. She was ready to fling herself between her father and the strong man but went back to her room. Gladiators ran to where her father was, and Cynthia feared that would start the bloodbath. What should she do? Call the governor or police? Perhaps the bloodbath began.

Dreams often wound us by choosing just the contents we

would prefer to overlook. When Cynthia thought she had gone beyond father problems, her dream threw her back into them. The campus was a container that had to deal with her father and impending catastrophe. Her father, once enormous, now seemed small and faceless, and Cynthia felt protective of him. It was important for her to be able to feel pity and compassion, but she chose to leave him and go to her own room.

Why was Cynthia's father represented as a hostage? Was I—so often tied in knots—her therapy hostage and she mine? At times, Cynthia felt that she used her body as trap. She seduced and controlled men with female containers. She pitied men while she held them captive and spoiled or washed them in blood. At such moments she enjoyed exercising the faceless compassion of the breast, at the same time that one of her greatest dreads was realized: how helpless we are in the face of our own destructiveness.

The movement of the dream was toward the obliteration of all psychic contents. Who would be left after the catastrophe? The governor and police were ineffectual remnants of authority. Was Cynthia safe in her room? Would she alone survive as witness? Was the dream heading toward a null point or the nakedness of a new beginning? To what extent was her container now self-cleansing? Did catastrophe help keep the psychic universe clean?

A definite advance was that fighting was in the hands of specialists (gladiators, kidnappers, the strong man). This division of labor suggested that more tension could be tolerated, even if it might be undone. The strong man was not seductive. Cynthia's sense of her body as trap did not exhaust his significance. His strong arm expressed brute force in life and how powerful–powerless Cynthia could feel and more.

The psyche is more than the sum of its products. The strong arm points to mysterious unconscious processes in which disaster plays a role. Our dreams repeatedly force us to build up a tolerance for disaster. Over and over, the age-old story of helplessness and catastrophe brings us to our breaking point. The self tries to humanize this predicament with its commingling of pity, panic, and aloneness. There are greater powers in life than Cynthia's father or everyday authorities. Cynthia's inner father and her relationship to him would be broken down and reworked. We learn to work with violent psychic processes as part of personal development.

COMING THROUGH THE WHIRLWIND

In and Out of Containers

Cynthia's next dreams (the night after the preceding dream, reported in the same session) provided variations that helped place her need for a container in perspective. In one of them, she drove a 1950s car that Wes had fixed up. The car rolled back on an incline. Cynthia let it roll too far, and it landed in a ditch filled with water. As water started to fill the car, Cynthia calmly rolled down the window. Her stomach sank. She was scared but methodically climbed out. She thought about the loss of the car and pictured how Wes would feel. She walked to the store to tell him his car was under water in a ditch. He'd probably be glad to see her after all. The ruin of the car was not so important as she feared.

Cynthia's overall feeling after telling me this dream was one of gratitude for reaching a level of life in which love was primary. She knew it was true that Wes accepted her regardless of her destructiveness. She had been careless with something old-fashioned that he offered her. She needed to test him to see if he valued her for herself, not for appearances or materialistic reasons. None of this was new but the dream enabled her to feel it more nakedly. In ditching the car, she felt she discarded a shell. She had been encased in metal armor. She could now give up a mechanical container and be reborn through the water.

Many questions remained. Was the car Wes's persona? Wes's body? A part of his ego ideal or an aspect of his individuality? And, through Wes, did the car suggest something mechanical in the containing function of Cynthia's mother? Did Cynthia's relief mask a flight from depression (the ditch)?

It would be unfair to see the car as merely negative. There is a mechanical aspect to life and our bodies. We invented machines because, in part, we are machines. Machines are valuable. A car enables us to go places. For many, a car is an expression of individuality. For many, it is linked with social status. But machines have their limitations: they break down, they do not feel, metal is not flesh.

Cynthia got a lot of mileage from Wes's car but it also acted as a barrier. When does a container become overly constricting?

When is it time for it to be discarded? No container is fit for all situations. Part of maturation involves the ability to use the containers we need without drowning in them. We rebel against the containing function in others and ourselves insofar as we find it suffocating. At the same time, it is difficult, if not impossible, to give up the containers we have valued. Shedding a container is not the easy, natural act of a snake shedding its skin.

In dreams it is possible to represent the rebirth one hopes to achieve. What is not needed is destroyed and one shines forth in naked openness. Cynthia stepped out of the water anxiously but became confident that props were extraneous. What counted was something intrinsic. A person-to-person existence was possible. Her most basic value was affirmed, but it was not a noiseless or problem-free affirmation.

Whether awake or dreaming, we do not stay at our best for long. The epiphany Cynthia achieved was necessarily temporary, although it continued to act as a reference point. Soon enough, doubts and anxieties returned. After the car dream, Cynthia reported a dream fragment in which she tried hard to answer questions and wanted someone to give her a sign that she had done all right. The husband of a friend nodded yes, but Cynthia wondered if his affirmation was genuine.

Cynthia linked this dream fragment to our relationship and questioned whether my interest in her was genuine or selfish. Therapy was hard and she tried her best. Was I helping or harming her? She looked for confirmation and support and wanted me to make her feel that she was on the right track. She wanted a sign that would be *the* clue as to who she really was. It would make it easier if I possessed (contained) the secret of her identity.

In her dream fragment and remarks, curiosity, dependency, trust, and mistrust whirled about together. Her need to explore herself was enacted with another woman's husband as interlocutor. The exploration involved in therapy took place across a distance, yet involved an intimacy tinged with a sense of the forbidden. She had Wes and I my wife. The points of triangles are sharp.

The need to trust often contains a hidden violence. The next and final dream Cynthia recounted in this session referred to the violence of seeking or being a container. No amount of love or trust can escape the problem of violence in growth processes.

COMING THROUGH THE WHIRLWIND

86

The dream was vague. In it were swords, a vacuum cleaner, and pecan pie. Cynthia felt these objects were connected, although someone told her they were not.

M.E. [I mused to myself that the sword separates and imagined the vacuum cleaner as mouth or anus. A swirl of vague sensations in which Cynthia's father, mother, Wes, myself, and Cynthia commingled. I said nothing.]

CYNTHIA "I don't know. I picture a dream I had some time ago: eating Indians."

M.E. "Do you think you're eating them again—with the vacuum cleaner?"

CYNTHIA "I see my father as a ship sunk with curved ribs. The pie makes me feel it's all wasted effort, chewing around in old things. I can't get rid of anything. I chew around in this old stuff looking for something worth saving, something I need. The car surrounds me so I feel free when I'm rid of it; whereas I surround the metal thing [the vacuum] with my hand."

M.E. "Do you vacuum—suck in—your father? Are you too surrounded by him? Not surrounded enough? Do you want him in you because he's so far away?" [The sunk ship with curved ribs made me picture Cynthia's father inside her. Since she mentioned her father, I read her imagery in terms of him and myself. Was Cynthia too surrounded by me? Not enough? Was getting someone inside any better than being surrounded? Were my thoughts examples of what Cynthia meant by chewing around in old things and not getting rid of anything?]

CYNTHIA [After a good silence] "What do you suppose is meant by father?" [She referred to the hostage dream as well as my and her remarks which linked father to sunken car and ship and insides of vacuum].

M.E. "A greater power. Anything greater that diminishes you and you want to feel greater than." [I felt I was following her imagery, her lead. Was I? I might have played it safe and thrown the question back to her instead of answering what came to mind.]

EIGEN

CYNTHIA "That's pretty much everything. I wanted to take father's ribs and metal and use them so I wouldn't be afraid. What happened to them is not so reassuring."

M.E. "You need the power [father's] you want to be rid of."

CYNTHIA "I dreamt once of eating metal waste. The hard metal in my stomach made me cry. I couldn't keep it down. Mother said they'd have to x-ray me to see if the metal is all there. She wanted me to keep it down."

M.E. "She wanted you to comply—a complicity between the two of you, three of you?"

CYNTHIA "Yeah. The vacuum—the water—the bloodbath will get rid of complicity. I couldn't—can't—stomach it. I don't want all that sweet [pecan pie] and hard [metal] stuff inside me. Not the way I got it—not the way they put it in. Sweetness and hardness are OK—but not this kind, not this way."

The picture that emerged in my mind was something like the following. Cynthia put on her father (reminiscent of putting on Christ) like a coat of metal. Her father was a car or boat which got her somewhere, armor to protect and contain her. But things reversed and he became small and powerless, while Cynthia became strong as she once imagined him to be. Cynthia climbed out of him and when she took him in again, she was the powerful container, the vacuum, to use and discard him as she wished. The metal that once propped her up gave way and she was left on her own, to find deeper powers. That she might vacuum up everything that once helped or harmed her (make a clean sweep, clean everything out) was scant comfort, since she would be left with nothing. Nevertheless, she refused to fall back on the false strength foisted on her by her mother, a wounding strength. She could not stomach the shit (waste) metal her mother fed her. She did not want her stomach (container) filled with hard or sickeningly sweet, alien matter. Perhaps she wanted to leave room for something truly worthwhile and digestible to happen. It remained to be seen to what extent she could do this, since the ability to live in a worthwhile way cannot be taken for granted.

Do such constructions take one closer or further from living experience? Did my mind prematurely give form to Cynthia's communications or did it help a healing process evolve? So many other alternatives were possible. Two people in a room together can only say or think what they are given to say or think.

Cancer, the Bird Man, and Marriage

Cynthia continued to depict catastrophes in her dreams but did not seem to be overwhelmed by them. Her dream catastrophes mirrored important aspects of her condition but also functioned as stepping stones in a growth process. The movement from bloodbath to sunken car dream above was not only from a more global to more circumscribed catastrophe. Cynthia worked her way to a sense that faith was a valid response to catastrophe. The self moved through the danger of being obliterated (annihilation by war or flooding) to the sense of value that comes from being lovingly known.

Cynthia's dreams of catastrophes began early in life and so antedated therapy. However, in therapy, they could also be taken as indicators of catastrophic aspects of the therapy relationship, including the impact of the therapist's defects and more general upheavals intrinsic to growth processes. To an extent, one comes through therapy as through a catastrophe. Everything depends on the quality of one's coming through.

No human being escapes dread of catastrophe and its consequences. Human personality is, in part, a response to catastrophic dread. Some people are better off than others, more carefree, easy-going, more loved and loving. But after thirty years of clinical work, I am all too aware of the bad dreams of good people and the breakdown of happiness ("I was outgoing and enjoyed life before this happened to me"; "I always thought of myself as a strong person before this"). The price friends and family (perhaps a whole society) pay to keep one person (or group) together can be staggering.

Dread of catastrophe may be wished away by calling worry

normal (although it may be normal). Ways we unconsciously process affects may stiffen or freeze or become too narrow or loose and diffuse. The sense of catastrophe does not vanish as therapy progresses. Catastrophe is endless. Therapy supports the psyche's ability to process what it can.

The great crude rock of formless dread is turned over and over in the belly of the psyche. Facets of it are broken off and metabolized. Electrifying, flooding, and mesmerizing dread may be churned and worked on so that emotions, feelings, images, fantasies, narratives, and thoughts contribute to personal growth. Unconscious processing of "the flood" or "torment of joy" or "global horror" becomes more firmly elastic (also see Grotstein 1979).

It is cruel to say that one becomes more resourceful in face of catastrophe. No one can be resourceful enough for the catastrophic dread that personality faces. Yet therapy does foster the capacity to work with catastrophe (particularly the catastrophe we call personality or character). Perhaps therapy's most significant contribution is to help the psyche have a belly which makes digestive processes possible.

Cynthia's next dream of catastrophe was followed by her announcement that she was changing jobs and marrying Wes in the spring. She dreamed that a ninety-year-old uncle with cancer fell down, hit his head, and died. Cynthia flew to him and stayed in a hotel room with her mother. She was his favorite niece and was named executor.

In this case, catastrophe was beneficial. An old, diseased element was cleared out so that Cynthia had a chance to exercise good feelings about herself. At the time of the dream, cancer was the most dread disease we knew. As an image of psychic life, it portrayed one's horror that the self would be consumed by its own malignancy. Cynthia dreaded that her life would continue to go around the same self-destructive circles. She would grow old with nothing to show for it, a victim of her diseased brain.

Instead of metabolizing trauma, affects, and thoughts, her psyche ate itself up or aimlessly multipled unconnected bits of experience. This state of affairs was circumspectly ended by a blow on the head, a fitting end insofar as psychic cancer is a mental disease. Cynthia could never have come to a decision about her life from obsessive, intellectual ruminations (which, to some extent, an aspect of therapy may have exacerbated). Her "head" had to be put out of play so that her "belly" could do some work.

We did not spend much time on this dream, although its importance can scarcely be overestimated. Cynthia quickly went on to tell me of the new, impending changes. Of changing jobs and getting married she said, "It's out of character to do some of the things I spend so much time thinking about." Her job would pay less. It involved helping poor people with claims against landlords. She viewed it as an initial step toward being a helper of those caught up in obvious injustices. She and Wes were moving to East Harlem. "I can't do what friends say, to get another job with a big firm and marry rich. I would have felt secure with a big paying job and gotten a lot of status. Now I must go on my own merits. I don't see how I can do anything else."

Where did these decisions come from? How were they made possible now? The abrupt finality of her tone surprised me. Did she mean it? Would she really follow through? Was her growing sense of worth sound enough? Would the psychic realignment she was undergoing hold up? What was this realignment? How did it happen? Was the therapy bubble really bursting? Were her decisions life-giving or catastrophic? Were her dreams of catastrophe preparing her for the catastrophe of marriage? For a life of relative duress and poverty? With more of a psychic digestive system, decisions grow from a deeper place and have more weight and resonance than those superimposed from "above" or "outside." Was this a decision from a deeper place?

Cynthia was taken by surprise, too. As she said, it felt out of character for her to take these steps. They were so substantial and definitive. It was as if she stepped out of her character and into her Self. Yet she did not throw everything over. She did not give up on law as she had the ministry. She built on what she had. She made a leap yet felt she was going a step at a time.

Although Cynthia's decisions were practical and realistic, her dreams went their own way. How dream and reality might be connected was not often obvious, yet Cynthia acted as if they were. Immediately after announcing her new decisions, she avidly launched into a discussion of the following dream.

Cynthia kissed a man with a round face and beak nose. He sucked on her tongue with a birdlike, quick, precise motion. Cynthia's style was to sweep her tongue around in broader motions. He may have been blonde and dressed in a suit.

CYNTHIA "My mother would have approved of this guy, as he was white. His face was flat like a sundial. His tongue felt like a washing machine. Robotlike. A baby nursing with the metallic quality of my father. I tried to push him to be more sensual. He has no substance in the middle. He needs to be strengthened in the midsection. Up close, he reflects me like a mirror, more moon than sun. Hey diddle diddle, the cat and the fiddle, it's the dish running away with the spoon. I was more a talker than walker as a kid. I shit in my pants a lot. Dad liked playing with me when I smelled good but not when I'd do something like that. I'm in a topsy turvy world where everything's a lot of fun anyway."

In her talk for the rest of the session there were few further references to her decisions. She dropped into the world of dream and free association, letting her mind travel where the birdman propelled her. At first, she associated the metallic, heartless, gutless quality of the birdman with her father and men in general: how difficult it was to establish a workable rhythm with real men. But it was also clear that every time she spoke of the birdman, she said something about babyhood. The birdman was also the relentlessly active baby without concern for the other's comfort. It did what it wanted. The entire intensity of its being seemed to be concentrated in its eyes and especially its beak and propulsive tongue.

At first, Cynthia felt irritated because his movements were sharp and quick, while hers were vaguely circular. She tried to make him fit in with her rhythm without success. He was driven by his own nature or will. A discordance between them remained, neither adapting to the other. Perhaps both rhythms were necessary for the cleansing effect to occur.

Cynthia also felt stimulated and relieved. She could count on the birdman to be himself. There was something freeing about his persistence, his unshakable otherness. Nothing she could do would compromise him. She felt that his staccato insistence mirrored her own tenacity, her grip on life. She was determined to get what she wanted from herself and others. She was not going to be said no to—most certainly not by herself. She was going to do everything she could to find out what she really wanted, to find her way. And like the birdman, her striving thrived on otherness.

To what extent did the birdman refer to my own phallic aspect, the insistence of therapy, and Cynthia's developmental needs? How often I brushed her aside to get to (or grab onto) something inside her! My background made it impossible not to think that the birdman was also the "combined object," breast-and-nipple, mother-and-father, a kind of primordial rape or intercourse in which mother and infant turned into each other. Who sucked on who? Tongue and nipple became each other and exchanged roles. The active side of mother and baby achieved a heightened intensity. Cynthia's mother and father were babies who would not let go and who would not take hold. Pick your favorite fantasy. The dream image itself is the fact. The quick, insistent sucking movements of the birdman: Cynthia knew this elan and determination well. It refused to lay down and die or behave or give in. The dream image broke into Cynthia's and my own life like a fetus ruptures its sac.

The Toothless Mother: Evolution of Aloneness

In the following session, Cynthia spoke of a new dream in which her mother had no teeth. Her mother's mouth was hollow. Cynthia kissed her. She described her as cavelike, deathlike, and weathered.

Dreams often evolve via polarities. The birdman's beak and tongue and the mother's toothless, hollow mouth were part of a yin-yang rhythm. Cynthia needed to assimilate active and passive tendencies with roots going back to very early in life.

Cynthia's telling the toothless, hollow mother dream triggered her memory of another dream she'd had the week before but forgot when she spoke about the birdman in the earlier session. In the newly remembered dream, a lot of sexual attraction was going on between androgynous-looking people. Affairs and infatuations were rampant. Cynthia felt people were attracted to her but she did not want to join in. *"There was a wall between me and the rest,"* she said.

CYNTHIA "I see a few people I like in my daily life. The ones I like seem in touch with thinking and feeling but shut down sexually. There are a lot of gregarious, sexual others, the majority. That was the group in the dream. I felt alone as a little kid. I thought that was because I was a little kid. I waited for a connection to happen. It happens with people who have a deep aloneness, too, who have been to the bottom of themselves and are not just following a part put out for them."

M.E. [Ought I emphasize the wall between us, the therapy wall? The walls of our personalities, mine and hers? Lifelong isolation, hers or mine? This would be useful but more was at stake. Her speaking about those who went "to the bottom of themselves" expressed a longing, a hunger. She was battling for the possibility of psychic space, its very creation and existence.] "What about the hollow space in people?"

CYNTHIA "I'm not used to seeing others as having a hollow space inside them, too. That's a whole new way of looking at and encountering other people. I assume the other doesn't have it and is trying to do something to me. I see the other as monolithic. I put out my vibes as a barrier to keep others away. But I feel I'm a failure if I'm alone. I misuse my feelers. I could put out my feelers to think about people I know—not to dismiss them. It's a relief to think everyone has this empty space. It's not like a stomach which needs to be filled but a hollow containing something which doesn't have to spill out or go along with others.

"We used to have chromium salt shakers. They were hollow inside. Chromium and hollow. There's a lot of room inside for whatever I want to do and a strong, indestructible exterior, with holes on top for things to go out, and holes in bottom for things to go in. Smooth all over. I think of Rilke. Love: two solitudes protect and greet each other."

The toothless hag and birdman were two sides of the mother–baby relationship. Toothlessness refers to an earlier phase of infancy than biting. The bounded hollowness of the mouth recalls the uterine container and may act as an image for the birth process. The idea of birth is kept alive by the daily exchange of fluids between mother and infant. At a later stage, the idea of birth is easily transferred to the anus. There are likely moments when mouth and anus are scarcely distinguishable. One experiences sucking and expelling motions with both and may be at a loss to know if one is taking in or letting out (e.g., letting out may sometimes seem like taking in).

Cynthia used body imagery to organize experience but her sense of relationship to the other went beyond the physical. She was most alive when she spoke about the creative hollowness in people. Then she spoke with the conviction of someone at the edge of discovery.

It is not simply real or fantasy body elements that flow in and out between self and other. Immaterial moods and intentions do also. One is encompassed by more than arms. The intangible atmosphere of the other upholds, challenges, or debases us.

For the moment, Cynthia reached a fresh experience of others and herself. How precious is the hollowness within yet what distorted and frightening forms it can take. The hollow space or spacelessness within (beyond) ourselves needs to be protected. A certain hollowness at the heart of experience leaves room for something more to happen. There is no guarantee that something more will not be something worse as well as better. We fear hollowness will lose or never achieve resonance and end in bitter emptiness. Nevertheless, Cynthia and I were enlivened by her vision of "something more" in people, beings with unknowable spaces to be thought about.

The toothless mother might be a witch. But she brought the shock of contact with the unexpected. She aroused thoughts of birth and death and made one grapple with what it means to be embodied and what the body is not. The toothless mother presented herself as someone to be faced and transcended. What made her so striking was not simply the dark space she enclosed, but the open space that surrounded her. She placed a limit on things, but that very limit enclosed and was surrounded by fathomlessness.

Rage: Making Space for Self

The next week, Cynthia spoke of a dream in which her father died, followed by a dream in which she was alone with her mother looking for a hiding place from projectiles. There was a massacre, bloody bodies all around. Cynthia and her mother were doomed.

Was this another instance of catastrophe cleaning the psychic landscape or would the aftermath be a proliferation of dead inner objects and a sense of personal deadness? Was Cynthia a psychological orphan in an empty, malevolent world? Did the mother–daughter bond kill the father off so that the latter sought revenge? Did the dreams reflect a wrong turn we took that momentarily shattered her psyche or were mother and father themes naturally alternating with and feeding each other?

I tried to leave things as open as possible and simply directed attention to the devastation. Cynthia replied at length.

M.E. "Why do you suppose there is so much destruction?"

CYNTHIA "I have to fight for space in my own head. I kill them off for space. Why isn't there room for everybody? There seems to be infinite space for beings. But in my own head there's not enough space. The presence of others is threatening, it's either destroy or be destroyed. I got this impression early. To please someone was to deny myself. To please myself, I must deny others. A power struggle.

"I see it in little kids trying to define what they want to say and do. I see them trying to create space to operate in. They operate under tremendous pressure—with adults modifying their behavior, ideas, what they say, even what expression to have on their face. Erase it.

"Mom wanted me to erase it. Dad kicked me in the butt—booted me out of his presence. He didn't tell me how to behave. He was more subtle. He didn't have anything to do with me when I behaved in ways he didn't like. I felt I could kill him. But Mom bound me more to her. Killing her would have been more dangerous to myself. My elusive quality came in. Mom was dead or down on something Dad said or did. I'd appear to be in solidarity with her but slip out the back way. It was really happening to her, not me. I could go down with her, then waft up again in the clouds or somewhere else—like a dream.

"I dreamt of a dog—by itself, exploring. It's good to be myself exploring—not with others as I usually am. Would this dog go out and kill? Like a demon, monster dog?"

M.E. "Why do you think it would be so destructive?" [I was thinking that dogs are often associated with affection and loyalty, qualities in children Cynthia felt were exploited.]

CYNTHIA "I can think of ripping their throats but not what would make me want to do it. I can't feel what it would take to do it. A sense of power, an alternative to not being. But it wouldn't seem biting peoples' heads off would be an attractive alternative to just sitting there. Sometimes I feel somewhat like a monster dog. Blind rage symbolizes that there really is no connection between what I'm doing and what led me to it. I go around just destroying things. Last night, I didn't like something Wes did in the apartment and got into a black rage about his always fucking up. Even when I found out he didn't do it, I still felt like destroying things. I was puffed up. I just get tired sometimes of trying to be understanding. It feels good to shut off my mind in this wall of fire and smoke and become a dragon."

Cynthia's rage cleared a space for herself. It was not the old hostility which thrived on blaming others for her troubles. She blamed Wes for something he didn't do, but when she discovered that she was wrong, she went on enjoying her rage for its own sake. She pushed past the need to see connections and assign causality. She undercut the quiet, sneaky way she won space as a child. As a child, Cynthia pretended to be in alliance with the feared-hated other, then slipped away when the other was too self-absorbed to notice her any longer. Now the rage she luxuriated in was pure, not tinged with self-pity. If her fury was still unconsciously attached to a sense of injury, she did not use her wound as a trap or hiding place. For the moment, she felt the freedom of her mad dog becoming a dragon.

Perhaps the dog in the dream simply was having a good time with itself and Cynthia tricked herself into thinking the dog was mad. Apparently she used this dog as an excuse to give fuller expression to her rage. It helped organize the inchoate fury she felt. Nevertheless, the dog which enjoyed exploring did not get lost. It surfaced in the good feeling and humor Cynthia had in the midst of fury. She could be a dragon without harming anyone. Is it odd to think that fury need not be merely hostile? Perhaps winning this kind of space was necessary in order for Cynthia to live with someone and feel fresh.

It seemed wrong simply to tie her rage to past wounds, to mother or father. It swept past her parents. The death and destruction in her dream underwent a reversal. Fury gave rise to life. She no longer held on to being a passive victim. For the moment, she felt herself to be the center of energy in a way which made everyone (including herself) feel better. Her rage cleared the air because it was not mad or small or secretive.

Cynthia's Last Dreams in Therapy

Cynthia went to California for a week's vacation. When she returned, she started her new job. She liked her work and enjoyed the challenge of making do on lower pay, although she hoped this would not be a permanent state of affairs. She could no longer afford therapy without insurance and did not ask for a reduced fee. Wes's business was better but not well. We ended therapy at the beginning of the Christmas season.

It felt odd not to be a part of so much that was happening in Cynthia's life. In the corner of my being, I must have felt that we were one, that we had a special bond or intimacy, that she would not leave me behind. The fusional feeling in human relationships, if it is kept in bounds and structured by discernment, is often healing. It played a real role in helping Cynthia feel valued. One might suppose that Cynthia broke off therapy to escape my clutches or because we could not possess each other more fully. But that would not do justice to the sense that her life was rushing forward from its own center and that we wished each other well.

We kept on working to our last moment together. She went through her week's dreams. One night, she dreamed of an old woman, followed by another dream in which a woman used her breast like a penis to stimulate Cynthia, who enjoyed it.

The following night, Cynthia dreamed of men amputating her leg inches at a time. She was one of a large group of prisoners taken over by malevolent forces. There was great tension as guards picked out a few people to be sacrificed each day. Her mother was a prisoner, too. Cynthia was told that her sister was a prisoner but her mother did not know it. Cynthia increased her mother's suffering by telling her, then felt badly about having done so. A gong was a symbol of doom in the prison; when it sounded, those who were inside a door were going to be killed by those leading them in. Cynthia was among those to be killed. She had a sinking feeling in her heart.

Two nights later, Cynthia dreamed of a red-haired man who was also her sister. She tried to get him to leave her alone, stabbed him with a saw, but he kept coming. Cynthia went into another room to dial 911. No answer. She feared he would stab her with a saw.

The next night, Cynthia tilled soil with something like a third leg. She cruised along creating furrows, skimming wires underneath. She had a sense of pride and accomplishment.

One night later, in her last dream in therapy, Cynthia was with her cat, Dinna, shopping in a big barn for housewares at a going-out-of-business sale. The cat was afraid of being in the store and stuck its claws in Cynthia. She saw another cat and feared Dinna would get sick from it. The male storekeeper said they had a place in the basement for Dinna. Kids and dogs were there. Cynthia felt Dinna would be OK in a cage off the floor where it was dry and clean. She went back to do her shopping.

In the first dream of this series, an old woman appeared again, then Cynthia was genitally stimulated by a breast. Her vaginal mouth sucked teat and enjoyed it. Life seemed nourishing. Her earlier birdman and toothless mother emphasized the mouth, a primal center of desire. Now the vagina was included. Cynthia wanted to put good things inside herself, top or bottom.

Punishment came—amputation, doom. What a price to pay for one's pleasures. Men were fearsome torturers and executioners.

But all ended well enough. Cynthia was capable and fruitful. She was active. She worked the field. She shopped. She took care of her cat. She let a man help her. She will leave the store and enjoy what she takes home with her.

Cynthia failed in her attempt to solve her problems by calling the police. How lucky that 911 did not answer. This dream ended on the border of nightmare but the lack of a rigid solution permitted more organic possibilities to mature. Cynthia did not merely whip elements of her personality into line or intimidate herself into being better. Cynthia grew in a fuller way. She portrayed herself as a farmer and a shopper for housewares, thus making her way out of the realm of murder and punishment. She did not cheat annihilation by imposing an external order. She helped things grow and cultivated her home.

At the end of therapy, Cynthia's life was incomplete and fragmentary. She did not leave with an idealized sense of herself or our work. She did not substitute a false self for real problems. In her dreams and sessions, she dealt with wounds, anxieties, guilt, and self-doubt. Her relationships were marked with terror, hate, and happiness. They were alive. Her life was beset with problems but her relationships with men and women and herself were intense and meaningful.

If I were to meet Cynthia today, I would not be surprised to learn that she broke up with Wes again, that she was on her own or dating other men, or that she settled down with Wes or someone else. How could this be possible after our work together? In spite of Cynthia's work on her relationship with Wes, I never felt it was resolved. She was still capable of reversing herself if the spirit so moved her. I felt in her an unconquerable light, an elan, a love of life and self, a faith. And it was this, above all, that therapy supported.

Her last dreams in therapy did not mean that she and Wes would stay together. They indicated that, in spite of her self-doubts and conflicts, she was moving more deeply into life. She was more capable of working with whatever came up. Cynthia's final dreams in therapy exhibit an ability to come through catastrophe, to land right side up. One might call our work a kind of "catastrophe therapy," insofar as it validated a basic pattern or rhythm in human life. Over and over, we fall apart and come together. We die and are reborn throughout our lifetime. The agonies of the self are never left behind but we are partly transmuted through them. We move further on our way, although we might be hard put to say just what our way is. We learn to work better with what we are given, to be surprised by our gifts, and to be less afraid of ourselves.

chapter
FOUR

Ben

The Truthful Insomniac

Ben entered my office about six months after his therapist committed suicide. He did not speak so much as spat at me or, rather, I felt sprayed by his words as by so many missiles. His face reddened when he spoke and looked like a raw, wet erection. I felt a twinge of embarrassment, as if I were seeing something I was not supposed to see.

The doctor who referred Ben to me warned against letting therapy become a battle of words. "He's a good talker, but that won't help him," this kindly man suggested. Ben spoke nervously and angrily with as much flexibility as a hammer. He was clever and even brilliant in his associative flow. Like a lawyer, he possessed the capacity to use anything I said against me. Yet he was flat-footed and blind, as if his verbal powers were stuck on one or two tracks. I imagined I could find spots to move in and out of in ways that might prove useful.

Ben complained that he had not slept well since the breakup of his marriage several years earlier, and his insomnia worsened after the death of his therapist, a year after his wife left. According to Ben, his open marriage was nearly perfect. He and his wife were free to have others, yet she supported him unconditionally. She praised him and took care of his needs. She was pretty, energetic, and ready for fun. She laughingly said she would wipe his behind if he wished, and he felt she was behind him one hundred percent.

The rub was that Ben felt she was superficial and urged her to go into therapy, which she refused. He was critical of her carefreeness, a quality that also made him feel good. He could not bear her lack of self-examination and was but dimly aware of how oppressive he was. Her leaving him completely surprised him since his narcissism obliterated signs of her discontent. He felt he was the center of her universe and could not believe she could lead life independently of him. Yet she was happy without him while without her, the plug was pulled out of his universe.

Ben spent much time in his previous therapy weeping and raging over the breakup of his marriage. He was very good at expressing his feelings. To show his feelings was one of his basic credos. It was allied with his sense of truth. He was capable of becoming quite rageful if others did not express their feelings as fully and lively as he did. In group therapy, he could mask or justify his rage as trying to help bring others out. He felt his past therapist appreciated his emotional openness and his need to make others be more open.

For several years I was disarmed by Ben's ability to weep and the way his weeping seemed to be allied with his sense of truth. He could be raging at his wife's or girlfriend's deficits, then suddenly burst into tears, deeply moved by something I said or by a realization about himself that hit home. His capacity to weep made me think that for Ben words were not empty but deeply connected with feelings. I was moved by Ben's grief when he was moved by a truth about himself. Yet I was not altogether comfortable. I felt an urge to maintain some distance and protect myself from bombardment, even when Ben appeared to be defenseless. His moods changed so quickly.

It took me a long time to begin to test out the thought that Ben's rage and weeping were inextricably linked. I recalled meeting people in bars or seeing bums on the street who raged and wept promiscuously. They slipped in a well-oiled way between a sense of persecution and self-pity. Ben did not drink and was far from being a bum. But there was something sloppy about his emotionality. It was too imprecise and ready-made. His stormy tears blurred the nuances of situations. If rage did not win the response he wanted, perhaps tears would. If he could not intimidate, he cajoled. Rage or tears momentarily swept away or melted the tensions and difficulties of life. Still I was moved by Ben's love of truth, even if it contained a large dose of sentimentality. It was not *all* bogus. Not everyone cares enough to be sentimental about truth.

Ben could not control truth by words or fury or tears. His problems exasperated him and kept him awake at night. Ben was tormented by the idea, as much as the reality, of his wife's leaving. The truth of her leaving woke him up. He did not like to think that he was the kind of person she would want to leave or the kind of person she *could* leave. Her leaving him was the biggest single blow of his adult life. He was proud of his marriage. In it, he seemed to outfox life and make the best of all possible worlds. He had everything he wanted. His ego was supreme, vindicated, and happy.

He did not like to think that he was the sort of person who totally depended on another for his well-being. He liked to think his wife needed him more than he needed her. He did not like to think that she filled a hole in his being. He liked to think she added to his sense of completeness rather than masked a lack. It bothered him that so superficial a person could get along without him. How could she give up so much? How could the lie they lived have been so soothing for him? Why was it he who lay awake afraid that his being was slipping away from him, that he was in danger of spilling into space? How could he have gotten such comfort from one who hated him so?

The death of his therapist added to his sense of self-doubt. Why had he picked someone who was suicidal? He saw this man for several years and felt he ought to have detected signs of depression. It aggravated Ben that he could be so blind. He wanted to think that he was on the side of life and not secretly drawn to death. Ben grieved for his therapist but often his sorrow was less important than the assault to his pride and good opinion of himself that resulted from making a wrong choice. How could he be so wrong—about his wife, his therapist?

In a short time, life had dealt Ben a series of blows to his sense of omnipotence. At the outset of therapy with me, he raged and wept over his wife, his therapist, and his girlfriend. In time, I would be added to the list, but not for awhile. He felt helped by his various therapies, including the last one. He had raged and wept in all of them. He was not ungrateful. He had had wonderful times in his marriage and could rage and weep over his loss and betrayal. His supports had been taken away and he hoped to replace them by his present girlfriend and me, whom he could rage and weep over in turn.

Ben's insomnia did not go away, and he felt tired and taut during the days. With his nervous tiredness came a fear that something bad would happen to his body, such as heart disease or ulcers or some horrible illness. More was involved than loss of support in Ben's insomnia and dread of physically disintegrating, although wounded dependency played an important role. Ben slept well before and during his marriage. He had lived and broken up with many women and lived through a number of attachments to therapists without ill effects. But he had never felt *basically* wrong about anything. He felt confident in his decisions. He was vital and exuberant and followed his enthusiasms. He ostensibly believed in himself.

Now Ben began to be haunted by the possibility that his luck had run out and what happened to him was not simply the fault of others. His "bad choices" must reflect who he was. The double betrayal—by wife and therapist—could be no accident. It must be an intrinsic part of his destiny, a mirror of his nature. For the first time in his adult life, Ben became frightened of himself. He was terrified that in some basic way he was catastrophe prone. At the same time, he tried to wipe bad feelings away and maintain his sense that he was basically good and right and viable. He would have liked to deny his sense that he was caught in something over his head. He felt more and more constricted and flooded. But Ben was a fighter, and he would not easily give in to the idea that there might be something wrong with him.

The Forest Primeval and The Happy Fight

"It is hard to imagine worse parents than Ben's." These were the words that formed in my mind when I thought of his childhood. I took these words with a grain of salt because they often formed in my mind when I heard someone try to convey the horrors of childhood. Nevertheless, the horror of Ben's upbringing felt real to me.

Ben called his mother a "wild animal." Life with her was chaotic and stormy. She might rage one moment, then praise Ben to the heavens the next. He was her sun, the star of her life. She would do anything for him. If the slightest detail were not to his liking, she could not rest until it was corrected. Yet she tyrannized Ben with her whims and impulsive outbreaks. The whole family revolved around her will, as she revolved around Ben's. Who was the greater sun, she or he? Ben became addicted to her stream of praise and stormy emotions. This was the reality he knew, the reality with which he had to work. It formed the background of his being and became as much a part of him as breathing. Ben was horrified by his own mother, yet adapted to his horror, so that what horrified him became the basis for his sense of what was right and real.

His father was a defeated man who described his life as one of misery and tears. His self-pity alternated with fits of rage that bordered on physical violence. He was often more bark than bite but managed to make Ben so fearful and guilty that Ben gave his father the better portion of his paychecks for years. Ben's father was secretly pleased yet extremely threatened by his son's successes. He refused to drive in Ben's imported cars and made sarcastic remarks about Ben's material possessions. But before he died, he went with Ben in his new car and admitted it was fine.

Ben slept in his parents' room throughout his childhood; in adolescence, he moved into a room with his father's mother. He masturbated several times a day as a way of handling some of the tension he was under. To do this required the greatest secrecy and stealth, since he had no privacy. Ben gloated triumphantly at his ability to gratify himself in adverse circumstances. In general, he became adept at getting his way in the face of unfavorable conditions.

Ben's grandfather was a warm male presence who sometimes took Ben's side in family fights. He was the only member of the household with a room of his own. His wife refused to sleep with him and slept in a room with Ben. For Ben, aloneness was a sign of rejection and weakness: his ostracized grandfather. Yet his grandfather was the only one in the family who showed signs of having a mind of his own. He cared for Ben and acted out of a sense of justice when he sided with Ben against parental excesses. Like the rest of the family, Ben looked down at his grandfather but felt loved by him in a steadier, less crazy way than by his parents.

It was difficult to reconcile Ben's relatively happy adult life with his traumatic family background. Ben claimed that his adult life had been happy and successful until his wife left him, an event that triggered his first major depression since childhood and adolescence. Ben described much of his adult existence as positively euphoric. "I felt turned on and high most of the time," Ben said, and not by drugs or alcohol.

How did the pain of a stormy, chaotic childhood, with threats of violence, turn into such professed good feeling? Was Ben kidding himself? Did he adopt a manic life-style? How did he do this successfully? Would his mania have collapsed without his wife leaving and his therapist's death? Was Ben so out of touch with himself that he could not admit pain or had he really found a way of solving or postponing his difficulties?

In Ben's family life, everything had depended on momentary whims. Whose whim won out at any moment governed all. It was a family of crazy baby tyrants. Ben learned what it meant to be catered to if the dice rolled the right way. The art of living consisted of getting the dice to roll in one's favor as often as possible. Ben became a fighter. He tried to manipulate conditions so that success and good feelings came his way. His frequent successes with his mother and the praise she lavished on him supported his drive to be number one. He felt he could succeed often enough to make life worthwhile. The intense pleasure of his triumphant moments carried him over more difficult times. The high feelings of his better moments spilled over into, blurred, and blotted out his worse ones.

There are psychotic patients who appear to be able to anesthetize themselves to pain. In such a state, dental extractions can be performed without the patient wincing. Human beings possess this capacity with emotional pain as well. We may numb or deaden ourselves in impossible situations. We may substitute good for bad feelings. Ben had been able to ward off the onslaught of bad feelings with a sense of glory. His family life forced him to become an accomplished social and emotional engineer or go under. I sometimes envisioned Ben's early family situa-

tion as akin to a primordial ooze in which microorganisms prolif-
erate, a swamp supporting all sorts of life forms. Ben grew up in a
crazy medium, but he and those around him possessed real
vitality.

The Truth Game

Ben's professional success supported his sense of glory. He
entered the mental-health field in his early twenties and became a
well-known psychotherapist. Fame was important to him, his
dreams were filled with movie stars. He loved to be admired for
his work and had a flair for getting others in touch with themselves quickly. He easily provoked moving therapeutic experiences. Many of his patients were actors who became stars.

As a psychotherapist, Ben could be the star of other people's
lives, at least for a time. He expected and needed to be kingpin,
and one way he did this was by "sharing." He got others to show
their feelings and he showed his. Therapy was a kind of show-
and-tell game that he was very good at. He especially shined in
demonstrations before large groups of people. Ben was on top
because he helped others, who couldn't share as well, speak up.
He was the role model who showed the way. *He* helped *them.*
Others learned to do as he did. For years, it worked marvellously.

Ben lived well—beautiful homes, women, friends. He had a
great capacity for pleasure and denied himself nothing. He followed his appetites. At the same time, he pursued truth in his
own way. For Ben, enjoyment of life was part of truth-seeking. It
would be a lie to want something and not go after it, to have a
feeling and not express it. Truth meant being honest about one's
desires and fulfilling them.

It was to Ben's credit that he stayed in therapy throughout his
adult life. Therapy was part of his commitment to living truthfully. Initially he used it as a way of pulling himself together and
directing his energy. It was also part of his career ethics: he felt a
therapist should be in therapy. For Ben, therapy was a way of
staying in contact with what he really felt or what he imagined his
feelings to be. He felt superior to people who shunned therapy.

Therapy guaranteed him an added depth dimension not chosen by everyone. Therapy helped Ben play the truth game better.

Ben mastered his childhood pain by triumphs in work, marriage, and his own personal therapy. It was not until his life fell apart when his wife left him, followed by his therapist's death, that Ben could begin to grapple with his fragility and perceive how much he needed others in order to hold himself together. Throughout his adult life, he thought he chose therapy out of a position of strength. Now he was forced to admit that he clung to it out of desperation. He could not handle being thrown upon his own resources. The paradox was that in the depths of his dependency and need, he really did love truth. He was devoted to finding the truth about himself no matter what the cost—up to a point.

The Killer Faints

After our first meetings, Ben seriously doubted whether he would stay with me. He felt I was strange, too low keyed, and that I spoke a foreign language. Second thoughts about staying with me persisted throughout our nine years together. Would I mess up his life? Was I wrong about everything? Was I a fake?

In those first months, I told Ben that he lived in a mother-dominated world that lacked a viable father image to balance his emotional chaos and narcissistic lawlessness. I related his terror of disintegrating to his worry that the universe may be ruled by an implacable and capricious mother goddess rather than a loving God. My treatment plan was to help Ben develop a frame of reference beyond his mother-bound existence.

"If I said such things to my women patients, they would kill me!" he exclaimed and pointed out that my words were filled with value judgments. At such moments, he seemed more concerned that I might get away with something that he could not than with the truth or falsehood of my statements.

Ben pointed out the limitations of my remarks: my emphasis on the father vs. mother polarity was crude; a calmer, more consistent mother would have made a difference. Was I mired in sexist values? Was my viewpoint psychoanalytic? Religious? I sounded suspiciously paternalistic, a throwback to the past; I spouted stereotypes.

None of his past therapists had taken a stand with him. They helped him maintain good feelings about himself and fulfill his wishes. They did not confront his emotional lawlessness. Yet I was not heavy handed. Ben wondered if I was inviting him to join a macho conspiracy, a secret society of men. Ought he dare to? Women would kill us if they knew.

My opinions were based on my impression of Ben as impatient, rageful, sensitive, devoted, and hungrily and self-righteously needing to have his way. They also grew out of my reading of Ben's dreams, which were filled with seductive, dominating females, violent men, and movie stars—a kind of bad TV-program dream world. Ben tended to be powerless in his dreams, which explained his rageful demands during the day.

Dreams often portray sex, aggression, and helplessness. In Ben's case, these themes seemed to be inordinately fixed and repetitive. The figures expressing these themes did not seem to evolve. They remained unsophisticated and undeveloped. Sexy and bossy women mesmerized or enslaved him. Spanish, black, or poor white delinquents threatened him with annihilation. Moments of glory came with the appearance of a movie or sports star. Women seemed to exert the greatest power. Men orbited around their wishes. An exposed leg could start a war. Men fought each other but succumbed to a woman's power. In Ben's dreams, women always won out.

Not one logos figure appeared. Often dreams produce a foil or balancing figure which maintains a working tension with primitive emotional states. For example, a philosopher or priest might play a balancing role. In the Oedipus story, Tiresias, the blind seer, carries an aspect of the gnostic function. In Keat's "Lamia," a philosopher destroys the snake goddess's hold upon a naive youth; through the philosopher's action, the youth finally *sees*. Ben's dreams did not even involve bodily oriented cultural figures, such as dancers or musicians. He distributed his sense of power among figures bent on domination and destruction in a very lowbrow way, a kind of materialistic reductionism.

I found the lack of philosophical, religious, and artistic images in dreams unusual in one who had had as much therapy as Ben.

COMING THROUGH THE WHIRLWIND

Did such a lack represent a failure on the part of Ben's therapists to exert a therapeutic function or a pervasive incapacity on Ben's part to allow experience to evolve?

Almost two years into therapy, an event occurred that suggested the logos element was growing in Ben's psychic life. Ben feared he would faint when he touched a book written by one of his favorite movie stars. He grasped the bookstall to hold himself up, then ran out of the store without buying the book. No book had ever exerted so much power over Ben before.

Ben said he was shocked when he saw the star's name on the cover. He did not believe this star could write a book. His admiration became boundless. Was there nothing this star could not do? Ben wished he could write a book that people would want to read.

This was the first of numerous spells in which Ben felt faint. They came and went for about a year, and most had to do with admiration, especially of a male. But why did these spells come when they did? Ben had many opportunities throughout his lifetime to admire men and find books written by movie stars. Why now?

Ben was aware that I wrote a lot. He read and admired my papers and wished he had the patience to sit and endure the effort that sustained writing exacts. Ben often began projects but did not follow through. He confessed that he admired what he called my agility of mind. He admired my ability to be able to think of something different from his thoughts yet related to his concerns. In this regard, he wanted to be like me but feared he would fall flat on his face if he tried.

At the same time, he needed to tear me down. He felt he might have a stronger personality than mine. He was louder than I and probably could do better in a large group of people. He doubted that I could do the sorts of demonstrations he did. He would have liked to picture me as a mental freak with little social or physical aptitude.

A series of comparisons began that lasted for years. According to Ben, he was more talkative and giving as a therapist. He was warmer and shared more of himself. Yet he was intrigued and irritated by the way I maintained a friendly distance. I neither catered to nor attacked him and perhaps was too standoffish. I did not glow when he admired me, nor cringe when he attacked, but maintained a steady ground and kept on working—or so it seemed to Ben. Was I simply putting up a front or acting from my center? Apparently I mystified Ben. I was not as transparent to him as his past therapists were.

Ben was fascinated by my otherness, my difference from him, and hung on my words and actions to see if I fell flat or pulled it off. It was unclear whether his greater hope was for me and our enterprise to succeed or fail. We met at several professional gatherings, and Ben saw me dance and talk to other people. I may not have been as garrulous or as much the social butterfly as he, but I seemed to enjoy myself. My lower keyed style (compared with Ben's) challenged him. Why wasn't I overwhelmed by him and others? How could I just go on functioning? It became clear that Ben feared that unless one was overbearing and maintained the upper edge, things would stand still. Things would not happen unless one made them happen. Life would vanish if one did not keep it moving.

My type of person never had validity for Ben. He probably would have overlooked me in a group of people. Being in therapy with me forced him to begin to take me seriously. He created a polarity. If I were real, he must be unreal. To feel real, he needed to stir up excitement. He loved to overreact. Exaggerated emotions were reassuring. "You make me feel that in order to have an effect on you, I'd have to kill you," I once told him. It was difficult for him to notice or believe in a feeling unless it were magnified.

If Ben felt wiped out by my existence, he kept himself in existence by wiping others out, especially Lucy, his girlfriend. He was often angry at Lucy for one reason or another and faithfully reported his rages. She failed to dress stylishly enough, take care of the house well enough, look happy enough, make enough money, and so on. If he wanted to lose her, he was heading in the right direction, and I pointed this out to him.

Ben did not know whether or not he wished to lose Lucy, but was incredulous that rage might force the issue. He felt his rages were a normal part of everyday interchanges. He had no sense of their wounding impact. Or, rather, he felt the other person ought to be able to handle hurt feelings and learn from them. He felt right in his rages. They were truthful. Others ought to heed his rageful messages and adjust accordingly or enter a bargaining process. He enjoyed the rage of others and felt others ought to enjoy his. Ben could not seriously entertain the possibility that this behavior might be repellent. He had not learned very much from the breakup of his marriage.

If Lucy had faults, she was deeper than his wife had been. Ben could not blame her for being superficial. He raged at her for being withdrawn. Was she more like me? Ben's rage and admiration mounted, although for the first couple years of our work, he muted his rage toward me. When I asked if he felt phony modulating his rage at me, he said no, he was not as mad at me as at his girlfriend or, if he was, his admiration for me kept his anger in check. Would he be more furious with me if we lived together? He thought so, but still, admiration might dilute his fury.

When I pointed out that Lucy showed strong signs of being uncomfortable in their relationship, Ben tried to hold some of his rages back. His success was transient and intermittent, but over the years his behavior improved. For a long time, he feared that if he held his rage back, he would become withdrawn like Lucy (or myself?). He also feared that if he held his rage back, he would damage his body. Ben did not want to compromise or injure himself by holding back emotions. However, through our work, it began to dawn on him that he might injure himself by not holding back.

Changing times also forced Ben to take stock of himself. Throughout his adult life, Ben lived for the moment and squandered his resources. He felt his source of supplies was limitless and did not save or invest his money. As inflation soared, it became more difficult for him to support his life-style. He had to struggle to pay his bills. Ben hadn't given money a second thought and now feared being swept away by social and economic forces. He began to wonder how he could have lived so long without thinking about the future. He believed that I was less showy than he but built myself a solid base.

Ben began to associate Lucy's "withdrawnness" and my "distance" with depth. In some ways, we were deeper than he, or so he felt. We did not squander ourselves. We spent more time with ourselves and did not so readily spill out. Ben masturbated frequently and spent a lot of time watching TV. He imagined that I spent my evening hours reading and writing or having meaningful conversations. He became more critical of himself as a therapist and felt his work was more superficial than mine.

The self-doubt, initiated by the breakup of his marriage, tended to organize itself around his relationship to me. My personality and life, as Ben experienced and conceived it, became the center of his envious self-doubt. This movement was, perhaps, one of the most important vehicles of change in our work together. Ben's interest in me forced him to participate in the possibility of intimacy with distance. In so doing, a father principle might begin to balance his demand that the world be an all-giving mother.

Ben's envy of me made him feel faint. He connected me with books, culture, and religion. That a book could make Ben feel faint suggested that his image of me was beginning to take on power. I did not represent for him merely another competitor for mother's attention but an alternate dimension of reality. No competitor for a woman would make him feel faint. Win or lose, the battle was one he knew about and was used to. What was truly threatening was the possibility that there might be something more to life than being the center of woman's great power. The power of the Word had its own claims and requirements which no amount of narcissistic success could buy off.

Ben grew faint when he glimpsed a reality beyond the ego and maternal rejection or applause. A logos element was beginning to take hold in his psyche or, at least, find support in therapy. It is possible, too, that trying to hold rage back made Ben feel faint. Traditionally, the head is associated with solar masculinity and the father principle. Fainting exploits a weakness in the head. One might say that intense emotions blew Ben's head off. Therapy was helping Ben to reflect imaginatively upon his explosive capacity. Imaginative reflection is a strain and blanking out provides relief.

Ben's envy of me was not merely hostile and damaging. His admiration expressed genuine sensitivity. He vibrated to my love of beauty and responded to some of my remarks with religious feelings long kept away by cynicism. My relatively even way of meeting him made him feel he did not have to overwhelm the world or be overwhelmed in order to speak or listen. He wished he were as well educated as he imagined me to be and began to read deeply in his field. To an important degree, his envious admiration spurred him to move in directions that made him feel better about himself. Indeed, that Ben should feel faint because of touching a book suggested a deep love of logos waiting to evolve. Ben's rage killed it off as fast as it could be born. Yet he glimpsed it and struggled to give it room.

I do not recall further reports about growing faint after a particular session near the end of our third year together. Ben began this session by saying that his mind was blank and dumb and he was in despair of ever having a mind. He pictured an ax murderer in his head, chopping up thoughts and connections. Images of two t-shirts facing each other appeared. A killer was on one, while a letter on the other symbolized mind murder.

"I've gotten by with half a mind," Ben said. "Look what I can do with half a mind. What do you think of that?"

"You want me to be your other half mind?" I replied.

"I'm reading Freud for a class I'm teaching. When I don't understand something, I get wiped out and give up, instead of realizing I understand most of it but have some questions. I have more of a mind than I think."

It is impossible to know with certainty why Ben stopped growing faint and what role the above interchange played. At this juncture, he was able to experience his killer and not simply act out. He could depict the annihilation of his mind as it happened. More distance from the killer had been achieved. The killer was not dead. He was as alive and active as ever. But a broader mental context began to situate or encompass him.

Ben produced three symbols of murder in short order: the ax murderer chopping thoughts and links; the t-shirt image of a killer; the t-shirt mirror image, a letter symbolizing the killer function. These represent successive levels of symbol formation. Ben's psyche depicted a self-destructive process that plagued it. The psyche built itself up by depicting its own undoing. The fact that it kept trying, image after image, to achieve a satisfactory outcome suggests that a communicative rather than merely evacuative process was at work.

After three years of work, Ben was able to visualize a series of states concerned with the death of psychic life. He could voice his chronic fear that knowledge kills: too much head kills spontaneity. However, he was now painfully aware that mere emotional expressiveness often aborts a more imaginative elaboration and subtle experiencing of emotional life. If knowledge kills, so can emotion. Beyond both looms the more horrific possibility of knowing and feeling fading out altogether, a total loss of mind and self.

Ben began to appreciate how his killer kept him in life, at the same time that aspects of mental functioning were killed off. He deprecated himself for getting by with half a mind, but was also proud of doing so. He mocked me by implying what he might do if he had more than half a mind. Instead of merely being wiped out by his envy of me, his appreciation of himself feistily came through, although with an emerging sense of limitations.

Ben grew more aware of dangers in psychic life. He realized how difficult it was to live without killing oneself off or dying out, yet he did not give up on himself. He became more intensely aware of the self's struggle to become viable. What direction to take at any moment became problematic in a far more radical way than Ben anticipated. He was shocked to discover what could be at stake in a shift of feeling. The very quality of his being was on the line, and Ben was determined to come through.

Black Father, Black Son, the New Mother

An important consequence of Ben's growing fascination with me was that a richer variety of male figures began to appear in his dreams. The father–son theme became explicit. Following is an excerpt from a session that occurred at the beginning of our fifth year.

> BEN "I dreamt of a black son and black father. The black son says, 'You're not really proud of me.' The black father doesn't say anything. I think the son must be hurt but also feel that deep down the father was proud."
>
> M.E. "You feel I'm not proud of you. You want me to be proud of you."
>
> BEN "Yes I do. [weeps] I never let myself feel that with my father. I said I don't give a shit but it hurt

tremendously. He wasn't proud. He'd make light of what I did, but I also feel he *was* proud but embarrassed to say so to me. He'd brag to others, 'My son is a psychologist,' but to me he'd say, 'You work with crazy people.' When I showed my paper [for a professional journal] to Pam [a colleague], she didn't say anything, and it hurt that you didn't say anything when I told you about it.

"In another dream, Ronald Reagan was held captive in Poland. My friend and I talk to him, but while we talk our plane leaves and we are terror stricken. I fear we'll be prisoners for life. A Polish woman pays attention to me, and before I know it, my friend is gone and I miss my plane again. I'm panicky that I'll never get back home.

"I feel calm telling you this dream. The humming in my ears lessens. [crying] My father was Polish. Without my Polish feeling, I would feel alone. I'm afraid to leave my captivity. If I'm too involved in what you think of me, I'm still in captivity. Here I lie asking to be validated, captive to your creativity, your mind. If you don't say you're proud, I'll feel crushed. I'm captive to what you say.

"I feel calmer than I have in a long time. The way I feel reminds me of a dream with an attractive, dark-haired, married woman. I don't remember more about her except that it was good to see her. She seems down to earth and good willed. In the next scene, my mother is in a diner. She is calm, not intrusive, very different than in real life. A friend of mine, Ron, offers me a peach and slices it. It's juicy. He and my mother are nourishing in the dream. Another male friend is there, too. He's friendly but I'm afraid they'll all find out I want to go to bed with the dark-haired woman."

M.E. "The dark-haired woman makes a difference."

BEN "I feel the dark-haired woman has made a difference. I *feel* when I hurt Lucy. Never felt that before. I feel more compassion and guilt when I'm nasty. I let myself feel it. I'm also afraid I can lose Lucy if I let myself love her more.

"I cut off my feelings about wanting my father to be really proud. I didn't let myself feel how much I wanted that. I want you to say more about my dreams. I want you to tie things up. You let things hang. I'm afraid I'll go too deep and won't come back. If I felt all my losses, I could've gone mad. My wildness is a kind of madness. The humming is louder now.

"I wanted to be really accepted by him [father] and allowed my wild, crazy behavior to defend against feeling what I really wanted from him, to be proud, to say nice things about me. Nice. 'Nice son.' Having a son would help me rework this. It would be different for my son. Feeling softer, open, less roles, less intrusive. Yet I'm afraid to get out of captivity."

In this session, Ben's dreams had a variety of nourishing male and female figures. Terror and violence remained. His pleas were heartfelt. He had come a long way in four years. Still his need for me to be proud of him was not free of coercion. It reflected a real deficit in his life, tied to a panicky need to control others. Ben was keenly aware of the rageful baby tyrant who must have his way and was more able to express the deeper longings which occasioned this rage.

Near the end of the session, Ben touched on two painful themes that were to be important in the years ahead. One was his wish to have a son. Ben had wanted to be a father ever since he could remember. He could scarcely believe he had made his way into his forties without a child. Perhaps nothing made him more aware of his mortality than the realization that he might grow old and die without becoming a parent. It was not a thought he had permitted himself to dwell on before.

The second portent of things to come was his allusion to going away and never coming back—his dread of insanity. Ben feared he was basically a madman. In his dreams and sessions and, especially, at night, he felt a danger of going out of control. Oddly, he never felt out of control in his daytime rages, at least not until our work was well under way. His rages made him feel

COMING THROUGH THE WHIRLWIND

more cohesive and whole. It was precisely when he was beginning to exercise more control over his rages that his fear of madness mounted.

After four years, I felt our work was just starting. I was heartened by the appearance of nourishing men and women in Ben's dreams. Perhaps they would encourage Ben to sustain a more thorough encounter with madness, childlessness, and whatever other painful realities were in store.

A Glimpse of Madness

Ben married Lucy and was disheartened to discover that his rage and panic were worse than ever. I do not know how Lucy withstood his verbal abuse of her. Apparently she understood that marriage upset him and was determined to see it through. To Ben's credit, he never stopped grappling with himself, and Lucy must have sensed this. He was as impossible to himself as he was to her but, like Lucy, kept coming back for more.

The worst of it lasted for the first six months of their marriage. During this period, Ben experienced a frequent ringing in his ears which he could not shake off. A nightmare helped turn the tide.

BEN "I came home from a lecture by Joyce McDougall about difficult patients and felt she was talking about me and maybe herself, too. My ears were ringing. Then I had one of the worst nightmares of my life. I was afraid I was going to die. I dreamed of heads floating in space. I woke up with my heart pounding. I was frightened for my life. I thought I was having a heart attack. Couldn't control it. No sense of penis or neck. Had to feel for neck to realize it was connected to my body. I was frightened to death, cut-off bodies, heads. I was in dread of dying.

"I'm afraid to fly to see my mother. To fly is to

risk death. To reach out to her might have killed me. I've cut off the world by not reading philosophy, poetry, literature—the great works. I never read newspapers for news, just to see who's 'making it.'

"It's me who's cut in pieces. I'm a body without a head and a head without a body."

M.E. "Or neither body nor head."

BEN "I've blamed you for my feeling crazy. It's crazy to try to hold back my anger. Holding back makes me feel crazy. But no, it's deeper. It's worse. My rage comes out of my craziness. It's part of it. It blurs how crazy I am. When I'm mad, I can't see myself. I see nothing but injustice and fury. It's like an explosion and head gets severed from body."

M.E. "Rage obliterates how split you are."

BEN "Anger doesn't cause the split. It blots it out and makes me feel whole. But when things settle down, there's more cut-off bodies and heads, bits of thoughts and feelings with no one to think or feel them.

"The nightmare continued long after I woke up. I can feel it now, but it's balanced by dreams I had the next night. Ron Reagan commended me for great courage. In another scene, I'm in a synagogue with my parents. I can't believe they leave without me, but I go myself when I'm ready.

"After these dreams, I felt better with less ringing in my ears. I guess I think I'm brave for facing that nightmare. I ought to get a medal. Not everyone can see his craziness. I can't take much of it but I got a glimpse. I didn't run away. I'm still here. I'm still with Lucy and she's with me. Maybe we'll make it. I want to make it. It was good being in the synagogue. It shows me I can feel things more deeply. I can stay there myself even without my mother and father. I've been pretending I'm more normal than I am. I've been terrified of getting into my thoughts. In that synagogue, I can take anything."

COMING THROUGH THE WHIRLWIND

Ben reached a point where fear of dying and fear of insanity fused. His nightmare mirrored a split in his personality. The origin of the split and its relationship to hate was theoretical. Did hate cause or grow out of the split? Did the split mirror something basic in his parents' personalities as well as his own? Did it mirror aspects of our culture in general? Of the human condition?

A pat on the back was needed and the president of the United States supplied it. Ben relied on famous figures for narcissistic supplies. Nevertheless, a more profound sense of life was growing. The synagogue supported him. He endured separation from his parents because of his link with God. Was this another sign of grandiosity or a maturational step? It was unclear at this point whether Ben feared madness or death more. But he let down enough to realize that his problems could not be solved by the glorification of his ego. Ben was a bit more naked with himself.

The Illusion of Wholeness

Ben's nightmarish vision of heads flying in space gave the lie to his ideology of wholeness. Ben expected to become whole by suffering through emotional difficulties. Each time he came through a crisis and felt good, he would think, "Now I've made it. I've finally come through. I'm whole at last." He imagined the good feeling would last forever.

His wish to achieve an everlasting sense of wholeness was more than a hope. It was a demand he expected to be fulfilled on this earth. He judged himself in terms of it. Insofar as he was not perfectly whole, there was something wrong with him. He had not made it; there was more to go. He treated wholeness like a commodity or possession that his self-esteem required. Once he had it, evil would be vanquished, and he would live in the promised land. He would be worthy and there would be no further falls from grace. For Ben, wholeness was a kind of static, materialistic perfection.

Ben's nightmare (above) depressed him. He had tried so hard in therapy, and his reward was a glimpse of how bad off he was. He felt injured that his dream did not reflect the fine work he put in on himself. Why should he bother, if the more he tried, the worse his dreams became? He consoled himself by thinking that he had become well enough to see how sick he was, but wished it could be otherwise.

Ben's idea of wholeness would have to undergo adjustment. To be sure, the image of heads flying in space implicitly refers to an underlying norm of wholeness. Head and body ought to be part of a common boundary and work together. However, Ben demanded too much from wholeness. He made it work overtime and thus placed too much stress on his psychophysical system. The facts of experience would not settle into his wish for wholeness. He did not allow for the falling-apart–coming-together rhythm of psychic processes.

In the session following the one in which he told me his nightmare, Ben linked his fear of madness with his ideology of wholeness. He used the term *nonintegration* to portray the fragmentation and incompleteness he wished would go away.

BEN [weeping] "It's against my idea of therapy that non-integration is a part of life. Where's the hope for integration? The paradox is my depression makes me calmer. Is my idea that I should be whole forever mad? I feel more in danger of madness when I think of not being whole. I'm afraid of disappearing. There are so many crises of despair. It's depressing.

"I'm envious of Lucy's dreams, afraid she surpasses me. It's like they come, they go. She seems to accept her feelings. I'm afraid my bad dream will never leave. It'll always be with me, weigh me down. It shows me what I'm not—I'm not integrated. I'm flying off. I'll never be whole. I don't know if I can take it. But it passes like the ringing in my ears. I feel better for awhile.

"I'm starting to be afraid of my unconscious, my dreams. I used to love my dreams—never used to be afraid of my unconscious. Always saw it as friendly. Now it's a potential attacker. I've no control over what happens in my unconscious and this makes me feel very weak. I thought by being in therapy, producing dreams, working hard, I'd feel more content,

COMING THROUGH THE WHIRLWIND

more energy. But I feel more drained. I'm more creative, teaching better, better with Lucy. I should feel happy and strong and do feel stronger in a way. I look better, dress nicer. But too much despair, depression, weakness. If I were with an ego psychologist, I wouldn't have to face and experience this. I could fool myself into being integrated. Cruel therapy—where's there solace and hope with all this nonintegration a part of life?

"You don't look like you go through constant waves of depression. You look more integrated.

"Sometimes I feel more whole in my depression. More sexual. Then all of a sudden a bad dream or experience and I'm sunk to the lower depths again."

M.E. "Maybe it's been too easy for you to get out of your bad places."

BEN "I don't seem to have faith I'll get out of it when I'm in despair. I'm afraid it'll never subside. I don't know whether to hug or hit you. I don't learn from experience. Experience teaches me depression lifts. The humming goes away. But when the bad feeling is there, I feel it will last forever. Also when feeling good—I've made it forever. I lose faith that the other side is necessary. I see it in my dreams—bad ones follow good ones, good ones follow bad ones. No one lasts forever.

"Today I dreamed a friend gave me a beautiful set of women's pajamas which were so big I'd need two years to grow into it. That's hopeful. I feel good about that. My femininity will grow. I won't just be flying off in space. You set me challenges but I'll grow into them. I hate you for it but it helps. I'm better off.

"I also dreamed of a song: 'I found you just in time / Before you came my time was running low / You changed my lonely life that lovely day.' You? Lucy? Just in time. I feel more hopeful, more loving."

EIGEN

In theory, Ben knew that growth is endless. But to work with this fact on a day-to-day basis was another matter. Ben wished to rush growth and be finished with it. The wish for wholeness was an enemy of growth but could also act as a spur, if it were not confused with the thing itself. Ben was beginning to suffer through an important bit of disillusionment. Wholeness would not save him from himself, but other rewards were possible, especially growth of the ability to love.

A Little Girl Baby, Death, and Balls

A little over a month after the preceding "nightmare" and "wholeness" sessions, Ben dreamed of a baby girl about to be born. He described her as a contactful girl with a wide, bulbous nose. "The nose knows," Ben added playfully.

It made sense to dream of a little girl baby in the process of being born after feeling more open and loving. When Ben experienced how cut off he was (the flying heads, the defensive use of wholeness), a more contactful attitude appeared.

The baby girl was matter of fact, not mushy or mean. She felt good just being herself. When Ben spoke about her nose and made comments about "following your nose," I spontaneously added, "What the nose tells you isn't dependent on arrogance or modesty." The little girl baby stood for the "just-so-ness" of experience.

In a series of dreams a month later, first Ben's mother died; then my head was slack on one side as a result of a car accident, but I still did therapy; and finally a large woman with a pretty face wanted to date Ben and reached for his balls.

Ben depreciated the pretty woman. "She wants my balls, she wants to use me," he insisted. He feared I would die like his past therapist but also felt I was in his way. It was as if I represented the law or conscience or something that he was not. "I feel I'm very good as long as you're not around," Ben said. Did he feel that I was judging him and that he could get away with things if I did not look over his shoulder? Did he perceive a genuine slackness in my personality?

BEN   "I think of the baby girl I dreamed of last month. Now she won't have a mother. Mother is dead. Maybe I don't have to hold on to my mother so much now that the little girl is coming. Mother's dying makes it possible for the baby girl to be born. Death and birth go together. Killing and dying and growing go together. Death is the final killing and there's no growth there.

"Now I've got you. You and all your creativity don't have an answer for the final blow. There's no growth at the end. We just die. Are we all growing to die? I want you to find some way out for me, to escape the final death. I'd like you to say you've found a place under the earth, and me and a few others can go there. Why am I angry at you? You didn't make the world. I'm angry at God. There's no growth at the end and there's nothing you can say about this. You're impotent like all of us. We all die, the geniuses and the nongeniuses. You're also vulnerable to death."

M.E.   "You don't want to find out you have balls."

BEN   "Ridiculous. You're trying to slip out of your helplessness."

M.E.   "It seems to me that the large, pretty woman is a pretty good figure. You think she's trying to take your balls away but maybe she's trying to point out that you have them. Maybe she appreciates you and is trying to help you."

BEN   "I have a fantasy of being a baby in diapers without balls. To have balls would be a castration of something—of not wanting to keep on developing. In the workshop I gave last weekend, my hands dropped on my lap and I secretly felt my balls. Feeling my balls made me feel closer to death. [weeps] Without balls, I can ward death off.

"The contract for my book came in the mail and it

scared the life out of me. Growing forces me to give up the feeling that I can control life. Feeling my balls has movement. I tell Lucy to touch them, touch them and I've a boner, see, see, feel it, feel it.

"I haven't had the balls to really live life in some way. I've been protecting myself, the open marriage [with his former wife], no children, not studying depth psychology. I feel enriched by my workshops and lectures most of the time. I used to think that thinking was a lot of elephant shit. I need to be castrated to feel my balls [that is, Ben's narcissistic illusion that mental life was simply elephant shit needed to be castrated, so that a deeper appreciation of psychic life could be born].

"Suddenly I feel like I have a tiny penis. If I have a tiny penis and balls, then I'm still a baby. If I'm a father, then I'm getting on."

M.E. "It sounds like you're getting closer to what you're so angry about."

BEN "I'm angry about having to have balls."

Easy Triumphs, Impotence, and the Striving for Fatherhood

A persistent theme over our next year of work was Ben's fear and wish to become a father. This fear-longing underwent a number of transformations. It painfully dawned on Ben that his need for easy triumphs and lack of children went together. Ben wrote a movie script but did not put in the work that would make it viable. He wrote a book on therapy but balked at the editing his publisher demanded. He could complete only short projects requiring one or two sittings. He looked for shortcuts and could not tolerate the tension of letting something build to fruition.

Children would be all right if they were not so challenging or if they could somehow emerge fully grown or take care of themselves. It was difficult to bear the idea that children would require a recentering of his existence, a reordering of priorities. Ben knew that he would be deeply affected by having a child. Children touched his heart. What would become of his vacations, his freedom, his career, his writing, and his fantasy of becoming a theatrical success—if he had to spend more time at home with a child? To really care for a child involved hardships. The art of husbandry would be no easy triumph.

On the other hand, Ben felt that doing what was necessary to raise a child would force him to be attentive to the kind of detailed work mature success called for. Perhaps a child would catapult him into a dimension ruled by a true sense of generativity. A child might make or break him.

Some of these feelings were worked over by a dream in which Ben played with all his might on the Giants football team. The female quarterback told him that the commissioner of the league praised his efforts, but she doubted they could win the game. Ben said it was important to keep trying, and she warmed up to him.

M.E. "You'd have to be a giant to have a baby in order to afford giving up so much. It's depressing. But maybe there are compensations."

BEN "It's depressing and exhilarating. I won't give up. I keep trying and give it everything I have. But it's a no-win situation. The female quarterback in me is despairing. Is she realistic? Or is she my mother who puts me down and wants me to give up? It's more complicated. I feel you're proud of my efforts. She likes me, too. She likes me to try, no matter what the odds. I get something from doing, from the work itself, although it's hard as hell. My belief in easy triumphs was a defense against feeling doom and defeat. I did not want to face the feeling of smallness."

To have a baby would be glorious and mortifying. Ben now focused on his sense of defeat and doom. He would lose as well as gain if he became a parent. Despair emerged more clearly. The idea of a baby's smallness brought out his own sense of smallness. The polarity, big–little, was constellated. For a brief interval, he tried to sidestep his despair and smallness by turning into me.

EIGEN

In a dream, I slammed and yelled at a crazy woman who refused to have a child with me. I screamed that I want children so badly.

Ben knew that I had recently become a father, that my wife in fact did have a child. In his dream, he pictured me as rageful and frustrated. His projected rage provided him with a transient escape from his wish to risk fatherhood, too. In part, he was in despair over ever pushing past his ambivalence about father-hood. Should he or shouldn't he? By portraying me as stuck in the same position as he, he got himself off the hook. If I could do no better than he, he was absolved from trying.

Ben's indecision and despair, a kind of psychological impo-tence, mounted. For a period, it transformed into literal sexual impotence. It was as if Ben's psyche was unable to sustain the pressure the idea of fatherhood exerted and short-circuited the equipment needed to achieve his goal.

Softness, Power, and the Unknown

When Ben became impotent, the females in his dreams changed. In one way or another, they accused him of abusing them or not listening to them. They wanted more autonomy and spoke for a wider range of feelings than Ben was used to. In a particularly important sequence, Ben's mother was upset and told him that he did not allow her to mourn. "Someone died and you talk me out of my feelings," she said. Ben could not allow females in his dreams to express soft feelings. He wanted them to be hard.

"I want to brush death aside," he said. "My dream mother wants to mourn. She lets herself feel the soft feelings. I want to rush past them. I'm angry and sad that some part of me died but I don't want to feel anything about it. I don't want the sadness. I don't want to be soft. I'm furious when my prick won't stay hard. It scares the life out of me, like dying."

M.E. "Your penis is forcing you to deal with softness."
BEN "I lose my hard-on when I go on top. This is new. It just started happening. As soon as I go on top of Lucy, my prick gets soft."

M.E. "Maybe you have passive needs which need to be gratified."

BEN "A dream comes back to me. A woman sees my long tie with colorful print and says it's the same tie as the sex strangler. She tells me to take it off, and I do to avoid being accused of being the sex strangler."

M.E. "So you're afraid you'll lose your prick if you stop being a strangler."

BEN [cries] "Lucy asked what she could do when I get soft. I told her to say, 'I can beat any woman.' I get hard if she says that, but when she stops saying it, I soften."

M.E. "I don't know. Maybe you need to feel you can beat any woman, that your prick is more powerful than any woman's power."

BEN "My prick feels small next to female wants. A woman's desire is so strong: I want you, slurp, like a ghoul, devouring. It's when I can hold them down that I feel good. There has to be some fight for me to get hard. Holding her down or her on me or her beating another woman. I have to face the hard fact that I'm soft. Did you know that I originally began therapy [twenty years earlier, in his early twenties] because of impotence? I forgot that myself. I forgot that I had problems with impotence."

M.E. "You got around it somehow."

BEN "Yeah. My feeling inferior reading your papers, my not finishing my book—you're forcing me to face my sense of inadequacy.

"In a dream, a friend of mine from high school said, 'I won't let women have me. I can't give myself to women.' Then I get into a balloon, and he holds on to the outside. We float up, then crash into Lucille Ball's window. She's upset with the mess, but we're grateful we're alive.

"I'm feeling good with what's happening to me, though it's painful. Everything is crashing. My inflation is crashing. It's painful not to be able to penetrate someone at will. This work helps unmask my problems but now I don't feel I'm a man. I'm not a man now.

"My mother is in mourning for me, for the awfulness of being inflated and crashing, for my not being a man. My wanting a baby makes me impotent. How's this going to look? I imagine someone saying, 'You went into therapy because you were impotent. You've come full circle. After all this therapy you're impotent again. You'll always be impotent. It'll never get worked through.'

"My mother is less crazy in the dream, less inflated. I never experienced this fear of woman's power. I never let myself dwell on it before. I'm a scared little boy when it comes to sex. I masked my fear with fantasies of women beating each other, one woman raising her legs higher than another. In my mind, I egg them on with macho bravado. I'm the audience, the judge, the prize.

"I feel like saying, 'Quick give me the remedy to get hard, some thought, some action, some thing I can do.' My impotence is an attack on my ego. How long can I keep sustaining these blows? [cries] How can I fuck a woman if I'm not that angry? Anger feeds my penis.

"I told Lucy to get lubrication. I felt it's cheating but at least I might slip it in that way. My manhood's at stake. I'm scared. If Lucy plays the tough bitch or I imagine I can beat up any woman, maybe I can do it. You're not saying anything. I'll have to go through this degradation of impotence, of not being able to penetrate a woman. I don't know if you've ever been impotent but it's degrading to me. What I want to do I can't do. I'm like a man in his forties going on a first date, wondering if he can get it in. It's crazy. I've had it so many times. Five years with Lucy. I had it down pat. I'm not a machine. I want you to say something. I feel stressed. What if I don't have intercourse for months? Maybe what I'm going through will take too long for me. How long do I have to be

COMING THROUGH THE WHIRLWIND

so degraded? My ego will suffer harm and never recover."

M.E. "Going through mourning will harm your ego. Going through mourning is degrading."

BEN [weeps] "I didn't see it that way. I got softer, less angry, but expected everything to stay the same. Everything should stay the same no matter what I go through. The inflated balloon crashes, and I should just go on fucking as if nothing happened. My soft penis is forcing me to pay attention to what I'm going through. It doesn't fit in with my image, my standards. It's a blow. I'm not on top of what is happening to me. I don't like to think that I'm at the mercy of the unexpected, that I don't know what it is that I must depend on."

Lucy's Pregnancy, Envy, and Ben's Fear of Aloneness

Within a year of the above session, Ben's impotence cleared up and Lucy became pregnant. Ben was joyful and terrified. He did not know what to expect. We were into our sixth year of work with many of the same problems, but Ben could now be heard speaking more about his fear of aloneness.

BEN "Our last session set off a lot of stuff. I can't grieve or have relief. I don't want to experience I'm separate or alone. I haven't slept through a night since my ex-wife left. I have to think of women crossing their legs high to sleep. My body feels like a steamroller went over it. I'm envious of Lucy. She's connected with the baby in her. The baby's not in me like in her. There's more merging for her. She's lucky. I'm more separate.

"If I don't have fantasies of other women, I'm sealed off in a coffin. It's death if no woman cares for me. I'm in a coffin without a woman loving me, with no one else around. In a dream, I'm with a woman who says she can love me. My hair is crumpled and my eyes are red with sleepiness. She's Irish with red hair."

M.E. "Do you want your own femininity? I'm not sure."

BEN "If I love my own femininity, I feel I'm betraying Lucy. In one dream, my friend Joan S. did a one-woman show, singing, dancing, enjoying herself. She topped it off by somersaulting into the audience, a fantastic finish to terrific applause."

M.E. "Is Joan jealous of Lucy?"

BEN "Yes. Joan has no children. She's all wrapped up in herself. I had so many dreams of stars and shows the past few days. My old friend Bill T. put on a father–son drama for my birthday in one of them. We got the results from the amniocentesis, and we're going to have a boy. I'm afraid of killing myself off in my sleep. Will I die if I become a father? I dream of all these stars and shows to feel like someone. I'll die if I have to be alone."

After the Amniocentesis: Ron's Dance

An amniocentesis is a test often given to pregnant women past a certain age to determine whether the fetus is likely to be genetically sound in certain respects. For example, it may tell you whether or not the baby you are carrying is mongoloid. Since Lucy was almost forty, she took the test and learned that, as far as the test was concerned, she would deliver a normal baby boy.

Ben could scarcely believe his luck. He harbored the belief that his child must be a monster. He did not believe he could have a normal child. Many potential parents share this worry. For Ben, it was tied up with his own distorted self-image. In some way, he felt he was a monster and that nothing he produced could be truly good. The results of the amniocentesis were immediately reflected in Ben's dreams and catalyzed a shift in his feeling about himself.

BEN   "In a dream this morning, you tell me my genes are normal. Then I'm in church and an all-male choir is singing. I didn't expect a normal report from the amnio. I *can* have a normal baby.

"In the most beautiful dream of all, Ron is dancing. We're going to name the baby Ron. In the dream, he's here already and has his own personality. I never believed in my own normalcy. I came from a crazy household and did crazy things. Ron's dance is the most wonderful thing in the world. It makes up for everything. It's life itself, the best of life.

"After I watch Ron, I meet a lovely woman. She's warm and friendly and kisses a friend of mine. I wish she'd kiss me, but I'm a married man. Then a beautiful fish comes out of the water, very close to land where I'm sitting. It is multicolored and changes into a bird, a beautiful fish-bird. The beautiful woman becomes a waitress in a restaurant and says my credit is OK. She's lovely.

"I'm afraid to tell Lucy these dreams. I'm afraid she'd be envious of such healthy dreams. Maybe you're envious, too."

M.E.   "You're proud of these dreams. A little high?"

BEN   "I've always shown off my distortions and nightmares. Now I want to show off my health."

M.E.   "Who is your audience? The sick you?"

BEN   "I guess I want to show the sick me I can be healthy, too. This competitiveness isn't in the dreams. In the dreams, there's no sense of trying to influence anyone. When I think of the fish-bird or the singing in the church or Ron dancing, I feel wonderful. The influence-and-applause business comes when I write it down or talk about it. Drunkards and rapists can have children. But to me, in my forties, a healthy child feels like a statement that I have some normalcy.

"I feel like I've been going through a test with you and you show me I have some normalcy. I've been going through a psychosis with you. I feel so grateful for the spirituality, the men singing in my dream. I feel grateful that good women are appearing. I've been so stuck with sexy, showy, hard women. I can't believe this is happening to me. I wish you'd say more but I'm shocked to have gotten this far."

Pissing and Grief

It was natural that Ben would feel a letdown after being so happy. In his next sessions, he developed a "psychological equation": depression = fatherhood = normalcy = limitation = death. Although Ben felt depressed, his good dreams continued. Both father and mother images continued to develop.

In one series, a woman in Switzerland served nourishing food. She was businesslike and unseductive. This was followed by Sid Caesar in costume trying to raise money for politics, but he is not funny. His days as a comedian are over. Finally, Ben told George Steinbrenner, "Besides the two breasts, a father is the one who can save you." George Steinbrenner agreed with him.

Ben's dreams had come a long way since the beginning of therapy. They were no longer fatherless. Men were not simply brutal or delinquent, nor women mainly demanding or engulfing. Ben no longer gloried in a clownish self-image. He felt good that George Steinbrenner had agreed about the importance of fatherhood. He described Steinbrenner as egoistic and tyrannical and hoped that these traits in himself were more modulated. We were also glad that the saving significance of fatherhood was affirmed without denying the importance of the breasts. Nevertheless, excesses were inevitable.

BEN "Lucy is lying down, and I'm pissing in the bathroom. We were warm together. Some piss gets on her bathrobe, and she says I should be more careful.

"In another scene, there's trouble at a camp. A father had custody of his two kids for twenty-one years and never let them see their mother. She's coming and is angry and maybe has a gun.

"I guess I've gone overboard with the father business, from too little to too much. Maybe I sometimes feel there should be no mother at all—only father, only me. Do I have to go to such an extreme to feel that father is important? Either parent can be a tyrant. There's a war inside me between men and women, mother and father. Is that why I piss on Lucy's bathrobe? Am I envious? I'll get back at her and keep her in a lower place."

M.E. "Maybe you can't help yourself. Feeling warm made you lose control."

BEN "I've had hostile images since last session. Warm feelings trigger off hostility. I think of Melanie Klein's baby wanting to spoil mother's insides with urine."

M.E. "Pissing also cleans you out."

BEN "I've defended against all these feelings. I couldn't look at what I've done with my life, why I didn't have kids before. I'm feeling more maternal. In my dream, a mother wants her children. I haven't wanted to see my maternal side. I feel sad having my first child at this age. I'm glad I'm having it, but I missed out on something very important. There's a well of sorrow in me. I feel my limits. I'm feeling uncovered. I didn't take life seriously enough. I feel a deep sorrow. I'm grieving for something that died, for something I never had. I should be happy I'm having a kid, but there's such a deep loss."

What are the links between urinating and grieving? In urinating, as opposed to defecating, Ben stood up like a man. While it is true that urinating can be a spoiling process and that Lucy is in a lower position, I felt it was important to emphasize the cleansing rather than destructive aspect of Ben's affirmation of his phallic activity. A sense of strength enabled Ben to experience grief more fully. The image of urinating played a role in an expansive process culminating in Ben's open expression of sorrow. Ben grieved over the loss his narcissism and spoiling hate inflicted on the course of his life.

The Saving Castration

In the two weeks following the "urination dream," Ben experienced an increase of energy and lessening of hostility. Mother and father images continued to evolve. In the first of an important two-dream series, a kangaroo (mother) burst through the tapes and ropes that held it and moved with terrific energy. In the second dream, Ben's penis dropped off into his hands. His father was calm and insisted it was important for Ben to lose his penis. "It's OK, very usual," his father said. Something in the dream suggested that Ben's mother was smarter than ever. Meanwhile, his father found an opening below Ben's belly button and reconnected his penis to it. "I felt solid, good, better than before, less limp," said Ben. "My penis was higher up. I felt a connection between my belly and penis."

I wondered if Ben were assimilating a positive aspect of mother, since the sequence began with mother's active energy. Did such energy threaten him and make him lose his penis or was he getting to something more basic and cleaner than threats of engulfment and implosion? His penis was reconnected in a way that emphasized a link between guts and balls. All this was happening under the aegis of his father. His dream father mediated a wisdom that allowed full play to maternal energy and intelligence yet was not swamped by it. Some of Ben's remarks echoed my thoughts.

BEN   "Something in me had to be castrated to get to this place. I was hysterical when I lost my penis, but father saw me through. I got reconnected through something female. I'm stronger.

      "A few days later [after the castration dream] I dreamed of a pretty, dark-haired girl. There's a warm glow between us. We go to a raceway where horses catch pink balls in their mouths."

M.E.   "It sounds like you're trying to overcome a deep body ego fear."

BEN   "I'm trying to assimilate my balls, my body feelings."

M.E.   "There's a connection between the two dreams, balls, penis. They balance each other."

COMING THROUGH THE WHIRLWIND

BEN   "Kangaroo force, energy, aggression. Soft balls, a feminine aspect of the body. Once when I was a kid, I screamed for my penis. I thought it went down the drain when I took a bath. I called for my father who said, "Stand up, let's see." It was there but I was afraid of baths ever since. I thought the drain sucked it down. My penis, my self vanished down mother's drain. In my dream, I have an opening that can contain my penis and not swallow it and make it disappear. Father helped me."

M.E.   "In real life, your father was fine when you called him. At least in this bath incident. But you didn't really believe him.

BEN   "How could I believe him? He was crazy. We were all crazy. I woke up the other day with the words in my mind, *psychosis liberalis*. Do you have any idea what that means? That whole morning, I kept thinking of an old dream in which miniature men get out of a toy bug car and say they're from the year 2000 and another planet. You can sum my whole life's story as digging myself out of a bug—craziness. I think of Vickie, my patient, whom I'm helping. She's coming through her psychosis. She has a long way to go but she's getting there. The toy bug car is a real bug trained to carry things on its back. It has tremendous power. You're strong when you're crazy. You're unbudgeable in face of everyday reality. That bug is amazingly strong. It can bear anything."

M.E.   "It's also a kind of slave."

BEN   "The bug can carry a toy car on its back but what about a real car? The bug's been more exciting for me than looking for real baby things. Lucy and I are shopping for real baby things. I love it, but it's not so dramatic as my crazy bug. Well, maybe it is. Can my craziness compare with Ron's dance? You know, this is not the first time I dreamed of my father helping me with my body. A few days before the "castration dream," I dreamed of a low down pulsating button, just above my belly. It buttoned my rib cage. I get hysterical when I see it, but my father says I need surgery. He seems to feel I'll come out OK. He's confident."

The father principle would see Ben through whatever vicissitudes of body ego were necessary. Ben was closer to noticing the fall-apart–come-together rhythm of psychic life, and he was developing a perspective in which male and female elements were given freer play. Most importantly, he was more able to see beyond the craziness of the moment and reform himself on what was most meaningful in his experience. Nevertheless, much work had to be done.

The Sick Self and the Therapy Fight

The Paranoid Marshmallow

After Ron was born, Ben changed dramatically. Ben's ecstasy at Ron's birth did not die out. It remained as a muted undercurrent informing his existence. His rageful behavior at home virtually stopped. He worked harder on developing a sound financial situation yet found ways to help at home. He was more reliable, sensitive, and creative.

However, when Ron became a toddler, tensions increased. Ron began staying up nights and rejecting baby-sitters. He demanded more time from Ben and liked to control what they did together. Lucy wanted Ben to help out more. Ben was not prepared for how demanding and controlling a child could be and complained of tiredness, frustration, and uncontrollable rage. In fact, he controlled his rage but feared he would not. Even more devastating was his sense of weakness. He feared he was not up to the demands life made on him and that he would collapse or in some way ruin everything.

Therapy gained enormously from Ben's fear of breakdown. The difference between therapy and Ben's life was never more marked. He began to use therapy as a place to deposit his worst fears and free himself to function better in the rest of his life. Therapy became a place where Ben could break down with impunity. Previously, he tended to think that all of life ought to be like therapy. Everyone should be his therapist, and he could be a patient anywhere. Now therapy became more concentrated. He seemed to save what felt wrong for therapy. It was as if therapy gathered up his dreads and rages and acted as a container for them.

For a long time, it was impossible to tell whether Ben was using therapy to evacuate his fears or whether real work was done. For the time being, it was not necessary to come to a conclusion about this. Even if it turned out that Ben used therapy as a place to discharge his anxieties rather than "solve" them, the fact that he could use therapy to protect the rest of his life was an achievement. That he could do so was due to his love for Ron and the deepening of values stimulated by fatherhood.

Holding back destructive feelings because of love for his son deepened Ben's vision of his predicament. He began to grapple more thoroughly with paranoid and addictive elements in his personality. In one session, Ben spent a good deal of time talking about his problems with a paranoid schizophrenic patient, then told the following dreams.

BEN   "I'm with Dan V., an amorphous, marshmallowy guy. I go with him up an elevator in the Institute. I couldn't swallow and go to the water cooler on the eighth floor. The floor is security prone—cameras, guards. I leave with an eerie feeling about the place.

"In the next dream, my father is an alcoholic and treats my mother abusively. My father is in despair. He tells me that therapy doesn't help. Maybe he should kill himself. I tell him he just began. Maybe he needs to go to a therapist who specializes in problems like alcoholism.

"I'm afraid of Lucy becoming alcoholic. I've always dissociated myself from alcoholism. I put it on Lucy. I love cold water in the refrigerator. It's the elixir of life. I always lived near water. Fresh water is a miracle. I hate alcohol. Sometimes I drink some wine and get tipsy. In real life, my father was mad but never drank. He was emotionally thirsty."

M.E.   "How are you alcoholic in spirit?"

BEN   "I squander myself with TV and jerking off or falling

asleep. I don't work hard on things. I sit in front of
the TV belching. At parties, I used to play the clown.
I'd put a lampshade on my head and act like an idiot.
I haven't seen myself as an alcoholic or drug addict
until now. In the dream, my father needs a
specialist."

M.E. "You're not sure I can do the job?"

BEN "You'd do great with addicts. But how come I still
don't sleep through the night and my book isn't
done? I've been on a bender. Where's my life gone?
How much of this is your fault? It's a comedown to
think of myself as alcoholic, the lowest of the low.
I'm angry that my dream made my father an alcoholic. It rubs my nose in shit. The dream is sobering
me up. Why haven't I written a best-seller? I wonder
if I feel it's criminal being in therapy and helped by
you. Water is helping me grow.

"I'm thinking of my paranoid patient again and
my paranoia. I got out of the Institute with its
surveillance."

M.E. "Couldn't bear your paranoia?"

BEN "I can't swallow how hysterical I am—how
psychodramatic."

M.E. "Afraid of what being sober makes you see? Doesn't
being marshmallowy and paranoid go together?"

BEN "Being sober makes me more autonomous. I've been
a drunkard who squanders all his money or gets
rolled. It's very painful and sobering to admit I've
been a drunkard. I was enraged and fearful about
Lucy drinking before bed or her sneaking a smoke."

M.E. "For her it's a drink, for you a way of life."

Ben was not happy about my remark but he left the session in
a thoughtful state. He was hard on himself and showed some
self-pity but also saw aspects of *the sick self* more clearly. He was
becoming less intimidated by himself. Yet there was a shrill quality in his voice, a kind of scream at what became increasingly
visible. He did not want to believe what he saw—what his dreams
made apparent. It was as if he moved from one shock to another
and his body tightened.

Mother's Famous Helper

Ben began the next session by saying he had more energy and that his publisher wanted to meet with him. He used some phrases from the previous session as a jump-off for further work.

BEN   "After last session, I felt sobered up. I had more energy. I've squandered myself like an alcoholic. We're marshmallow men, marshmallow paranoids. It scares me to see you and me this way, but I feel stronger. I've hired a secretary to help me get what I've written in order. I think my publisher wants to help me get over whatever stops me from finishing the book.

In my dream, I take baby Ron to see his grandpa [Ben's stepfather] and my mother. Vickie [the psychotic patient Ben spoke about] comes into the room. I realize Ron is black. Vickie is skinny and withdrawn but has a force that's filled with life. I can't believe I produced a black baby. Ron runs the gamut of emotions. He's honest with his feelings. Truth shines out. If he's cranky, then he's cranky. If happy, happy."

M.E.   "It sounds as if Ron is your and Vickie's baby." [Vickie is a dark Puerto Rican].

BEN   "Vickie helps her family. She's for family all the way. She's an entrepreneur when she's not too ill. She sells real estate. She makes sure everyone close to her has a good place to live. I'm concerned with something down-and-out in me. Vickie's sick but has a lot of energy and heart. In another dream, Mondale says he'll help a dangerous area prosper. I wonder if I should believe him or if he is just another bullshit politician. I've been afraid of my darker side. A bombed-out area is getting help.

"I felt scared of my energy after the alcoholic session. Afraid of exploding. After a tiring day, I was alive with a confidence which lasted hours. I was afraid I'd burst. Are you a bullshit artist or are you really helping me? When I feel so alive I get frightened.

"I dreamed that a TV star goes off to a beach with a whiskey bottle. He seems lonely and vulnerable. I see he's an alky. All his fame is connected with intoxication. He gets a three-minute ovation just by coming out. The audience is drunk with so much applauding. He's a lonelier, more vulnerable figure than I realized.

"In the next scene, my mother tells me to get her a plastic fork, then finds one herself. I keep looking. Finally, I see she has one and I'm angry that she didn't say so."

M.E.   "She's wasting your time? Doing something for her is a waste of time?"

BEN   "Yes. Doing something for her has to do with fame. For her, it wouldn't be enough just to write a book. She wouldn't understand it. Fame she'd understand. Pulitzer prize, Academy award—writing a book to make me famous. It would have to be very dramatic and embellished.

"In my recent videotape for cable TV, it surprised me that I was less a star than serious articulator. After my TV show, I dreamed I gave a clinical talk that was well received. You're next to me in the audience and you're very supportive. I tell a story about an illegitimate Indian boy's long search for his father. His father finally acknowledges him.

"I've been without a father. As you've often said, I lived in a mother world. My father wasn't in the picture in some way. She bamboozled me. I felt illegitimate. Now she calls me by my stepfather's name and calls him by mine. She never wanted to separate. I'm seeing how crazy it is to be married to her. How crazy it must be for my stepfather, how crazy it was for my father. And for me! The Indians were ripped off. Their land was taken over. I was ripped off in not having a father. Weren't Indians ripped off?"

M.E.   "Isn't there something nice about your Indian father [the dream father]?

142

BEN   "Yes. He doesn't lie. He admits the truth. I'm trying to break my mother's hold with these dreams. Vickie's a schizophrenic who's struggling. She's trying to be truthful. My mother ended in a fantasy world. Vickie is struggling to come out of a fantasy world. Vickie is facing herself. The American Indian also is a lonely figure. The American Indian stands alone, a lonely kind of minority group. You're a supportive figure to help me connect with father. Father with a capital F."

M.E.   "With what tone did you say that?"

BEN   "Cynical. Thinking there's more to life than mother makes me laugh. Heh, heh. A devil laughing. There's no father, only mother. I don't really believe there's a father. You make me laugh."

M.E.   "You're mocking me?"

BEN   "Yes. But something's coming through."

My Best Patient

Ben began our next session by exclaiming how lucky I must be to have a patient like him. Was he mocking me or enjoying his grandiosity? I felt a mixture of pleasure and mistrust. I knew it would be out of order for me simply to burst his bubble. His dreams of the last session were very much on his mind.

BEN   "You've been very supportive of me in my dreams lately. It must be gratifying to you as an analyst to have a patient like me. There aren't too many patients like me. I'm one of a kind. Only a handful of patients really search themselves."

M.E.   "You'd like to have more patients like you."

BEN   "Yes, I would. A very good patient. I would like to have more patients like me. That wouldn't be bad. What do you think of my Indian dream? Do you agree it's schizoid, lonely? I don't like to be identified with an American Indian father. So isolated. Not in the mainstream."

M.E.   "You've often said things like that about me."

BEN   "I can see you that way. Not in the mainstream.

EIGEN

You're part of a small group in a tent. Maybe you lead a small group in a tent."

M.E. "You've often complained about that."

BEN "How do I know you're on the beam? How do I know you're not on the wrong track? What is this off-the-beaten-track business? A genius? Crazy? A crazy genius? A scholar? If you're so great, why don't you have more recognition in the mainstream? Someday people will realize what you have to say."

M.E. "Are these things you feel about yourself, too?"

BEN "Yeah. I feel rejected at the Institute, where people are so-so. A handful of people value me and say nice things about me. My publisher thinks I'm innovative. But people are not flocking to me. They're not following me like Kohut or Kernberg or Searles. I know you've helped me, so why can't I say I'm lucky for finding and recognizing you?

"For my mother, I'm not real if I'm not famous. Or is that my picture of my mother? I think that's the way she really made me feel. That's the way it really was. I was her little star. She put that into my future, too. How good you are is based on how many people are at the box office. Ghost Busters does great—kid stuff. In my dreams, you're appreciative of me. I don't want to make light of it."

M.E. "Maybe you feel I *am* appreciative of you."

BEN "Yes, I do."

M.E. "And that you're appreciative of me."

BEN "Yes, I am. My Indian is not alone on a mountaintop. He's in a tepee with others. He has a strong face and integrity. You have integrity. You haven't sold out or reduced things to make a quick buck, a catchy technique or something. Being with the American Indian and seeing through mother—seeing through being mother's desire—scares me. I try to ward things off by not sleeping. If I don't sleep, our work won't go on at deeper levels. I've been masturbating more and imagining women compete for me by crossing their legs high."

M.E. "Don't minimize the effects of your publisher's call."

COMING THROUGH THE WHIRLWIND

BEN "He's asking me to change the title and meet the production manager. I say I want people flocking to my doorstep but when someone calls, I ask who am I? His calling takes away my envy. If he called you, I'd have something to envy. I feel bad I can't be envious. He's a prestigious publisher. I've read good people he publishes. It scares me. Maybe I can help you. I'll introduce you to him. I've a sense of power. I've been with you seven years. You're the first person who wasn't a fake father. You're my first father figure. You're cutting and supportive. My old friends ask, "What are you doing in analysis so many years?" I joke and defuse things. Maybe I fear people will envy me. They'll envy me my relationship with you and my publisher. It's better to envy than be envied. If you envy others, they won't attack you. Who can attack you if you're a little piss, a little shit. I'd be opening myself up to attacks if I made it. If I'm not successful, I can attack you. If I'm successful, you can attack me. People do that with playwrights. I do it with Chris Everett Lloyd. If she's not #1, she's shit. It's safe being a little shit. What do you think of what I said, Mike?

"I feel good about what I said. [weeps] My inadequacy wants your applause but also fuels my hate. My publisher's call pulled the rug from under me. I've got a publisher. I've got to put up or shut up. It was after he called I started to think about who's better than who, who beats who. I got away from him wanting me to complete my book and change the title. Who can I envy if I'm successful?"

M.E. "Then you'd be alone like me."

BEN "I don't think I could stand it."

What a Good Meeting Can Do: From Monsters to Nuts

Ben continued oscillating between his own grandiosity and idealization of me, together with depreciation of us both. His feelings became even more intense after a successful meeting with his publisher, Louis.

BEN   "I had a good meeting with Lou. Then suicidal thoughts. I kept picturing myself jumping through my office window. It was more than a picture. I had an urge to do it. I thought of joining my old therapist and my father. But that didn't feel right."

M.E.   "Maybe you couldn't bear a barrier lifting by itself. You had to try to control it by doing the breaking through."

BEN   "There's more. The devil wants to kill me rather than have me write this book. I dreamed of a snake shedding its skin but in my notebook I wrote *sin* instead of *skin*. I also wanted to write *life renewal* but wrote *lie* for *life*.

"In another dream, one of my favorite movie directors screamed at me and called me a monster, Frankenstein's monster, for asserting myself. The director is Gene Wilder—it must mean "wild." To be assertive is to be a monster. I picture my father with a hammer, threatening to bash my head if I disobey him. Aggression can kill. I'm afraid if I stop neighborhood kids from swimming off my beach, they'll break my windows. Monsters. People will attack me if I publish. There's a hysterical part of me that acts wild.

"Last night, I dreamed of a thin, black man, haggard, in tattered clothes. He asks for money. I call the cops, who clip his fingers. He promises he won't do it anymore. All I think of is money, money, money. It's a mania. My world is caving in. I sink everything into my house. I ought to get rid of it. I'm not making enough. Oh, to have a best-seller. I can't stand always being behind. I'm masturbating less though, much less.

"In a dream, I see a movie actor with a big prick. I ask him how his wife, Carol, could leave him if he had such a big prick. I think he's creative but not too good with women. Carol was infantile."

M.E. "Maybe she couldn't take a big prick." [I think of the phallic side of creativity and human relationships. Perhaps the dream refers to a deficiency in Ben's feminine aspect, insofar as he admires, denigrates, but cannot really tolerate or make full use of his own or others' active powers.]

BEN "I had a hard time with Lou's kudos. He mentioned well-known authors who publish with him and talked about their problems. They have much bigger pricks than I."

M.E. "Your Carol can't take it."

BEN "Yes. It was nice of Lou to say they had flaws. I think of one of my dreams after the interview. I pissed in a movie-house bathroom. Another pissing man comes to watch me. I go to another urinal. The man smiles at me. He sells insurance.

"Louis is interested in my prick power. He asked if I had other ideas for books and made me feel good. But I get uneasy if people feel I have a big prick. The guy who watches me sells insurance for the future. Coming to you these last seven years is like paying off an insurance policy. Great benefits: a prick, a baby, a book baby, a solid marriage. Therapy is insurance for a better future. I'm grateful. You valued my prick. I'm confused between my mind and prick. You use your mind as a prick. You have sex with your mind. I can see you make girls come with your mind.

"I dreamed of two brothers flying a plane. Each was to make a solo flight. One brother could, one couldn't. The brother who did it consoled the other. The latter was afraid of taking off and really flying. A scared part of me is afraid to fly and an aspect can take off. I can and can't do it.

"In a later scene, I'm sitting on a toilet bowl. White almond nuts are in the bowl. Should I flush them down or pick them out? I can't decide and ask Lucy. This is the dream I like least. I wish you'd say something about it."

M.E. "Isn't it about time you got those nuts out of the toilet?"

BEN "It would be good to see how nuts I am."

M.E. "It might be good to learn your balls give milk, too."

BEN "How'd you get that, Mike? Are you saying that my nuts are nourishing? I'm not clear where you're coming from. Nuts are crazy. I really need help here. I'm angry at you. Tell me where you saw that. Don't leave me hanging here. I'm frustrated. You dangled something. Where are you coming from? You make me feel disconnected when you don't respond and say something like that. I feel dizzy. I don't know where I'm at. I'm furious that you don't respond. Does the dream mean that my nuts are good and tasty or that I'm crazy? My nuts are tasty, too. I'm angry you're playing with me. I hate to be left hanging. Clarify it. I don't fucking know if nuts mean I'm crazy or nourishing. I need to know."

M.E. "Well, hasn't the whole theme of the session been how crazy you get when your nuts are nourishing?"

BEN "Yes. White shelled almonds. I could eat them all day. I get confused when there are two tracks: nuts = crazy = nourishment. After my meeting with Lou, I wanted to fly through the window. I think how nice it would be to masturbate about one woman getting her legs higher than another, one beating the other. When something nourishing happens, I go nuts with it. I can't tolerate nourishing things. If I straighten out my finances, what will I worry about? It scares me to think of being without this worry, this struggle. You scared the hell out of me when you said nuts give milk."

M.E. "You fell apart. Instead of staying with your feelings and whatever my remark evoked, you wanted me to take over."

COMING THROUGH THE WHIRLWIND

A Crumbling World and the New Feminine

Ben felt shaky over the next several weeks. His shakiness alternated with bursts of good feeling. It now seemed that moments of well-being stimulated terror. This was very different from his past pattern of maintaining good feelings at any cost. He complained that he felt grubby. His world was crumbling. He had to sell his house.

But he also was hopeful. One day, he spoke about how impressed he was by Yogi Berra, who once again was going to manage the New York Yankees. He saw Berra as simple, excited, social, and able to enjoy basics, a body-ego figure with detachment and humor. Berra took demotion from manager to coach, then promotion to manager again. His love of the game (of life?) embraced ups and downs. He bounced back.

After speaking about Berra in this semi-idealized but useful way, Ben dreamed that his mother returned a pearl with a bug in it to Carrie, a woman friend of his. Carrie conducted a sale on the roof of her house. Ben's mother went downstairs and left. Carrie was upset that Ben's mother returned the bug-pearl.

Ben felt good about this dream. His inside mother was getting better. Something defective that Carrie wanted to sell was rejected. In her actual life, Carrie was married but refused to live with her husband or have children. She kept her own separate house and lived for her work and friendships. Ben saw her as a feminist with a vengeance, yet afraid of life. Her aim was to be complete in herself. He used to admire her but now felt relieved that he did not envy her path. Whether or not her style of living was right for her, it would be terrible for him. If he were like Carrie, he would be cut off from what was most precious to him. He was happy his dream mother wanted to walk on solid ground and no longer was taken in by buggy, rooftop sales. Carrie no longer offered the pearl beyond price.

In his next dream, Ben was in a car with his wife, Lucy, who wanted sex. He penetrated her and perhaps had an orgasm. Police took them to the station. On waking, Ben had the frightening thought, "Now my patients will know I'm normal."

EIGEN

BEN "What a contrast between Lucy and Carrie. Lucy isn't complete. I'm incomplete. We don't pretend we're more than we are in this dream. The police take us as we are. Now everyone will know about us. This could never happen with Carrie. She would never compromise herself that way. Not that she's above it. She's just too adult. She acts so grown up. She doesn't want to need anybody. I don't want to be a joker—but I wonder if she really has a body. I don't want to be like her.

"I've been her in so many ways. My patients think I'm wealthy. I get a charge when they see my place. A secret glee, as if I'm putting something over on everyone. Now I'm eating crow. Lucy has a bread-and-water mentality. She could live anywhere. She's content letting others see her as she is. When I think of moving, I get shaky. What a comedown it'll be. Everyone will know I'm not what I seemed to be."

M.E. "You won't be the bugged pearl anymore."

BEN "God, no. I only hope I can let that dream do its work. I hope I can live up to it. I'm thinking of starting my own clinic. I'm asking others if they're interested in starting one with me. The thought of it paralyzes me, but I pick up the phone and go out and meet people.

"I don't know why, but that reminds me of a dream in which you and a cowboy, my younger brother, were about to fight, like in *High Noon*. After the fight, my younger brother kisses you on the cheek. You suggest that he also kiss our father and he does. You know I don't *really* have a brother so it must be a part of me, something between you and me."

M.E. "A picture of some part of our relationship over the years?"

BEN "Yes. We brawl and come up for air. You want to mediate the father. You want me to believe in our Father. I've felt out of place with men. I never took their concerns seriously. When men talked about money worries, how they were going to keep up with mortgages, taxes—I'd laugh inside. I never worried about things like that. I never let them get me down. I didn't pay taxes for years and now the government threatens to put a lien on my home. Why did I dig such a hole? I think I'm above these things. I don't have life insurance. Lucy wants me to get it. I think I'm above death. Each year I pin a medal on myself for getting by without dealing with what ordinary men break their balls over.

"I used to think you had grown children. I was sure you had a son in college and a three-year-old daughter. My sense of loss makes me think these things.

"In a dream, I'm with a cute woman who likes me. I can't commit myself to her, perhaps because I'm married. She goes with me to a bizarre acting troupe. The actors talk about murder and death with glee. They're like the crazy me. The woman is something nice about me, some self-liking. I can't take it for long and turn on my madness.

"Then your wife appears. She's wearing a lovely necklace—no bugs. She's nice. I'm so glad she appears. There *is* something nice inside me. I'm not all bad and crazy. She helps me see through the actors. I see how cruel they are."

M.E. "Now the feminine helps you see."

BEN "Yes. I am *so* helped by these feminine figures. The psychotics I treat obliterate their femininity, their ability to receive. I've been so like them. I've never let myself really receive the world, really see it or see others, or really receive myself.

"Now I see you with a long cock and I'm sucking it, then give it back to you. Mine is small by comparison, a baby penis. I picture Ron touching my penis and laughing. I felt shaky and dead when I came here today but now am ignited. I feel ideas for papers and books brewing. Something's getting ignited with all these cocks and new feminine images. I feel less tricky and more up for business. I can take a little more of myself. I see through some more monsters. I want to work on my book."

Ben juxtaposed his wish for perfect self-containment and actual neediness by means of different female images (Lucy and Carrie). That his own mother returned the bug disguised as a pearl, which she once foisted off on him, was of momentous significance. Perhaps Ben could see more deeply into, and be less helpless in face of, the mixture of madness and nourishment (precious and buggy) in his maternal heritage. A gradual shift in values and perception was taking place. Ben no longer scoffed at the worldly efforts and problems of ordinary men — or, at least, saw that such a scoffing attitude betrayed a grave deficiency. In his dreams, he valued the kindness of simple women and discovered that their presence enabled him to work more effectively with himself.

In part, the growth of his feminine side enabled him to make better use of the big cocks all around him, like myself, as I appeared to him in this sequence. We could fight and kiss and make up. He could kiss a father. He could nourish himself and become invigorated by phallic power. The growth in some rudimentary feminine capacity went hand in hand with a sense of heightened phallic creativeness, first mine, then his own. He transferred some of his grandiosity onto me so that he could constitute and live out feminine elements in relation to an idealizeable figure. At the session's end, he took back the heightened phallic energy I held for him and felt more ready and able to use it. The feminine force, which supported the new upsurge of phallic/logos ambition, seemed more benevolent and interactive than his righteous self-sufficiency, allied with cruelty and showiness.

In the present instance, the therapy fight was encompassed by fundamental good feelings. Often enough, good feelings ward off hostility, and that may also be the case here. But my sense was that something positive was trying to be born, and that expressions of love (Ben's younger brother kissing me and the Father) did more than mask hate. Love provided a context that made fighting useful.

The Impostor, Solidity, and Grace

Whatever love existed between us could not be taken for granted. It had to be tested, strengthened, and modified in many unforeseen ways. Love is no more final than rage—or perhaps both have a certain finality. Both are rock-bottom givens of the human heart. There are always complaints and problems, something more to be frightened and angry about. However, if things work well enough, the "I love you" bobs up again, and one is grateful to recognize oneself and the other anew.

Such a benign outcome is not won easily. Ben's ambivalent feelings for himself and me gathered more momentum. He had to deal with loss of self in his identification with me and his misuse of the unconscious.

BEN "In my dream, someone greeted me at my door and said she was Lucy. She was nice, but I knew she was an impostor. Lucy was afraid to say this woman wasn't her.

"I like seeing this woman but also feel unreal and enraged that she would pass herself off as someone she's not. I don't even know her. I never saw her before. It scares me to think that she might be my wife after all, that she might be very close to me, yet so unfamiliar.

"I used to take comfort in my unconscious. I felt it part of me. Now I'm afraid of my unconscious. I never know what it wants to tell me. I've lost control over it. More than anything I'm furious at you for this loss.

"How does the unconscious know so much about me yet seem so unfamiliar? It is an impostor. I feel ripped away from myself. I'm in love with my unconscious. I love my dreams. I don't want them taken away. They are not impostors—they are me. A strange woman tells me, "I live here." In *my* house. *I want to be the only Ben there is.*

"I'm afraid to say, "*I'm not Michael Eigen.*" Inside

myself, I see you and say to you, "You're not Michael Eigen; *I'm* Michael Eigen." I'm you somehow. I want to be you. But I also do not want to be you. I'm afraid to say I'm not you. *I'M NOT MICHAEL EIGEN!* I must fight for who's me. My dream preserves my sense of difference."

Ben fought against, yet appreciated, his growing sense of the gap between him and himself, as well as others (me) and himself. To his surprise, over the next few weeks, Ben's fury and fear, associated with his sense of loss, proved tolerable. He functioned well and felt better than he expected. To feel shaky, sad, and angry, yet still basically good, was a new ability for him. He was learning to stay open to shifting emotions while maintaining a certain solidity.

BEN   "I've got to admit, things are turning out well. In a dream, you show your book to Mayor Koch. He pays for a copy. I feel you love me. You give me one for free and autograph it. The binder is broken into four books.

    "Today I dreamed of a three-year-old boy winning a tennis tournament. Martina Navratilova is there. The boy and Martina like each other. I'm amazed that I see Martina as feminine and the boy says she's sweet. I've always seen her as masculine and tough."

M.E.   "You're surprised that 'no bullshit toughness' leads to something feminine?"

BEN   "Yeah. How can someone be tough and sweet? But there it is. I guess I've always known it. I ran from toughness. It's too demanding. You've got to shape up for this toughness. If sweetness comes through, it's not bullshit sweetness. Maybe I can take more toughness because I feel special to you, although often I'm hurt by you. You're too hard on me. Am I accepting that you or I can't be one thing? Is that why I go through changes better? You're not just hard on me. You could have thrown my grandiosity up to me, rubbed my nose in it—a three-year-old

M.E. "*Four* books?"

BEN "Four—not one. I can't believe how complicated we
are. There is so much to us and it keeps on coming.
Now an image of a woman with a 1920s hairdo. A
sophisticated, elegant kind of grace. I can almost feel
her on the couch. I think of an old dream I had of
oriental dogs pounding on my window. They were
half deer, half dog. I frightened them away. Now I'm
sorry I scared them off. I feel a little more ready for
them now."

winning a tennis tournament, you giving me a book
Mayor Koch bought."

We seemed to reach a point in our work in which a deep inner
fight was in progress between Ben and himself and between Ben
and me. Yet this fight was scarcely visible. It progressed more in
dreams and as a hidden growth process than overt rage and argu-
ments, although the latter were not lacking.

Ben had always been a fighter. He felt squashed by his father
but also hated his father for binding and frightening him. Ben
repeatedly returned to the memory of his father threatening him
with a knife. This happened once and only for a moment. Ben's
grandfather intervened. But the image remained as a reference
point for his father's madness and potentially uncontrollable violence. At the same time, his father's self-pity tied Ben in knots.
Until he married, Ben gave most of his wages to his father as
repayment for helping him through college. He thought this was
the right thing to do. His father wanted it this way. Ben's rage at
his father festered for years.

The pool of rage and fury is inexhaustible. No matter how
much fury is overtly expressed, more remains. Ben had been in
body therapies in which he had banged (with hands and stick) the
couch and wrestled with his therapist. He kicked and screamed as
much as he was able. But the rage went on, past all physical
limits. My hope was that in our work together Ben's fury could
interact with another, subjective presence in complex and sophisticated ways. It was not a matter of what we did or did not do, so
much as the atmosphere we created together. I never expected
Ben's rage to be "cured" or fully expressed. Perhaps it could not

be fully tolerated. But perhaps it could find its place and blend in with the rest of him and make its contribution less fanatically.

The Fight Climaxes

The subterranean fight that structured much of our work temporarily reached a climax in the following dream.

In prison, two Japanese men fought with knives instead of fists—a boxing match with knives. Instead of landing blows, the men pierced each other. It was gory. At the end, the winner, like the loser, lay in a pool of blood. After witnessing this brutal contest, Ben got out of prison.

M.E. "How has your life been like the dream?"

BEN [weeping] "My father's blowing up. My getting back. A dog-eats-dog world. It's the first bite that counts."

M.E. "Why the first? Why not the last?"

BEN "The first blow gets the advantage."

M.E. "But doesn't the last blow win? You think first guarantees staying power? Impatience wins?"

BEN "I'm teaching at a new place where all the students are connected with therapists. There's no place for me. Who gets there first wins. It's my hysteria. I think no one will ever work with me. There's no room left. I beat others out for my house. Now look at the financial mess I'm in. But I believe it—the first to get there wins. I take on more than I can handle. Each time I pay off debts, I do it again. It's a fight. I'm always fighting someone. I walk down the street and think, "I've been here nine years and no one's kicked me out." I expect a fight. I won and lost with my house. I have to get a cheaper one and am furious. I'm furious I have to trim down. I feel I can knife somebody. I'm furious I have to leave. It's a humiliation. I'm surrendering. I can't leave with dignity. I can't get the price I want. I've given up. I've surrendered."

M.E. "Surrender?"

BEN "Yes. Surrender. What would you call it?"

M.E. "Defeat. Surrender is something else. What is surrender?"

BEN "Surrender *can* be giving oneself up without anger. Accept a helpless position and grin and bear it. Sooner or later, students will choose me as their therapist. Sooner or later, the house will sell at a better price. What would you mean by surrender? If you're furious, you're still in a war. Surrender means you stop the war. [weeps] I haven't surrendered. I lost a battle. I'm still warring. I put up a white flag, but there's still an arsenal left. I've still got my cannons, grenades, knives. I'm ready for a last-ditch effort.

"You knifed me with your book. I wrote mine first. But yours came out. I started first, now you're ahead. I see life as a battle. Killing. Gladiators. It's a vicious world. If I don't get what I want, I want to knife. I view life as one combat after another. You knifed me and left me bleeding. I'm constantly knifed. Surrender is accepting I'm knifed and not want to knife back, not wanting to knife and be knifed again? I don't know what surrender is."

M.E. "Perhaps the only thing now is to note that you don't know what surrender is."

BEN "I'm so angry at life not giving me what I want. We knife each other. I knife myself. I'm identified with my father's knife. Now I feel boxing is relaxing.

"I feel attacked by what I can't get. I've always had this feeling of wanting to get even. In the dream, even the winner is a loser. Both lie bleeding. There are no real winners. I've got the mentality of gladiators. I wave a white flag, but there's no real truce. With real surrender, the war is over. There's still a war inside of me. I give myself credit for seeing all this. You've been compassionate, not just a killer. I envy you and feel good for you. I'm not a shit. There's a lot of good things in my manuscript. I'm not denigrating myself. It's a deep form of Oedipus complex, these guys lying in blood. What would I lose by surrendering my ego? Shame? I get out of prison after witnessing this brutal contest."

The great fight in therapy is to sustain an evolving vision of the sick self, yet push on to what is sound and life-giving. One sees more and more of what is wrong with one. One may be fascinated, horrified, or crushed. But one keeps moving through the fight with parents, culture, therapist, and self, past the sick vision. In this movement, fighting and surrendering converge. Exertion is needed but one is surprised by an openness one scarcely believed possible.

Getting One's Own Legs

Different Kinds of Strengths

Several months after the bloody fight dream and upon return from our summer break, one of Ben's "perversions"—perhaps his main one—occupied the therapy stage. As mentioned earlier, Ben watched to see how high women crossed and swung their legs. He imagined women were fighting for him. The highest crosser and swinger won. He wanted his woman to beat the others. For example, if Lucy did not cross her legs higher than any other woman in the room, Ben might become disconsolate, depressed, and furious. A woman crossing her legs high enough could actually bring him to orgasm. This could happen in a room full of people with no physical contact or on double dates in the movies under cover of darkness. Other fighting fantasies often accompanied these scenes.

Why this pocket of perverse activity should become central after the bloody battle dream was not clear, although a connection between knives and legs was obvious. Were we like two women fighting with sexy legs? It was Ben's first session after summer vacation and perhaps he resorted to perverse fantasy to hold himself together. Perhaps we failed to deal with Ben's aggression successfully and his fury was expressed perversely. Or perhaps the sick self was met with sufficient empathic resonance to be able to bring out more of what plagued it. Was Ben trying to show me another way his development went awry? He presented his obsession as the focus for work during a session in which he spoke about vulnerability and megalomania in new ways.

BEN "Why is it so hard for Lucy and me? Others have it
easier. Ron is such hard work now. His energy is
unbearable. My friends' kids are grown up. I hate
Ron's age [approaching two]. He's so demanding. He
interrupts everything. I don't know what he wants.
How do people have four or five kids? I idealize the
Rothsteins—their facade. They have a kid, yet go lec-
turing and traveling. They act as if all is OK.

"I dreamed that Lucy bumped her head getting
out of a car and Ron fell. I got angry at her for not
watching Ron more carefully. She's so clumsy. I see
lacks in Lucy and me. We're both hysterical and get
upset easily. I think the Rothsteins are so great, but
they can't talk to each other. Whenever anyone tells
me how great their life is, I die. I think Lucy's friends
handle their families better and easier. Lucy doesn't
want a nanny. She wants to do it herself. She doesn't
want to miss out on being with Ron. Her friends
seem great to me. I inflate them. I live off my inflated
feeling.

"You wife [Ben met my wife, Betty, on several
occasions] and Lucy are more vulnerable. They have
less facade and cover-up. Betty's a walking target for
vicious animals. She is too raw and vulnerable and
open. Betty and Lucy walk with their vulnerability on
their sleeve. It's embarrassing. I want to protect
them. I see Betty as lost. Have to guide her some
place. I don't see her strength. In marrying you, she
couldn't be a marshmallow. She'd have to stick up
for herself and fight it out. She'd have to hold her
own or be whisked away. She must have a hard core
that stands up and won't take your nonsense. Either
a person looks so great or so vulnerable. Betty and
Lucy are wounded birds. Yet they are not really
weak. They're honest. I don't want to accept the idea
that someone can be vulnerable but not weak. I simplify people's mentality and character.

"I'm seeing through inflated narcissism more. I
thought everyone would be enamored by mine. If
there's no frills, I fear there's no room for manipula-

tion and embellishment. What you see is what you get. With Betty and Lucy, there's less of a split between the image and realness of the person. I live off the split. It gives me some kind of security. There's more to a person if he or she is split. I dreamed of a simple, solid woman. She was simply what she was. I felt embarrassed for her. She was OK but there was nothing else to her, just her realness and strength. She was too straight. Not enough room for the imaginary or manipulation or seduction. I need someone to say this but mean that. There was no other person there—just her, just the her she was. I need more to play around with. Seductive women give me more to play with. With someone who is straight and solid, there's a loss of playing space in my mind—Winnicott's space."

M.E. "Winnicott didn't mean seduction and manipulation by play space. Do you mean perverse space?"

BEN "I dreamed Donna F. died, yet came alive to cross her legs with Lucy. I was turned on. They competed. Maybe her death means a lessening of seduction. A big part of my exciting fantasy life is ending."

M.E. "In the dream, Donna comes back to cross legs. Perhaps she dies as a person and comes back pure legs."

BEN "I want Donna to want me more than her husband. Their marriage isn't so great. I can't believe she doesn't jump at the chance to see Lucy and me more. She takes her time about it. For me, the competitive thing goes on. She doesn't dump her husband for me. I use the imaginary, my crazy way, a perverse, creative way. It's not all bad. Look. Donna died and I dreamed of a solid woman."

M.E. "You had moments of being the woman [the solid, nonseductive one] you feared."

BEN "Yes. Like Betty, she's so very real. That reminds me of a terrifying dream of tigers and lions. A whole area of my town had tigers and lions lurking about. One clawed my arm. Tiger and lion power is nonseductive. My seeing through the Donna F's let the tigers

COMING THROUGH THE WHIRLWIND

and lions in. I don't want to see that if I scratched Lucy or Betty, they'd growl back."

M.E. "Their tigers and lions are real."

BEN "They scared the shit out of me. They could rip me apart."

M.E. "As long as you're manipulative-seductive, you won't be ripped apart."

BEN [crying] "That's right. I want to think that Betty and Lucy are easy prey. My lion could rip them apart. They're no match for me. Manipulation is a defense against ferocity—mine and theirs. Against being ripped apart.

"I admire the way Mayor Koch is straight with women. He says what he feels. I become a sweet, little, seductive boy, not saying what I feel. I'm afraid of women. In the past, I've seen lions and tigers as negative—they prey on the weak and vulnerable. I need lion and tiger power so as not to be so seductive. If I'm seductive, who's going to claw me?

"Do you know I forgot to tell you one of the first dreams I had this summer was of all sorts and sizes of penises. Long, hard, getting hard, tiny—all with good humor. No man is one thing. I'm accepting different types of strengths, different penises."

Caught Between Parents, Between Sexes, Between Big and Small

Ben began the next session unhappy about having a paper rejected by a journal. I pointed out to him that he had written on a topic he knew very little about, and papers that grew out of his real experience did better. I was curious why he had written this paper and what he expected of it. In the course of our discussion, it became clear that Ben once heard me lecture on the topic and, in identification with me, felt he could write about it. He felt his penis very small next to mine and wondered whether having a real penis of smaller size could be better than having a make-believe big one.

EIGEN

The imagery soon became fecal. Ben reported a dream in which Donna F. went to her husband, although Ben was on the toilet making a bowel movement while talking to her. This was followed by several dreams in which women like Ben but do not leave their husbands for him.

BEN "I expect to be admired for shitting. I'm really surprised Donna doesn't stay with me. I can't believe women really love their husbands. I think all women will run to me but they have babies with their own mates.

"I thought I could write a paper just because I listened to you give a talk. Another paper of mine got accepted. It's my own, and it's a good one. I don't have to be you to be good. But I'm you a lot. How can I be you and me at the same time?

"When I was a kid I felt father—not mother—would kill me. Me thinking I can seduce women to leave their husbands is part of my fight with my father. It's easier to deal with women. Men are harder to seduce. It's scary to think I got hooked on seduction because I was less likely to get killed by mother than father. It was too terrifying to be alone with my crazy father, and I ran to mom. She was kind when I was sick. She'd nurse me. He threatened me with a knife. Staying fused with mother keeps me crazy but I fear annihilation with father.

"I let women show their legs while I sit back and watch. Wow—look at the courageous baby. Let them fight it out because I'm too afraid to show my penis. Let them show their legs. It's heroic to compete. I show off. But showing off is like shaking legs. Look what I'm doing everyone. That's different from real phallic action. Being a performer is easier than really expressing myself.

"When I cried afraid of father I feared body disintegration. I ran away. Crying over my fear of father scared the hell out of me. How scared of anger I really am. Something's lacking. I woke up last night afraid of disintegrating. I partly feel you're a fucker who's going to leave me at the mercy of my father instead of making me feel good and less frightened.

"I dreamed of a woman sleeping her life away. Am I afraid I'll never wake up if I sleep fully? I dreamed I swung on a rope like Tarzan on a vine over water. My body felt good. O. J. Simpson wanted to play with me but I wasn't sure what to do.

"Donna F. crosses her legs when we're together. She swings them high. Higher than Lucy. When I watch her, it's as if she says: 'I have your penis for you and will fight your battles for you.' I won't have to be massacred by father. I can fuse with mother. Women protect me, though I lose my penis in the process. She fights my battle while I sit back and come in my pants but give up power. Father would [threaten to] hit me with a hammer if I spoke up and showed my feelings. I wouldn't risk it. Fusion protects me but robs me of power.

"Donna F. says: "You'll never have to be castrated." I think of her and indulge all my fantasies of legs crossing. I get into a rage and scream, "Beat her. Whop the shit out of her. Knock her socks off."

"I'm caught between not letting mother overwhelm me and getting killed by father. I want to overpower mother or her to overpower me or else it's annihilation by father. There's no safe space except maybe in my fantasies. I'll either be overwhelmed or killed so I have to protect myself.

"I feel all alone in this—caught between a vicious, annihilating father and overwhelming mother who partly protects me. My body's cold and shaking. Where am I in all this? Against a problem like this you have a small penis, too. How can a small penis like you help me with such a gigantic problem. What do you say? I treat you like a little cocker, like my parents did me. My father felt small. It helped him feel big to rage. I feel small and attack you. You're just a small penis like me."

M.E. "Do you think I'm afraid to show my small penis?"

BEN   "I think you waver between being big and small. Like me."

Two Power Sources: Anus and Phallus

Ben used body imagery to express and promote different aspects of self-feeling. In the present instance, manifest phallic imagery went along with Ben's contempt for his mother as "a weak ninny." He associated her weakness with anal imagery, but in work with anal imagery, he discovered a hidden source of power. The interplay between anal and phallic imagery was increasingly amplified.

BEN   "My father put my mother down as stupid. He acted as if she were an idiot. He laughed at her antics, and I fearfully joined in. We were triumphant over her. She was shameless. She'd do anything for me. Often she wouldn't make sense. Her chaotic rages terrified me, but I thought she was a nincompoop, a real asshole. In my leg fantasies, I give her power.

    "I dreamed that Donna F. was on top of me. I feel she has guts. She's powerful. I feel secure."

M.E.   "You need a powerful woman as a container. Your rage will blow up mother if she is too weak and there will be nothing."

BEN   [weeps] "Donna is the most powerful of all. I only bow down to the highest crossed leg. She's the champion. I feel turned on. She's superior, I'm inferior. No woman alive can beat her. You're discouraged I'm choosing Donna over you."

M.E.   "There's not enough room for both Donna and me?

BEN   "I'd lose my mind if I had to bear both of you. Lucy's a wimp. She's like my weak mother, an asshole. I dreamed of sitting on Lucy's lap in the nude. My ass is exposed and she lubricates my asshole. Her cunt lubrication starts to get into my ass. I get turned on and feel like having intercourse. I'm surprised because usually I hate assholes, even my own—the smells. Something is penetrating my behind—Lucy's cunt wetness. I'm getting fucked from behind."

M.E. "I wouldn't exactly call this getting fucked. Do you have your and Lucy's asshole mixed up?"

BEN "You think I'm getting sanctified by her oils?"

M.E. "When was the first night of Chanukah?"

BEN "Saturday. I had the dream Saturday morning."

M.E. "Sounds like you were getting ready for Chanukah."

BEN "The asshole is disgusting. This is unnatural."

M.E. "Aren't you happy you're finally letting Lucy in?"

BEN "You're fucking me with your interpretations. Like Lucy in the dream. You're infuriating."

M.E. "Yes. But Lucy doesn't fuck you in the dream."

BEN "She lubricates me. You're probably disappointed because I choose Donna's legs over you and Lucy. Donna's the biggest turn-on."

M.E. "This is what the dream says?"

BEN "Donna's more powerful."

M.E. "Donna's legs are a resistance to Lucy's lubrication. Or maybe they're in tension with it. You can jerk off a hundred times this week thinking of Donna's legs, as long as you spend a few minutes thinking what Lucy lubricating your asshole might mean. You seem to be shutting Lucy's lubrication out."

BEN "Why do I have to make it one against the other? Maybe both have something for me."

I felt both did have something for Ben. On the one hand, he needed to assimilate the "leg power" associated with women. His obsession with female legs might express his sense that women are the most powerful creatures in the universe, as mother is physically more powerful than the infant. However, as the present session suggests, Ben also wished his mother were stronger. His obsession with legs may function to guarantee her strength in a quasi-controllable fashion. Legs are well bounded and circumscribed enough to function as well-packeted bits of maternal phallic power. They are not amorphous and messy like the anus.

Ben associated his mother as debased, weak, and contemptible with the anus. Until the present session, Ben was relatively phobic with regard to actual anal matters. Now something positive about anality appears. His anus is anointed by Lucy's vaginal secretion. It is as if Lucy is trying to help Ben's anus become psychically usable and valuable. In colloquial terms, this might lead to Ben becoming more loose than tight-assed. His focus on legs smoked out an anal dimension, which led to a potentially positive vision of anality. Ben's emphasis on legs kept attention away from his asshole. Lucy's care of the latter may open the way for the anus to function as something more than a trap or instrument of abuse.

The Wound, Egocentricity, the Kiss

It was not surprising that after the above sessions, Ben would bring up the idea of female genital as wound. According to Freud, the belief that woman has a penis functions to deny her penisless (castrated) state. Ben's case bears this out. However, the image of the phallic woman also expresses the experience of woman's active power, a position also true for Ben. Ben first broached the genital-wound image in a Freudian key.

BEN "I've been up nights. Last night, I had a sensation of a gaping slit. A wound in woman. I never thought of female genitals as wound. I read about it but never experienced it myself. Now I feel my obsession with legs denies her castration. Now I remember when I first went out with women, I was anxious about their slit. I wanted to get my penis in as fast as possible. I was afraid of finding a wound. I couldn't bear it. If Lucy actually had a penis, she'd be a freak. In lieu of that, she'd have to show some kind of phallic quality, some strength to feel good about. Women are castrated and wounded. But I'm inferior.

"When I finally got to sleep, I dreamed I confronted Karen B. about how egocentric she is. Then she asks me to kiss her, but I have to buy a ticket to do it. I'm afraid I might get turned on, but I fear her fury if I say no. She appears in the next dream writing a book. She's very creative and full of life. I'm fumbling in the dark."

M.E. "Perhaps she felt more womanly and saw you more as a man, after you told her how egocentric she was. You confronted her even if there were difficulties and you didn't know quite what to do."

BEN "Creativity would also be confronting something. You work, confront something, put it up for criticism. I'm afraid to have a point of view and be up for criticism. Creativity connects with my fears of dealing with people. I know how cruel people can be. I've been the same way."

After Ben thought of woman's wound, he confronted her vanity. It was as if seeing the wound enabled him to see through egocentricity. This, in turn, led to the perception of a genuinely creative element, a real bit of aliveness. Fumbling in the dark recalls his earlier associations of fear of women's genitals. But in the present context, it also refers to his fear-envy of creativity, his own and others'. His reference to the dark is self-deprecatory but also suggests a link between creativity and groping. Creativity involves perceiving gaps in knowledge and the ability to respond to gaps with tolerance, patience, passion, and work.

Beyond Perversion: Gratitude

An increase of gratitude followed Ben's new relationship to his anus and female genitals. It was a relief not to have to always defend his "asshole." His anus had been used as a kind of missile launcher. From early in our work, he had spoken of his urge to "shit on everyone" and have his shit worshipped. The dream of Lucy's vaginal secretion lubricating his anus marked a new position. In this image, he is vulnerable rather than destructive or constricted. Something gentle is happening to his opening. He is not annihilated by being vulnerable.

Similarly, Ben's sense of female genitals as wound suggests a letting down of fecal phallic defenses. Such a sense involves a phallocentric perception of female genitals, but implies a growing awareness of vulnerability. Not only are females wounded, Ben is wounded. Ben permits Lucy to glimpse him without his fecal penis. They see each other's wounds. They do not destroy each other or, rather, they survive each other's destructive attempts.

BEN "I feel grateful to Lucy for having a child. She stays with him and doesn't shut me out. It is a relief to feel grateful. I reduced my passions to masturbation and legs instead of experiencing the limitlessness of love. It's similar with the courses I give. Will I let myself follow my passion for knowledge or show off? Creativity brings out how much I don't know and don't control. I'm afraid of how voracious my passions really are. Masturbating over legs is a way of controlling the mysteriousness of love and knowledge.

"I dreamed of a spacious, elegant mansion with lit chandeliers and winding staircases. A celebration is going on, but I arrive in undershorts. I tell an uncle I'm in real estate part time, although I mostly do therapy. No one comments on my underwear in this elegant place. I go up to a room and put a suit on. I can't wait for Lucy to come so I can show her this elegant mansion. I envy the people who own it.

"The dream has something to do with my new relationship to psychotherapy training institutes. I'm doing well now. Students and colleagues like and respect me. I'm going through normal channels. I've tried to get around things. I've not fitted in—my shorts, too informal. You're not exactly a conformist either but you do what you have to. You don't live beyond your means. But you have a rich inner life and I've gotten involved with a rich inner life through our therapy. You're helping me fit into society in a way that works better for me. My life is more normal. I have a wife and a child. I would have missed all this. I have to pay my dues. I put in my fair share of work. The institutes are connected with formality. Maybe family feeling is too—I'm a working part of a family structure. There's formality to intimacy—it's not just someone taking my shit. I have to put a suit on. It scares me to think how I nearly missed the boat. For years, I thought the trick was to do away with any sort of structure. I'd perform and people said I was brilliant and they'd kiss my ass. I did anything I wanted.

"Why do I feel more alone now? More connected and more alone. The more people you meet, the more you lose. What happened to all my friends from high school? From college? I've lost a lot of friends since being in therapy with you. Will I lose the friends I'm making now? It's lonely not to know where growing will take you.

"Masturbation is under my control. You can't control what people are like or what time can do. I feel very lonely over my lost past and not having a child sooner. The future scares me. I missed out. I'm afraid of the future. Death scares me. I feel very alone. Yet I feel grateful. I feel grateful but I don't like to feel so alone. Your work helped break my fusion with mother. Now what do I do for connection? Yet I'm freer—really freer."

Saving Limits

Who Is God?

Ben's talk about women's legs temporarily diminished and issues concerning limits took center stage. Speaking about his secret sexual scenario made Ben realize how lonely he was. He felt he twisted life out of shape to achieve impossible aims. The orgasms he had while watching women swing their legs higher than one another were spoiled by anxiety and furtiveness. He might be found out and exposed for what he was—a pervert, a voyeur. But even if the women shared his secret and conspired with him, his pleasure would be marred by the knowledge that somewhere, someone else could swing her legs higher. The true champion was always elsewhere. One impossibility followed another.

EIGEN

BEN "I spoke up at an institute meeting but didn't say everything. Others piggybacked on me but I didn't try to take over. I held back but it was worth it. I made the points I wanted to and didn't bludgeon them to death. I left room for others. That's new for me. Usually I feel I've got to say everything or no one will notice.

"I still felt I wanted the others to ooh and aah when I spoke. I want them to give their lives up to me, like James Jones. I expect others to lose their selves, their egos when I speak. I see myself on a throne and choose this woman today, that woman tomorrow. They'll fight it out for me like cats fighting it out over who's going to be fucked by the emperor. I'm a regular Nero.

"A solid life with real goodness goes with limits. But I still have a feeling I shouldn't pay taxes and all the women at a party should only want me. I have a hard time calling a woman for business reasons if I feel she hasn't flattered me enough.

"When I gave therapy demonstrations, I thought people would give up their lives to stay with me. "You kiss my ring, kneel, take several steps backward." My identity is God. I want to be worshipped. I have no relationship with God. I'm identified with God, being *the* God. Being in relationship with God would be lesser than, like I am in relationship to the institute. Being in church and hearing the chorus and organ music makes me feel small. I'm small in comparison with the Holy Church, the universe, God. I've reached a limit. Being one of God's children is much different than being God himself. One of many is different from being the center of all.

"Why can't I be God and have other people look up to me? Why do I have to be one of the children and not the God of Gods? If we're all God's children, what makes *me* special? Do we all blend in with each other? Why should I only be one of God's children and not God himself? I want you and all the other children to look up to me. It's a terribly depressing fall to have to make a living and do more work at lower fees than I want. It's upsetting not to be the one in control. Waking up and finding that I'm not the center of everyone's ego throws my whole world into a spin.

"I have a fantasy that I can control my psychosis. To know oneself should give one a little handle. Knowledge is power—control. Where is this power? Is the idea that knowing oneself provides power—a handle on oneself—a fantasy? Where are all the people I've known throughout my lifetime? We go through something together and part. Most are out of my life. There is loss. I still behave like a madman. I still have insomnia and crazy sexual needs.

"Is it a fantasy that friends are friends for life? Is it a fantasy that I should be less hateful than I am? After all this work, shouldn't things be better than they are? Should I cut down therapy? Can I do without it? What would I lose? If I'm more aware of myself, I'd expect to have less difficulty. But awareness has its disadvantages. I'm more alone. Therapy is not all it's cracked up to be.

"I used to count my friends. There was pride and safety in numbers. The more there were, the better you looked. Most of them I couldn't talk to. I couldn't have the relationship with them that I do with Lucy. It was a popularity contest. Image. Vacuous compared to my marriage. I want to talk more with my friends now. Maybe that will happen. Maybe what I have with Lucy can spread a little.

"Lucy was crazy today. She was furious with me then apologized later. We can be cruel to each other. The bad times pass more easily. But I'd like to sleep fully, complete my book, have less angry outbursts. It's honest of you to say that these things never go away. But when am I going to sleep through the night? I've stayed in therapy more than most. I hoped there would be more after all this. I'm angry there isn't more. I'm angry it takes so long.

"When Lucy and I blew up at each other, I felt we

were back to square one. But we got through it. We got somewhere. We worked with it in a way we couldn't have several years ago. There's some change. I'm a better person now.

"If I left therapy I'd want you to miss me."

Ben was angry that I did not cure him. Did cure mean that he would finally be the center of the universe? That he would be free of needing to be the center? Or that he would develop resources to help him move closer to his own center? He was mad at me because I did not have the key to free him from his perverse fantasies or insomnia or temper. In a way, I could not blame him for wanting to leave me. Therapy is not all that it is cracked up to be. Yet what is it cracked up to be?

We *would* miss each other if he left. It was good he could let himself feel his connection with me and his disappointments. As Ben said, there is loss. Had he lost his hope for therapy? His wish to be everything for everyone suffered another blow. He repeatedly saw through his ego's wish to be God rather than be in a relationship with God. Was the pain of not being God the greatest loss of all? Perhaps it was no accident that Ben wished to say goodbye to me when he was saying goodbye to so important a part of himself.

The Trap of Gratitude

Only after seeing that the ego is not God was it possible for Ben to see through the trap of gratitude. Ben had the tendency to feel grateful to others who wounded him, if only they showed some sign of regret or commiseration. All someone who slighted Ben had to do was offer a meager excuse, and Ben would jump at the chance to exonerate the offender. On the surface, it seemed that Ben was generous, loyal, and trusting. But now this behavior bothered him. He felt it desperate, a grasping at straws. He would swallow anything to maintain an illusion of being liked.

He could not believe in the reality of slights because he had not faced the possibility that his ego might not be the center of all existence. Now, by seeing through himself more thoroughly, he could also see through others. Crudely put: "If I'm not God, you're not either."

BEN   "Ted and Barbara were late for the show. They didn't show up until the first act was nearly over. We left tickets for them at the box office. Do you believe they were pissed that we didn't wait for them? Later Ted talked about financial problems. He was annoyed at having to pay for the taxi he took from the train station. He went on about his money problems, and usually I would have let him off the hook and felt sorry for him. But this time, I let him know that Lucy and I were looking forward to seeing them. We had gotten a baby-sitter and got to the theater on time ourselves. We bought the tickets.

"Ted and Barbara have no children. They don't know what it's like. They take us for granted. Just because they were there for me when my first marriage broke up, I've always made excuses for them. I was grateful they didn't desert me. They were supportive. No matter what they did to me over the year, I'd think: "I owe them." I would have fallen for Ted's rap about his problems. But now I see he's self-absorbed and pissed at having to do anything inconvenient. [The play was in Connecticut, which was closer to Ben and Lucy than to Ted and Barbara. The play was Ben's idea.]

"Something similar happened at work. I'm grateful to Sal for filling my hours. But I have to stand up to him when he gets intrusive and bossy. He's an angry man and puts everyone down. I don't want to collude with him. I want to get away from that kind of hostility. It's as if he's good to me so I can side with him against others. A while ago, I would have gone along with him without knowing what I was doing. I would have been so grateful, I wouldn't have noticed. I would have cheapened myself out of gratitude. I felt I owed you my life if you helped me."

M.E.   [The trap of gratitude must apply to Ben's relationship to me, too, but I waited on this.] "You keep expecting something else from people?"

BEN   "I'm shocked by the narcissistic and evil nature of people."

M.E. "Why are you shocked?"

BEN "I didn't think they'd treat me like that. I didn't think they'd do it to such a nice guy. My parents treated me as so special. Who wouldn't want to be with me? Whatever I say is golden. My parents idealized me in a way that's unreal. It seems to work in reverse. I get disarmed by the confessional aspect of others. I feel loyal and grateful when they seem to share something of themselves with me.

"I can't believe someone who likes me has another side. How can someone who likes me be evil or competitive? I've been warned about Ted. I've been told he's a cut-off guy. But I think, with me he'll be different. With me it's special. I'd have fallen for Sal the same way. This feeling of being special blinds me from seeing people as they are. I'm blinded by the other liking me. Ted or Sal says one confessional thing and I'm grateful. Even if someone is really good to me and helps me, I'm grateful far beyond what's needed."

M.E. "Your ego is a sacrifice to the loving god."

BEN "Yes. Like with father. Because he put me through college, I got myself in the position of giving him my paychecks. Ted said he didn't want to pay for the [show] tickets and I'm supposed to be grateful he showed up at all. After my child was born, Ted didn't come around anymore. I couldn't believe it. I wouldn't be that way. I get confused. I think everyone's like me. If he had a child, I'd want to visit. That feels natural. Ted doesn't have feelings for kids. He distanced himself from Lucy and me. I didn't let myself take this in. I just assume others feel as I do or I think they're the opposite and get angry."

M.E. "Life should be a fusion of gods."

BEN "If the god is not like me, it's against me.

"I don't know why but I think about my mother now. I see her showing herself off after coming out of the bathroom. She'd snap her stockings in her garters outside the bathroom door. I feel the connection between this and being overwhelmed by women

COMING THROUGH THE WHIRLWIND

when they kick their legs. When I see my wife put on her stockings, I fall to my knees and get so hot. I'm so beholden to her. With my mother, I was turned on and couldn't express it. Most of the time, I hid it. I still hide my excitement. I invent games to manipulate women. My mother got me in some way. She could make me feel so powerless, so helpless. When I tell Lucy, 'Beat her, beat her,' I'm telling her to protect me from my mother. I'm so afraid women will take my breath away. I should enjoy it but I'm terrified."

M.E. "Fighting mother and worrying is better than going under."

BEN "How I must have worshipped her legs—and despised them. Maybe this is one reason I always had to have fabulous homes whether or not I could afford them. I wanted my home to be praised, to be looked up to and worshipped—like my mother's body.

"But doesn't every boy want to fuck his mother? Doesn't every kid have to divert his feelings? The difference for me was getting so hot seeing her come out of the toilet instead of the bedroom. She was sloppy. I have to scroonch my nose. 'Why don't you clean yourself? Why don't you fasten your stockings and come out fully dressed?' A shitty connection between legs and toilet.

"My heart's beating rapidly. Terrified. Furious. If not for my fury, where would I be? Her skin terrifies me. I'm losing myself. I refuse to lose myself. I'll be garbage, nothing, lost. I feel so little with mommy. I put Lucy in my place. She's my stand-in. Let her fight mother. Legs against legs. Fire with fire. She must beat mother."

M.E. "Beat mother at her own game."

BEN "If Lucy gets beat or overwhelmed, at least I can have some distance. This is my rock-bottom feeling. Bottomless really. My fear of being overwhelmed by females—mother. I'm scared of my turned-on feel-

ings. I don't know how to handle the erotic dimension. Should I be a eunuch or have an open marriage? Neither works. I'm a little boy. When a woman
shows herself, my soul cries out, 'Mommy, I'm
yours.' I hear my mommy saying, 'Look at me,
sonny.' My mother annihilated my sexuality—normal
sexuality. She annihilated me through sexuality.

"When a woman brushes up against me, it's like
feeding me crumbs. I look to see if she's going to
show herself. My heart starts pounding. I can't think.
I get obliterated. I force myself to act normal. As a
kid, I forced myself to go on being a little boy. I
didn't entirely give in. I made it. I grew up. I'm here.
I'll be here tomorrow. But someday, I won't be here
any longer. I get death mixed up with my mother's
body and excitement. You know that saying, "I get so
excited I could die." That's not just a saying for me.
That's the way it is—what it feels like.

"Maybe that's why I hang on to therapy. It saves
me from mother. It's not the same kind of excitement
here. It's quiet here, too quiet. I get a chance to hear
myself. You don't overwhelm me, not usually. I
guess I want to overwhelm you or want you to overwhelm me. I want you to be fabulous and think I'm
fabulous. I can't stand it when you hold back. I want
you to get in there and fight."

M.E. "You want me to kick my legs high?"

BEN [laughs] "Ha. But you don't play mom's game, and I
want to pull your hair. I want us to be girls fighting in
the mud. Then I won't have to worry about therapy.
There'll be no challenge. But if I win, I'll go under.
There'll be nothing left. I want you and don't want
you to kick your legs. At this rate, I'll stay here forever. I know a lot about myself now, but does it
help?"

M.E. "You want us to play the knowledge game?"

BEN "If knowing won't do it, what will?"

M.E. "Perhaps you'll have to stay with me forever."

As I write this, Ben is still with me. We are more than half way through our ninth year and our work is moving along rapidly. We have not reached the point of diminishing returns. How long can we continue at this pace? Are we missing something? Why does therapy take so long? Are we totally misdirected? Will we go until one of us dies? Is there a way out?

In our work, we go deeper into a mixture of megalomania and clinging, the point where pride and vulnerability meet. In Ben's case, this natural duality was exacerbated by the extremes of adulation and denigration to which his parents subjected him. In the above session, it became clear that Ben feared obliteration after obliteration. By riding on extremes of emotions, he kept himself in life.

After all this time in therapy, the theme of mother's dreaded power was still basic. The reappearance of basic themes throughout therapy can make one feel that little is happening. Yet Ben's erotic problems became more explicitly linked with fears of annihilation, fusion, and the fact of mortality. Whose omnipotence is greater: his, mother's, God's? Does he live in a world where bullying has the last word or is life precious for its own sake? Can anything be more real than tricks of power and excitement? Ben had to face the realization that therapy had limitations, just as he did. This idea terrified and mortified him. If therapy did not make him all better, would mother win?

Addendum

After this chapter was written, I discovered that Ben had not spent his entire adult life in therapy. The image of being a dedicated patient was a myth he created. He fooled himself all these years and was startled to realize that he was making this myth come true.

BEN "I was in and out of therapy. I never stuck with anything. I don't know why I thought I did. I guess I wanted to feel I did. I acted as if I were a great explorer. I got others into themselves. I'd torture

them with truth but help them, too. You're the first
therapist I really stuck it out with. Perhaps I was
ready. I believed in you. You're not a phony. If you
turn out to be wrong about things, I don't think it's
because you put one over on me.

"Maybe I should wonder if you're a hoax, too?
Maybe you're fooling yourself? Doesn't everyone?
Why not you? Am I letting you off the hook because
I'm afraid to be critical? Am I too grateful? Blind? I
feel faith here. I'm angry at you that things aren't
better, but glad we've come so far."

Ben's devotion to his work with me expressed itself in his
commitment to family life. The overall structure of his life
changed. He lived within his means, became a father, and after
years of hard work in his marriage, showed signs of becoming a
husband. Perhaps he was becoming a patient in the full sense of
the word: one who suffers the claims of existence and wins
through.

chapter

FIVE

The Sensitive Self

Coming Through the Whirlwind: Our Basic Sensitivity

In the Bible, a whirlwind is often associated with the leveling of arrogance. Evil is swept away by the storm. After the storm, there is fresh air, the light of God, and human goodness. The whirlwind cleanses the psychic landscape. Also, the voice of God may speak out of a whirlwind, or a vision may come out of a whirlwind, or a saint may be swept by a whirlwind to heaven.

The image of a whirlwind or storm aptly depicts what an individual goes through in therapy. Emotional reality is turbulent. Intense feeling may be experienced as violent. In therapy, we become aware of subtle ways in which we violate or do violence to ourselves and others. The violence of birth and growth processes and ways the self undergoes distortion may be experienced as catastrophic.

Cynthia and Ben became familiar with the sense of catastrophe. First of all, they learned more about ways in which they felt misshapen by their upbringing. They perceived parental distortions that affected the shape of their own personalities. Colloquial language teaches us that the sense of shape makes a basic contribution to the language of the self. We experience ourselves in better or worse shape depending on a variety of conditions. We instinctively link the term *shape* with pattern (e.g., personality pattern or patterns of upbringing).

178

In the course of therapy, Cynthia and Ben became more sensitive to the shape of self from moment to moment. They became better able to follow twists and turns of self-feeling through the threats and challenges of personal interactions.

At times, they went back to the past, spilled out present worries, eyed the future, or stayed with the reality of our meeting or failure to meet. Each session was a potential catastrophe. Perhaps nothing would happen. Perhaps the wrong thing would happen. Perhaps a realization would arise from which there was no going back. A false move on the patient's or my part and the self might explode or become distorted. A good move might also prove explosive.

Science tells us that the physical universe is explosive and may have an explosive origin. Explosions cool and conservative processes have their areas of operation. Are the explosions of spatial bodies joyous and orgasmic or agonizing and destructive? Are they indifferent? How do we encompass them in human terms? How do we understand one change of state after another? Is it surprising that we should find explosive and conservative processes at work in ourselves?

Babies scream. They explode and calm down. In therapy, we find that the screaming baby does not go away. A person comes in and says quietly, "I want to die. I'm already dead. I have no hope, no love. All there is is agony. I want to end the pain." She speaks with quiet hysteria. She is not completely dead. There is agony. Life still torments her. She is right to say that she is already dead, yet wants to die. She died out a long time ago, but not completely. In her death, the rise and fall of life is agonizing. Anything is too much. Her agony is a scream that refuses to disappear. Her talk is a quiet scream. It is almost deafening. She speaks so quietly to try to turn down the volume and, finally, she can no longer hear herself.

We have been given a precious sensitivity and awareness of our sensitivity. Yet what trials this sensitivity and awareness produce. We live from wound to wound and joy to joy. One moment we are too sensitive, another not sensitive enough. Because there is such a thing as sensitivity, we are aware of callousness and brutality. Sensitivity is the basic fact, the baseline and criterion that make moral discriminations possible. Sensitivity to pain and meditation upon that sensitivity leads to humane values.

Every therapy session challenges us to relate properly to our sensitivity. Because we are sensitive, we may feel maligned. If we feel maligned, we malign ourselves and others. To feel maligned is to nurse the sense of injury and carry grudges. Babies appear to pass from one state to another. Injuries come and go and do not harden into a maligned attitude. Wounds are not yet permanently coated by hatred. Individuals come to therapy because they have hardened in wrong ways. Psychic injuries have set in wrong directions. Something has gone wrong with a basic sensitivity.

Some individuals wish they had more insulation. They are too raw, too tightly wired, too exposed. Others wish they could feel or express more. There are those who bull their way past injury. They do not want to wallow in sensitivity and play the victim. A person may oscillate between deadness and hypersensitivity and wish to strike a better balance.

No wonder that so much has been written about the tension between stormy passions and controlling intellect. For ages, the notion of control played an enormous role in our picture of ourselves. From the perspective of the ideology of control, we are wild animals or brutes or volcanoes of will or desire which need to be tamed or cooled, or we are cauldrons of seething excitation that need to be channeled. Parents tell children to control themselves, whether or not the parents are able to do so. Children behave for awhile, then explode. Perhaps parents behave for awhile, too, then explode.

The ideology of control may reflect and reinforce a far-reaching dissociation between thinking and feeling. To try to solve our problems merely by controlling ourselves can hasten the further hardening of psychic arteries. The notion of control tells us little about what is being controlled and what is doing the controlling and what we can expect the results to be. To control sensitivity is not the same as cultivating it. All in all, our methods of emotional education are primitive.

Psychotherapy has grown up as an attempt to further emotional education. The complexity and subtlety of therapeutic processes teach us that simplistic notions of taming and training can be misleading. In therapy, a child's or parent's outburst gives rise to a host of meanings. The therapist struggles to help each person find the key to his own evolution. Psychotherapy evolves as the living subject evolves. Psychotherapy, too, is crude and inadequate as an educational tool. But it is struggling to free itself of the trap of pitting one side of the self against the other. It is exploring in new keys how inspired dialogue and nonverbal interactions may heal.

Many raw materials of experience are announced in the first passages of the Bible. The first line of the Bible begins with the theme of God's creativeness. We try to envision the beginning, the first cause, the origin of things. At the outset, we are permeated by a sense of creativity. Our sense of creativeness is expressed through images of darkness and light. Spirit hovers over the formless void and light is ignited. It is an act that goes on in every living soul.

We are sensitive to darkness. We are sensitive to light. Our sense of creativeness moves between them. We dip into or hover over formlessness and create forms. It is a relief to give up our formed personality and fall through the cracks of our official selves. It is a relief to be no-thing. Yet how good it feels to come back, to be upright again and filled with light, to be new. The spirit of God hovers over the formless void and lights up all things. The story of forms begins. Soon enough, we will feel the sting of desire and be stained by envious imaginings. But we have our sense of a primordial beginning to return to, our movement between darkness and light, our ability to shake ourselves off and dip into formlessness and begin afresh.

The Bible mirrors our explosive sensitivity. In the form of a history of a people, it portrays journeys of the soul. The stories of the Bible are the stories of each day. We begin each day fresh in the Garden of Eden, but before we know what happens, problems arise. We become swept up and worn down by the pressures of existence. Unforeseen tensions disturb us. We do not handle a situation right and it mushrooms. The rub of other wills keeps us off balance and we become mad or intimidated. We make compromises that enhance or poison our integrity. Our freshness is eroded. We regroup and try again.

In the Bible, God repeatedly tries to correct self-poisoning processes. Man has the capacity to repent, to be like Cain. As an act of purification, Cain built a city in which he would not remain. He could not stay anywhere permanently or the toxic process would catch up with him. To stay clean, one moves and builds.

The flood cleanses. Plagues sweep away arrogance and hardheartedness. A hole opens beneath one to swallow up evil impulses. Moses takes the slavish self beyond limitations in an ascent through a series of purgations, a journey from corruption towards the fulfillment of promise, a journey very much in progress.

We are wiped out and start again. The forms that define our daily business do not entirely define ourselves. The opposite is as true and significant. The vision Moses mediates at Sinai raises our daily business to something inestimably precious and potentially sacred. Everyday life wears us down but is an arena for the interplay of the darkness and light that begins creation.

The Bible is a momentous narrative and legal expression of our basic sensitivity. It seeks to educate sensitivity. It is sensitivity reaching beyond itself to a love that encompasses and transforms all possible impulses. In its stories and laws, sensitivity to self, neighbor, and God are cultivated. The ideal of fair play and charity in human relationships is stressed. Each chapter jolts us into further awareness of the holiness of life and of the sacred drama at work each moment as we grow in integrity and/or corruption.

Cynthia began therapy aware of the link between her life and biblical reality, but she was far from seeing just how far-reaching this link was. As she turned herself inside out, she began to see how every nook and cranny of her psychological being was stamped by problems of spirit, and spirit was stamped by problems of psychology. Ben began therapy oblivious, even hostile, to the religious dimension of existence. His "religion" was a kind of humanistic, psychological materialism—a universe of "honest" selves out for fulfillment in egocentric terms. Cynthia had to separate from her use of spirit to blur psychological impasse, and Ben had to go further than hedonic and willful use of psychology.

In therapy, Ben and Cynthia focused on their own emotional reality and the circumstances of their lives. Insofar as they drew near themselves, they described the self in turmoil, at sea amidst catastrophic dangers, at the mercy of its own sensitivity. Drama was everywhere. Would the self become more fully constituted or drift into disquieting oblivion? Would oblivion prove restful or purifying? Would the self come back fresh and ready or be reduced to a semi-anesthetized state? Would tolerance for intensity grow or would one remain explosive? If explosive, must one be abusive? What kinds of changes are we capable of making?

What does psychic aliveness mean and entail? In each case, raw sensitivity struggled for integrity. The self needed to evolve in accord with principles that led to the kind of freedom that mattered.

Cynthia's Whirlwind

Cynthia felt tossed back and forth by emotional currents she only dimly apprehended. She oscillated between periods of promiscuity and a stultifying relationship. She wanted to live in accord with God's will for her but did not know what that was. Her nature moved in opposite directions at the same time, and whichever way she went seemed wrong.

Nevertheless, she saw God everywhere. She kept losing Him and finding Him. She found Him in her promiscuity and in her stultifying relationship and lost Him in both. In the former were peaks of radiance and in the latter a taste of caring depths. She felt estranged in both and had to discover God in the abyss of her estrangement. She did not give up on herself even though she lost herself a little more each step she took.

The therapy relationship had to bear the pressures her life could scarcely handle. There was the temptation to have a sexual relationship, a spiritual-erotic feast. Cynthia's radiance was thrilling. We both seemed like beings the other wanted but could not have. In her life, the usual result was a sexual encounter. Would therapy break down or not get under way properly?

What would a breakdown of therapy mean? Would it symbolize the collapse of Cynthia's personality, a partially collapsed state that long existed and was not acknowledged? Not to give in to the sexual pull might bring incalculable boredom. Therapy would become stultifying. The result of giving in or not giving in would be the same. The relationship would have to end, at least for a time. We oscillated between tantalization and deadness, between closeness and flight.

One way or another, the pull of opposites characterized Cynthia's life from an early age. Both parents were remote and warm. She experienced areas of closeness and utter alienation with each.

Her memory was stamped by extremes of experience she could not digest.

The aborted sex play with her brother exacerbated a split between sexuality and communication. Sex with her brother was stopped at its peak and all communication about it was broken off. More generally, Cynthia's father was intolerant of her impulses and lapsed into silences that left her hanging. Cynthia's mother seemed to feel out of place everywhere except in her garden. Communication was possible under very limited conditions and mostly in silence. The gap between word and feeling was immense.

Religious experience was one area where word and feeling might converge. But the world of religion did not organize and give meaning to Cynthia's impulses. Her attempt to find herself in a religious world exploded. Her sexual misconduct was discovered and rejected by the larger world, which played the role of the incomprehending father. Her sexual radiance failed to find a container and Cynthia suffered exile.

Perhaps the field of law would be firm yet broad and flexible enough to provide a place for Cynthia in the world. In fact, the field of law was tolerant of Cynthia's personal affairs but emphasized communicative skills rather than communication. Her exile continued in another key. Her sense of social-physical awkwardness, insufficiency, and weakness came into the foreground. People were interested in performance, not inner states. How would she maintain herself in a world where persona was more important than being? She tried to find a way to practice law that would be true to her basic values. Slowly but surely she found room for herself.

Would therapy allow sex and communication to come together? How could therapy do this if it was conducted in a sexually aloof manner? How could it do this if communicative distance broke down? Could therapy last long enough for Cynthia to discover a path that did not culminate in a self-destructive outcome? The sense of inadequacy, noncommunication, and the need to wipe everything out was interlaced with sexual and religious radiance, the need for motherhood, family, and professional life. To what extent could the therapy relationship open a dimension in which the varied ingredients of Cynthia's life added to the evolution of self?

EIGEN

Ben's Whirlwind

Ben had a strong drive for emotional truth, a love affair with truth. But he also used truth to bludgeon others and hide his own waywardness. He wanted things his own way, and his lust for truth helped him get them.

He was a superior psychotherapist who used his sense of truth to open others up. In public demonstrations, he enabled people to feel deeply quickly. He felt safe and free in the helping position. To stimulate the emotional life of others was a great source of gratification.

In personal life, a succession of blows forced him beyond his position of control. His submissive wife left him. His therapist died. Economic inflation made his impulsive financial style untenable. He thought his new girlfriend would be malleable but she did not bend to his will.

Ben became agitated and could not sleep well. He was no longer satisfied with his work. He began to see his ego. For a long time, he raged at the tricks life played on him. Life was unfair. His mother spoiled and wounded him. He was terrified of his father's rages. He lived in a mad world.

His parents were self-absorbed and self-sacrificing. They worked like slaves to maintain a household. They were uneducated and did not realize that what seemed practical might be harmful. Ben slept in the same room with his mother or his mother's sister until he was an adult. The family joked about what tortured them and chronically lampooned each other. Ben's father rejected yet was secretly proud of his son's attempts to make something of himself in a wider world. In his mother's eyes, Ben could do no wrong but she treated him with the familiarity of a part of her body.

Ben found ways of making portions of the world cater to him like his mother. He treated others as if they were parts of his own body. Nevertheless, he needed to go beyond himself. He did not give up on therapy. His second marriage was to a woman capable of deep feeling and loving commitment without sacrifice of autonomy. He grew in his work. His soul vibrated to truth.

Where did Ben's love of truth and need to go beyond himself

come from? His father's father was a warm and loving presence in the household. He maintained himself outside the family storms and genuinely respected Ben. Ben tended to look down at him because he seemed to be weaker than the others. He did not rage or blame or have orgies of self-pity. He was a weak and blind old man who lacked authority. But at moments that counted, he intervened with a respectful and caring presence that did not fit in with the family's madness. His voice came from the heart.

Ben also received religious training in childhood which he mocked. The training was authoritarian and crude but stimulated the idea that God, not his parents, ruled the world. There was or should be something more to life than the rule of human egos. For most of Ben's adult life, this idea was lost. In everyday life, the play of egos won the day. If God was thought of at all, He was seen as a kind of giant ego, the biggest ego of all. From this point of view, God was the biggest cynic, pleasure-seeker, and materialist of all.

Nevertheless, Ben sought the emotional truth of his patients' lives in his way, and his own therapy could draw on his wish to discover the truth of his own life as well. In therapy, Ben dropped into the war of inflamed and distorted egos, his own, his parents', God's. Everywhere he looked, he saw aggrieved and shrieking egos. Over the course of many years, Ben began to follow traces of intersubjective experience beyond the tortured and mangled ego. His life began to be more solid and fulfilled.

Mental Ego and Body Ego

The division between mind and body has obsessed Western epistemology and played an important role in clinical language. Indeed, it has marked human experience from time immemorial. In one form or another, "primitive" and "higher" religions grapple with the doubleness that pervades experience. A sense of soul or spirit or transcorporeal reality marks our bodily existence.

Our doubleness makes it possible for us to feel unreal to ourselves. We may ally ourselves with the ineffable or immaterial over/against the visible and material or vice versa. Our allegiance to different dimensions shifts. In physical illness, I-feeling can leave the body. In mental illness, I-feeling itself may vanish. Our sense of reality is uneven. Some capacities and dimensions seem more real in one area than another.

Freud (1918) related the sense of unreality to splits between thinking and feeling. Federn (1953) discussed various forms and degrees of depersonalization connected with divisions between psychic and body ego feeling. Winnicott (1971) linked feeling unreal to oneself with splits between psyche and soma. Jacobson (1964) discussed depersonalization and depression in terms of splits between the mental self and physical self. Kohut (1971) distinguished between a mind-mind and body-mind. Elkin (1972) wrote of splits between the transcendental and body ego.

Freud (1940) noted that an observing I can remain lucid in the midst of a psychotic breakdown. The individual may bear witness to her psychosis and helplessly speak about it as she undergoes it. In an early paper (1973), I described a megalomanic, occultly detached, and active schizoid ego remaining as the rest of the self reached a vanishing point. My book, *The Psychotic Core* (1986), explores variants of a split between a steellike mental ego and a diffuse, clinging, and explosive body ego. I suggested that such a split may be characteristic of the psychopathology of our age.

The patients in the present book exhibit characteristic mind-body dissociations and deficits linked to a subtle sense of not feeling real and a sense of falsity and unfulfillment. In the following sections, we will explore these splits, deficits, or distortions and the struggle to embrace, transcend, and come through them. Although some repetition of earlier chapters is inevitable, a detailed discussion emphasizing mind-body problems will be profitable. As in earlier chapters, dream material is seen as particularly helpful, inasmuch as dreams often deal with personality divisions, deficits, traumas, and conflicts.

Mind-Body Splits: Cynthia

Pity and Eating Death

Cynthia's discussion of her "eating dead Indians" dream (pp. 74–77) brought out a mind-body split that kept her personal life at a standstill. In this dream, she was embarrassed to eat dead Indians in front of live ones and was especially stopped by an Indian who elicited pity. In our dialogue, Cynthia stressed that pity stopped her oral activity.

Pity was associated with seeing: she saw one pitiful Indian whose face made her feel guilty. A tension arose between seeing and eating, between "eye mind" and "mouth mind" (Elkin 1972). Seeing associated with pity and guilt inhibited motor activity. On the surface, this seems natural enough. The baby learns to inhibit his impulse to put what he sees in his mouth. He has to be selective. Not all things are good to suck or eat.

In Cynthia's case, pity was associated with repulsion. Eating dead Indians was disgusting. The repulsiveness of the act was associated with her mother's body and her mother's emotional deadness and her own deadness. The pitiful Indian was her mother's "pity me" look, which stopped Cynthia cold. A baby at the breast might ignore that look in the heat of active need, but it was not a look that would add to its pleasure. In time, such a look must take its toll. In Cynthia's case, her mother's wounded look prompted her to turn off or give up. It also provoked rebellion.

In ornery fashion, I told Cynthia to eat the dead Indians. What could be worse? I stuffed my ideas and words into her. In response, she spoke about how suffocating her mother was and how she needed to spit her mother out. Her mother's alarmed and piteous look stopped her cold. Cynthia was caught between dead body feelings and a pitiful face. She became cold as a corpse in her attempts either to spit out or take in. Her body ego became paralyzed by what she saw.

In actuality, both Cynthia and her mother were many-sided. Her mother was not simply a guilt-inducing corpse, nor was Cynthia simply cold. Both were warm human beings who wanted to lead good lives. Nevertheless, Cynthia's dream and our reactions were drawn to elements that kept important aspects of Cynthia's life at a standstill. A paralysis kept Cynthia's body ego going in circles. In important ways, she could neither take in nor spit out. Active self-assertion was often inhibited or destructive.

It was not only that Cynthia felt guilty for killing mother with her active urges. Her mother's injured expression induced pity, guilt, and disgust for a death that preceded Cynthia's activity. Later in our work, Cynthia's fear of murdering and being murdered came up. Then, too, she had to deal with a pity-murder polarity. However, the present dream said nothing of murder with regard to the dead Indians she was to eat. Death here was deeper than murder. The basic deadness Cynthia had to deal with could not be encompassed by treating it as an effect with Cynthia the cause. Deadness was part of the atmosphere in which Cynthia and her mother lived. Cynthia lived and breathed the death of her mother who, at moments, was very much alive. Cynthia was inserted into a death that preceded her and doubtless preceded her mother. The deadness that tied Cynthia in knots was part of her mother's childhood as well.

Cynthia was more mobile than her mother. When deadness threatened, Cynthia ran. She could not tolerate the deadness that was part of alive relationships. She stayed in touch with areas of body aliveness by bouncing off dead spots. It was natural to use sex to keep herself alive. The ideology of her peer milieu fostered sexual freedom. The age-old analysis of the destructive side of Eros was ignored, forgotten, or never learned. Her life became a revolving door of men and a boomerang relationship with one of them. She could not skip from life-feeling to life-feeling and skip over deadness with impunity.

Fear of death is instinctive. It is part of the body. Freud associates disgust with the upright posture, a movement away from the "smell mind" to the dominance of panoramic vision. The eyes are over the nose and mouth. In the human creature, the gaze is liberated. It scans the heavens. It goes higher than the sun and stars. It takes man upward and inward beyond all visible limitations. It catapults one from disgust to pity.

In pity, one possesses a transcendent empathy for the body. One transcends the physical and emotional plight of self and other. Pity is part of our human equipment, like guilt. We are diminished without it. Nevertheless, pity can work against us, just as sex can. It may secretly nurture a sense of superiority over the body. It can keep us above or seal us off from the facts of life, rather than enrich our predicament. In Cynthia's case, pity perpetuated flight and avoidance. It kept death outside of her. It kept her distanced from life.

In Cynthia's dream, pity and embarrassment kept the dead Indians at a distance. This is normal enough, yet it is precisely by eating this deadness and making it part of her that a tolerance for

Page 190

a fuller life might grow. Only by confessing, owning, and facing the deadness that terrified her would she become less afraid of living. Death must pass through her and she through it. She could not fly above it forever. She would have to sink roots into life deeper than death, not over or to one side of it. She would have to eat what she most feared—and live. Then her pity for the Indians would be freeing. In the transcendence that frees, we become more, not less, than we are. We do not seal ourselves off in flight.

In the eucharist, we eat the blood and body of the God who goes through death, through whom the fact of death is turned into a greater life. Cynthia's dead Indians did not complete this journey. Perhaps her job was to help them; by doing so, she would strike a better balance between transcendence and immersion.

as possible. She believed in the *living* God, the God of the alive moment, the God who worked with, between, and within people, the God who made people sparkle.

It is not fair to say that Cynthia's intellect was useless. It obsessed over life's possibilities and helped envision better and worse directions. It helped her get into therapy and become a lawyer. However, her sense of embodied spirit provided the background mood and context of values that informed her strivings. Unfortunately, her spirit as well as intellect suffered a paralysis. It, too, was helpless against destructive psychological patterns. Her sense of spirit added depth and meaning and made her more dedicated, but it did not stop her from going around in circles.

A turning point came when she realized in a decisive way that her head was not the answer. Cynthia dreamed that a diseased old man died from a blow to his head (p. 89). This referred to the traumatic blows, from childhood on, that knocked her out. However, it also pointed to a transformation process transcending intellect. An old diseased element died upon stopping obsessive head work. The aggression that went into obsessive head-banging now appeared in a more elemental form: the birdman's propulsive sucking mouth and tongue (pp. 90–92).

Head replaced head but with what a difference. The man with round face, beaked nose, insistent sucking, and propulsive tongue represented aspects of the primal baby. Through the birdman, Cynthia came in contact with her own elemental active urges. The tongue links head and body. It evaluates—it tastes experience. What tastes good becomes part of one, what tastes bad is spit out. The tongue can caress or fight. It complements the eyes as a vehicle for saying yes or no.

The birdman expresses embodied spirit in a rudimentary active form. It is totally unsentimental. It has a will of its own. It thrusts into life without pity or guilt yet does no harm. It goes its own way yet stimulates others, mouth to mouth, tongue to tongue. Its eyes and beak and birdlike nature keep it distant, yet it can scarcely be more intimate.

Contact with the birdman's spontaneous self-assertiveness (insistently taking life *in*) gave Cynthia the strength to experience a deeper emptiness. The mouth is a kind of cave or hole or enclosure which provides a base of operation for the tongue, a primal organ of sentience and cognition. The tongue-mind decisively changes one's experience of openings. Whatever else an opening may mean, it is the place where intelligence resides. From the vertex of the tongue, hollowness is a place where intelligence lives and works: intelligence pervades hollowness.

Thus dreams of the birdman were followed by dreams of the birdman's home: the primal oral cavity (pp. 92–95). Cynthia experienced the entire human body as an oral cavity, a place for intelligent work, the home of the flexible tongue-mind, the intelligence that runs through intellect and spirit alike. Hollowness or emptiness would never be the same—it would never be without possibility.

To a certain extent, the phallic tongue can change shapes and direction, unlike rigid teeth. It can surprise and cause laughter. It can express chagrin. No other organ combines flexibility and control so thoroughly. The tongue as a model for psychic functioning subtends obsessive rigidity. It is a guardian of the body. It stands at the passageway and inspects the credentials of whatever enters. It grows from the darkness within, yet is related to the outside world in a special way—it gives taste to life. Contact with the *tongue-mind* points to further development of the relationship between in–out and up–down. In Cynthia's case, it peeled away the obsessive intellectual coating of a dimension she deeply valued. She truly lived by the taste of things. Her dream gave her permission to make fuller use of a capacity that felt like home.

After this dream, Cynthia made momentous life decisions. She changed from a showy job to one that expressed her true values. She moved toward marriage and left therapy. She experienced her might together with new awareness of the space within and between people.

In her last dreams (pp. 97–99), Cynthia suffered through a series of catastrophes and came through better than ever. The phallic tongue had many parallels in her final dreams: the mother's breast as penis in intercourse, the cut of amputation, the stabbing saw, the third leg ploughing furrows, the cat's claws. Her final dreams objectified a major thrust of Cynthia's therapy: transformation of the phallic self.

For Cynthia, phallic imagery was associated with spontaneously active, self-assertive tendencies. Since antiquity, phallus has symbolized active aspects of spirit-mind and sovereign power. Cynthia's phallic images involved fear and fertility. They were wounding yet generative. They kept her tied to the earth and daily intercourse. Getting cut up is part of risk-taking, if one does not hide from the sharp side of others. Nevertheless, phallic weaponry must be controlled. One's cutting edge must find or create a context which incorporates but goes beyond egoistic strivings. Cynthia's dreams did this with images of tilling the soil and shopping. The phallic self, which for Cynthia was an important part of embodied spirit, found a way to situate itself in a context of helpful interchange.

Cynthia's mental ego pity had inhibited body ego strivings. This can be a virtue insofar as compassion guides impulse. For Cynthia, however, we saw that compassion also was tied to deadness within and between people. It reinforced a fear of life and, in particular, a sense of inferiority–superiority with regard to life. Cynthia also was horrified and disgusted with the deadness that tied her in knots. Facing deadness opened up a self-assertive tendency, as if deadness masked spontaneity. Split-off phallic elements appeared and were gathered up in therapeutic work. The result was a better working relationship between compassion, evaluation, and self-assertion. A deeper phallic movement created or discovered the resonant space (e.g., the mysterious hollowness within and between people) that made generative linking possible.

Mind-Body Splits: Ben

The Brilliant Swamp

Words like *lawless* and *capricious* come to mind when I think of Ben's descriptions of his mother's behavior and his own egomania. The word *egomania* is a good one, insofar as it focuses attention on a blown-up ego—an ego that has undergone unconscious magnification. The unconscious often magnifies. Wounds are blown up. Slights become nightmares. Threats become disasters. It is often hard to tell whether reality mirrors nightmare or nightmare mirrors reality. External events are molded by state of self, just as self is influenced by external events.

In Ben's case, "lawless" did not imply criminality, in the sense that Ben did not get a gun and hold up a bank or shoot someone. He was a good person trying to build a good world. His parents were good people. His son would be a good person. Goodness was handed down from generation to generation, goodness motivated by a loving heart. Yet it was a loving goodness mixed with madness.

Ben's parents were uneducated and struggled to make a living. They were coarse and emotional people who did the best they could. The loving thread that knit the family together was permeated by a sense of the toughness, if not impossibility, of life. Mutual scorn, self-pity, envious hatred of the successful, ridicule, a sense of humiliation, self-sacrifice, promiscuous adulation, erotic tantalization, explosiveness: a swamplike mixture of such ingredients set the tone for daily life. They wormed their way into Ben's ego. Ben's ego was nourished by a swamp.

Ben's ego was a bloated tick. He would attach himself to someone or to an enterprise and run through the swamplike mixture of emotions that governed his childhood. He would be inflated, coercive, manipulative, enraged. He thrived on flattery. Others existed to boost him up, to make him high.

The tick was permeated by sensitivity. Ben had a knack of worming his way into feelings and expressing states of self. His brilliant sensitivity thrilled him, and he needed it as much as he needed flattery. He loved to be praised but especially for a job well done, a brilliant insight, a moving moment. He gloried in his knack of touching live nerves of the soul. "That was great!" rang in his ears as he moved from insight to insight. Applause supported his movement into feelings. He could not be alone. He could not meditate or take walks or just be. He could not avoid feeling that his work was superficial.

Dizziness while touching a book was one of the first significant symptoms generated by our therapy. A book made him faint (pp. 110, 113–114). This went along with nightmares of headlessness or head cut off from body. Functions traditionally symbolized by head were lacking in Ben's life. His dreams lacked cultural figures, just as art, literature, and religion were missing in his conscious life. His mental life seemed to rise and fall with the moment. His thinking aimed at feelings but was unreflective. It came and went as feelings came and went. As a result, he could not tolerate the buildup and evolution of feelings any more than he could tolerate the gestation and development of thought. For Ben, mental life was as ephemeral as a TV show, and its results were no more enduring than applause.

Perhaps the most enduring creation of Ben's style of thinking-feeling was the image of himself as a terrific therapist. He found ways of patting his image on the back and getting it in front of people for the mirroring he craved. He was addicted to his image and found ways of masturbating it throughout the day.

His dreams hinted at the dangers to which he might be exposed if his masturbatory TV show failed. In radical contrast to his need for mirroring, his dreams were filled with violent threats, attacks, explosiveness, and erotic tantalization. He was in grave danger in his dreams. They mirrored his sense of helplessness as a child, when he felt taunted and blown about and smashed by blind parents and forces beyond the family. He threw his powers into building an image of himself that afforded some safety and satisfaction. The image covered holes and wounds and deficits. His need for mirroring reflected a deeper need for empathic responsiveness and respect. Breakdowns in the support of his image opened up the holes and lacks of a stunned, torn, and hazy self.

His mother's primitive adulation—son as idol—was channeled partly into being a shining star of a therapist. However, as a therapist, he could keep an eye on what was wrong with himself and others and attempt to heal himself, his parents, and his world by proxy. His hunger for truth gathered momentum. As fast as his masturbatory image covered the shattered self, a truthful eye picked at wounds and winced at damage. He could hide only for brief periods and could sustain truth only for brief periods. He lacked power to link truthful moments together and build a better foundation. He was caught between being too abrasive to himself and too congratulatory. He produced pearls but the binding thread was missing or faulty.

The fact that Ben's thinking was attracted to feelings was a virtue. His thinking was glued to the main currents of his life, to what was wrong with him. He could not give up trying to set things right. At times, truths were used as cement to bind his narcissistic image. At times, they cracked through falsity and he had to undergo dizziness, splitting, anxiety, paranoia, depression, and hysterical mood swings. He tasted the swamp and madness of his childhood—everything his parents pushed away or lived but could not handle.

A love of emotional truth survived the horror. That touching a book could make Ben faint testified to a deep love of knowledge, perhaps wisdom. That he could dream of a missing head (pp. 118–121) showed that he longed to make use of a function that intermittently thrilled him. He did not want it to remain missing, random, ephemeral. He had perseverance in that he returned to moments of truth repeatedly, but lacked resources to weave them together. His thoughts evaporated, his mind went up in smoke. It was as if he grew and lost a head each time inspiration knocked.

Ben saw me as capable of sustained, reflective imagination, and this empowered him. He admired my head. Envy maddened him but drove him to deepen himself and make himself the kind of person that could better absorb and use his own products. My use of head differed from most people in his life. I loved intellectual imagination that took depths of feeling further. The way one thinks about feelings may determine what feelings are experienced and whether they develop. Thinking not only puts a brake on feelings, it plays a role in gestation. Ben lacked models to stimulate thinking-seeing-speaking gestation. He skipped over psychic gestation in rushing from birth to birth.

Ben's lack was not only associated with head functions. The work that went into binding self-idolatry kept his body tied in knots. To an extent, Ben lacked a body as well as a head. His body was imprisoned by stiffness. He held himself too tightly. It was as if he kept his image up by gripping muscles. Too much body life was used up supporting an image of greatness. The result was a short-circuiting of the range and nuances of experience. Too often, budding feelings became explosive because Ben's body and psyche could not absorb them and let them grow. Too little head and too little body went together. Nevertheless, Ben had enough of each with which to do a lot. He had footholds that could grow.

Ben's love of truth was parasitic but elements of love and truth transcend and make use of parasitism. His love of truth attached itself to therapy like an ill and hopeful child, too weak and cruel to lift itself out of destructive ruts. Therapy provided an incubating-refining medium fostering gestation-generativity. Ben's love of emotional truth could be nourished and educated. With care and extended use and testing, the voice of truth becomes helpful rather than mean, as one's personality resets itself in better directions.

Little Bits of Body, Little Bits of Mind

It was important for Ben to learn to tolerate little bits and pieces of himself rather than aim at a marvelous sense of wholeness. All too often, he used a sense of wholeness to blur psychic reality (pp. 120–123). If Ben was to break through the idealization of his ego, he would have to respect fragments of personality that slipped through ego's cracks.

This happened partly by means of female dream figures (the dark-haired woman, p. 116; the baby girl with the bulbous nose, his mother's death, the large woman with the pretty face who touched his testicles, p. 123). His dreams had been mired in stereotypical images of erotic tantalization, violence, and stardom: blown up TV-show dreams. Now females who were not showy became important.

The new female figures were receptive to whatever was part of their natural direction. They sensed their way through things without inflating or deflating existence. Ben devalued them or paid no attention to them or fought them off. They did not make him feel bigger than life. As soon as he let them in, their importance became apparent. They affirmed psychic functions in body-language terms in ways that were nourishing yet assertive. The guiding function was not a transcendental figure but the nose. Ben was called upon not only to have a head, but to have balls, to be generative. He was called upon not to spin in outer space, but to move on earth a step at a time.

Ben's new female dream figures carried the voice of concrete physical intelligence, a love of what is. This attitude conflicted with Ben's judgmental way of functioning and did not cater to his blown-up ego. For one thing, if he followed his nose and used his balls, he would become a father. This would make him proud but shatter his existence. He would no longer be the most important person he knew. His ego would no longer be the primary or only center. Nose and balls took him beyond ego.

Ben became impotent as what was important to him came

closer. He feared and longed for fatherhood, but as the possibility became real, he became obsessed with the frailty of the body and mortality. By becoming a father, he would be like everyone else. He would be no better than the guy down the street who raised a family and paid his taxes. He would lose his specialness and be subject to death.

Ben's ego had placed itself above birth and death. Fatherhood would insert him into the generational chain and force him to have a historical location. He would have to understand himself in terms of the generations he was between and not be the last word. Impotence stopped the clock. It enabled him to postpone the moment of truth. No penis, no baby. At the same time, it undermined his system from within. If it stopped the march of time, it also intensified his awareness that he was not lord and master of his body. Impotence defeated him at the same time it saved him. It undercut his narcissism as a male performer while it maintained his splendid isolation.

Along with Ben's impotence came a dream of a slack head— my head was slack as a result of a car accident (p. 123). This could be understood as a displacement upward and outward. Sexual intercourse was damaging but so was therapy intercourse. Destiny built upon a series of damaging accidents. The result was not birth but a slack head. Ben wished my head would stop working as a result of our meetings. If my head could be put out of commission, perhaps time would stop as well. As consciousness ebbed, the pain of existence would diminish. If Ben stopped therapy, he might stop life. He could beat the tension of life calling to life. Slackness substituted for upsurge.

The image of a slack head was more than a displacement. It represented a double tension or failure of tension. Ben tried to hide from the fact that he had balls, that he could be generative. He could not support the double tension of balls and head, the double phallus, the phallus below and above. Or to put it negatively, he could not support the awareness that he had neither head nor balls, and that it was his job to develop and use both. Neither balls nor nose nor head supported Ben's ideal picture of himself. If he was truly to exercise his powers, he would have to do so within a context of limitations.

Little by little, Ben's dream figures became more varied and dream activities more intriguing. A baby kangaroo (p. 135) depicted an upsurge of playful body energy. Ben's father performed an operation connecting Ben's penis to his guts (p. 135). The father carried forward work initiated by female images. Slowly a psychic apparatus capable of sustaining more intense psychophysical functioning developed. An image of Ben's son-to-be shined with radiant narcissism but also was more than narcissistic (pp. 131–133). It gave joyous expression to the mind–body dance that Ben began to taste.

The Mocking Devil and the Good Soul

Through the birth of his son, Ron, Ben's narcissism took a new direction. He felt identified with Ron's aliveness and uplifted by the buoyancy of a fresh soul. He knew the ecstasy of fatherhood. Yet as Ron grew, Ben was appalled by the vastness of infantile clinging, demandingness, and self-centeredness. Dualities, like the double tendency to cling and search, tore him apart. He wanted growth to go smoothly and not be too messy.

Ben was especially threatened because he had just begun to get a handle on his own self-centered and explosive demandingness. His son exercised the same rights that Ben was abandoning. It was galling and frightening. Ben was indignant at the same time that he gloried in his son's expansiveness. His son's urges to withdraw or cling threatened him even more than rageful demands. Ben had a hard time getting used to the excesses of childhood emotionality. It struck too close to home.

Dreams of addiction and alcoholism symbolized the clinging aspect of Ben's nature that he dared not recognize. In real life, Ben loved to drink water. It symbolized life and a pure and clear nature. It cleaned him out. Freshly flowing water washed away inferior tendencies. He could not bear his wife taking a drink of liquor. He was afraid she would become sloppy or drink herself to oblivion or death. That his father appeared as an alcoholic in a dream (pp. 138–139) brought home the weakness of his father's character: his sloppy self-pity and boundless sense of being victimized. Ben recognized how his own ego bathed in self-pity and played the megalomanic victim. The nakedness of his son's feelings tore off Ben's mask. He could not bear to see his own clinging, demanding, sloppy self. Water would not wash it away. He could not make himself go away.

Yet Ron's strength and goodness and radiance shone through everything. No matter what he went through, the good radiance resurfaced. This was a sign to Ben that all excesses were encompassed by something more basic, something true and good and wonderful. Emotional storms and weakness came and went. The true self came through. His son became a model. If his son could do it, so could Ben.

However, Ron was not beset by lifelong rigidities. He fluidly passed through a variety of states. Ben felt stuck each time he moved from one position to another. When he was parasitic, demanding, clinging, explosive, he feared he would be so forever. When he was blissful, he hoped he would be so forever. This harks back to an early sense of timeless emotionality, when each state seems as if it will never end. A child moves from one eternity to another. The difference is that Ben's psyche had rusty hinges. It creaked and cracked when moving from state to state. It did not shift identity feelings as readily as a child.

Ben repeatedly underwent a profound sense of disorganization. A new seeing gradually permeated body ego tendencies (e.g., clinging, temper tantrums). The consciousness that permeated his body feelings was allied to the sense of Ron's basic goodness and radiance and, by proxy, Ben's own. A radiant goodness came through body ego dispersal and fury. At the same time, a mocking voice tried to exploit body ego weakness. A cynical devil would look on and ridicule Ron and Ben. "You really are not so good," it would say. "You are weak and puny. You will fall apart forever. What's the sense of coming together if you will only fall apart again? Look how furious and clinging you are. You are broken. Your goodness is a sham. Evil glows as brightly as goodness."

A malevolent attitude spread through head and body and aimed at Ben's sense of basic goodness. Good and evil attitudes intertwined. The voice of the inner critic and judge became the spoiler and demoralizer. Yet Ben could see in Ron something more basic than anything the bad voice could spoil. Ron brought Ben in touch with a psychosomatic fluidity and interweaving that undercut mind–body dissociations, especially the cynical, self-pitying mental ego aimed at body ego clinging, explosiveness, and dispersal. Through Ron, Ben would learn to refocus himself and find a deeper center.

Nuts and Bugs

Ben's top–bottom confusion became more explicit as the war between goodness and mockery deepened. After dreams of penises and talking about my mind as a penis, Ben said, "I'm confused between my mind and prick" (p. 146). His feminine aspect was not developed enough to assimilate phallic tendencies properly. This put him in the position of externalizing phallic aspects of self and envying his projections. While envy partly aims to incorporate its object, it also maintains the self in a semi-estranged attitude from envied objects or functions. Ben's dream of milky nuts in a toilet bowl expressed the devaluation and dissociation associated with envious idealization (pp. 146–147).

Nuts condense manhood and madness. The fact that they were white or milky suggests that masculinity can be nourishing as well as fertilizing or, rather, that the fertilizing aspect of masculinity (nuts = testicles = generativity) is nourishing. To an extent, madness can be nourishing, too. On the other hand, masculinity can be mad in lower and higher ways. "Nuts" is a body ego image but also represents mental ego derangement and madness in general. In becoming a father, Ben could not tell whether he was manly or mad or both. Did fatherhood make his life more sound or raise his madness to a higher level?

The very fact that his life was more sound had a disorganizing effect. In a sense, Ben felt safer without nuts. His dream suggests that he was used to flushing or, at least, throwing his nuts down a toilet bowl. His father had spoiled balls and so did Ben. His father felt powerless, and Ben saw him as crazy. Ben was not used to good, clean balls in his life. He partly compensated for an underlying dread of powerlessness with egomania and now his egomania was breaking down. The experience of a more real goodness, as expressed in his love of his son's radiance and spontaneity and vulnerability and resilience, made scared egomania seem hollow.

In the Bible, almonds grow out of Aaron's rod and signal the difference between holiness and phoniness, between basic goodness and cynical manipulativeness. Good and evil attitudes permeate all human functions. All aspects of the self potentially make a positive contribution, if properly situated or transmuted. The strand of the self symbolized by Aaron's rod comes through the test that consumes pretenders. In Aaron's case, the rod represents active creativity in bringing the self closer to God and peace, as opposed to being consumed by mockery and trickery. The meanings condensed and juxtaposed in "nuts" suggests there can be a hairbreadth between generativity and madness, between nourishment and destruction.

Issues brought into focus by analysis of the "nuts" image were deepened by work with Ben's dream of the pearl with a bug in it (pp. 148–151). The pearl stands for the soul in its psychosomatic unity, prior to mind–body splits or dissociations. It is associated with a feminine aspect of peace but goes beyond sexual imagery. Ron was Ben's pearl of pearls. Ben's pearl surfaced in response to Ron's. As a result of becoming a father, Ben became more maternal. The mother in his dream was healthier than his mother in real life. Ben cared more about his patients and less about using them for ego glory. This grew out of his caring for Ron.

The new mother in him could see that something had been wrong with his soul. She saw the bug in his pearl. The bug in the center of his pearl was the madness that consumed him. From the pearl as center, it split off in opposite directions: the scornful, superior mental ego, and the parasitic, explosive body ego. The bugged pearl and the splits that emanated from it could now be seen as fraudulent and misleading. Ben had been attached to a sick center and its consequences. The healthy elements that were growing tried to free themselves from the sick center.

Self and Other

The sense of self and other arise together and make each other possible. Mind–body relationships often reflect ways that self and other are related. Mind–body and self–other relationships structure one another. My preceding discussion of mind–body divisions and vicissitudes implied the play of self–other relationships, which will now be made more explicit.

Self and Other: Cynthia

A Sense of Benevolence

There was much in Cynthia's background that supported an underlying feeling that life was basically good and that this was God's world. Cynthia's father's quiet warmth and her mother's peacefulness in the garden combined with the rhythm of farm life to give her a taste of heaven. She knew that love existed. She loved the earth and sky, the sight and smell of the country, animal warmth, night and day, and the change of seasons. She felt embedded in and encompassed by a sense of benevolence. A warm and bountiful background Other made it possible to care.[1]

Cynthia's encompassing benevolent background Other pervaded Nature. Cynthia experienced a sense of spirit-in-nature that was akin to the Native American's sense of the Great Spirit. Her dream of eating dead Indians bore testimony to this kinship. Some of her Indians died in the process of personality development. She was ashamed and afraid of incorporating and re-owning them. To do so would break the unconscious fusion with the benevolent background Other. She would emerge as a figure capable of digesting her background. Her background would be part of her, rather than she part of it.

Cynthia went to church as a child. Religion came naturally to her. It fit and elevated her feelings: "Holy, Holy, Holy is the God of hosts; the fulness of the earth is his glory." As a teenager, the Sermon at the Mount struck a nerve. It brought her background sense of benevolence to a new level. She felt God's love for all humankind, especially the needy and downtrodden. God's love was more than the glow of nature. It spoke to the human heart and uplifted the soul. It united every person in the world. Every single person was of infinite worth. We are all connected to one another. Why, then, was life so painful?

---

[1]The locution "background Other" resonates to Grotstein's "Background Subject–Object of Primary Identification" (Grotstein 1981, 1982; Eigen 1986, p. 160) and Elkin's "Primordial Other" (1972).

The Violent Other:
Icy Stiffness and Nullity

There are many kinds of violence, some more obvious than others. Cynthia was well acquainted with the violent aspect of natural processes. She witnessed the birth and death of animals and the dependence of the farm on weather conditions. She knew about fighting and staking territory and that physical pain was part of life. Animals tended to deal with pain well. They went through what they had to and moved to the next state. Pain did not stop them for long. From time to time, catastrophe hit, but life went on. A sense of basic goodness surfaced through loss.

Parental scolding and threats of spanking also seemed natural when not in excess. She understood and took them in stride. They did not seem to traumatize her sense of self. A certain amount of parental exasperation was part of the flow of things. The sort of violence that stopped her cold was harder to pin down. Images of her father's quiet sternness and her mother's vacant stare chilled her more than angry threats. She took it for granted that her parents would not abuse her with their anger. They would not beat her or neglect her or harm her physically. She took for granted that she lived in a basically safe place. The dangers that paralyzed her were more covert.

The image of her father's face, upon discovering Cynthia and her brother doing something sexual in the barn, stood out. How quiet he was. His rage and hurt and fear were embedded in shock. Usually his quiet was warm and caring and comfortable. This time the silence was chilling. His icy shock spread through the barn. He gathered himself together and sentenced Cynthia's brother to silent exile. Something in Cynthia clamped shut. Something horrifying happened to her soul. His face was stiff and gray as a corpse, and her soul became that way, too. No one collapsed or screamed or became hysterical. Everyone stiffened.

The stiffness grew into a paralysis that never left her (or her brother). Previously all emotions were part of the flow of things. Now the flow stopped. It did not stop permanently or completely. After awhile Cynthia grew calm and active and alive once more. But it was as if the stream of life within her flowed around an icy stone. Sometimes, as life carried her along, the stone could not be felt. There was plenty of room to navigate. At other times, she could think of nothing else. There, in the center of the waters, was an unbudgeable rock, like an apple stuck in her throat. It determined where the waters could not go. At times, it made the water icy or polluted. At times, it threatened to act like a sponge or suction hole and swallow the waters entirely.

The image acted like a magnet and gathered together earlier and later moments when her father reacted with soul stiffness and icy condemnation. Perhaps buried within her were memories of other terrible moments beyond words—stiff, fearful glances at naked, baby ways. The chilling look was a part of her expectations which interfered with her highest hopes. The fear of being dropped, abandoned, frozen, and crushed led to an automatic recoil in work and relationships which often was self-destructive.

It became clear that her father's chilling look in the barn epitomized the cumulative effect of an aspect of his disposition. Cynthia appreciated his warm silence. But a chilling silence was also part of his being. It was a quiet, intermittent, chronic part of the atmosphere. Cynthia associated the cold stiffness with messy emotional intensity. If she physically expressed her emotions in "wild" ways, his face might stiffen and become somewhat ashen. Most people would not notice or dwell on such a subtle change, but over the years it had a cumulative effect.

Cynthia's father mostly suffered in silence, and his ability to do so contributed to an underlying sense of security. He took life as it came with muted optimism. Cynthia felt she could count on her father to be steady under pressure. She could not make him cave in or become wild, and she was thankful for this protection. However, an icy aspect of his self-control became part of her, so that her emotional life instinctively tried to fight past an inner chill. She was not protected from her protector. Her promiscuity, in part, was an attempt to fight past this iciness. It was as if with each man she tried to thaw out her father's chilling look, the chill in her heart. She needed to bring to a successful conclusion what went wrong in the barn. More generally, she needed to get past her father's fear of his-her feelings and thaw out the frozen aspect of his-her soul. By being promiscuous, she was saying that she was not afraid of herself, that she could do anything, that she could feel the maximum.

Cynthia's mother's stiffness was not stern or disapproving,

but self-absorbed. She was more obviously discontent with her life than Cynthia's father and stiffened against it. She set up barriers against the bombardment and tasks of daily life and quietly disappeared as she fulfilled her chores. Often her disappearance was elusive. She could be interested in and pay attention to life around her, yet be somewhere else.

As rich and caring as Cynthia's childhood was, it was stamped with a sense of the other who was not there. Cynthia grew up with a sense of something missing—the other was missing. This disappearing other did violence to Cynthia's self. The other who was not there gave rise to a self that was not there as well, at least in certain important ways. Throughout her adult life, Cynthia created dramas of the missing other and missing self.

It was hard to know which contrast was more devastating: the contrast between the caring and chilling silences of her father, or between the peaceful garden mother and the disappearing mother. Both sets of contrasts entered Cynthia's bones. Cynthia experienced a very full and rich sense of self and other. Yet this fullness often met with or was encompassed by chill and vacancy. It was as if at the height or center of richness was an electric shock that made her recoil or an absence that nullified all frames of reference.

Both sets of polarities contributed to the patterns of recoil and nullification that characterized Cynthia's adult work and love life. Cynthia might be electrocuted at the height of excitement or closeness. She might drop into nothingness if she entered the heart of peace. If she moved toward the father, she risked shock; if she moved toward the mother, she risked irritable formlessness. Cynthia found ways to conspire with circumstances in order to run from shock and nothingness. No work situation or relationship could build past the danger point. Either Cynthia shut down or caused an explosion which left her safely insulated. It was as if she provoked or colluded with the dangers she most feared, perhaps in hope of mastering them or because she was trapped.

When she reached the point of chill and nullity, Cynthia touched the worst elements of her parents' marriage and the aspects of the inner parental couple that kept her at a standstill. Aspects of her parents' marriage and the inner couple were generative and caring. Yet too often the mood was one of quiet discontent. The partners fell away from each other in seething blankness so that communication of needs even to oneself became impossible. The marriage itself seemed to be missing.

Cynthia tried to revive the marriage within herself, first of all by experiencing needs as intensely as possible. Sexuality lent itself to surges of intensity. Cynthia's promiscuity, in part, was a way of reviving the waning inner couple, of making them sexual. Similarly, she tried to keep herself alive vocationally by changing positions. She would not give in to parental deadness. She would not live her life in one place—in any sense. Cynthia's sexual and, to an extent, vocational promiscuity was tied to a determination not to give in to nullity within and around her. She would not let her needs die out like her parents.

Cynthia suffered a tradeoff in her will not to become like her parents. For a long time, she lost sight of the fact that her parents subordinated many needs in order to raise a family in a stable home. Their achievement gave Cynthia's life a sense of meaning as well as paralysis. Cynthia tried to resurrect what died out in her parents. However, a life of riding sexual currents missed more basic needs in her personality, the things she wanted in the long run. She did not want to suffer the fate of her parents in order to have a family, but her own solution was a dead end. Perhaps if she went deep enough, she could find the joy that is the underpinning of parental sacrifice. Before that point, there was layer upon layer of stiff and quiet angry deadness. She was afraid she would die out before touching the joy underneath. Was it necessary to trade one violence for another? Cynthia searched for other ways to reconcile conflicting needs.

Rebirth Through the Other

It did not take long before therapy mirrored aspects of the bind that characterized Cynthia's life. We soon were attracted to each other with fantasies of blissful fulfillment. We each possessed a commingling of qualities that evoked longing in the other.

She felt I might save her: someone like me might be the answer. I came close to spanning the spectrum of qualities that she wanted a partner to have. I combined religious, aesthetic, and personal sensitivity and tried to listen to her. At the same time, I was successful and responsible in worldly terms and decent enough physically. I was also funny. The polarities of her nature might find a home in me.

In real life, men did not listen to her. If they did, she did not truly feel so. Men liked her sexually and socially but she did not feel seen or heard. The few men who might be responsive to her in a deeper way were misfits or infantile or in other ways lacking. Relationships did not go anywhere, although they usually felt good. Her longest relationship was with a ne'er-do-well incapable of sophisticated, empathic, verbal communication. She was angry that she could not do better.

For me, Cynthia had the advantage of being a dream person outside the stress of daily interchange. We did not share the job of bringing up children and surviving each other on a daily basis. Her glow uplifted my life and smoothed the wounds and demands of working and loving. She, too, felt close to God and sought God. She loved life and wanted more life. Her light left a trace on the path she cut through worldly dangers. She did not lose her soul in the world but lit up parts of the world as she tried to find her way. Also, she was beautiful. My best self felt seen and appreciated by a lovely, searching woman.

For some time, it appeared that therapy might founder on our mutual longing and idealization. It quickly dawned on me that our bind must be relevant to her impasse in life as a whole, but it took time for me to assimilate the emotions aroused, at least enough to begin to work with them. The work had many strands.

The obvious and most immediate danger was sexually acting out. That would end therapy and cause difficulty in my marriage. Our relationship would become another of a long string of sexual enactments, in which sex was substituted for problem solving. Sexual intensity may keep faith alive. But in Cynthia's case, it also devoured personal possibilities and kept her life at an impasse.

It is always possible that this time might be different, the real thing. A real relationship might enrich us or be salvific. The real sin might be to pass it up, to say no to what is offered. Which voice should one listen to: the therapy voice or divine erotic longing? Isn't life more important than therapy? Perhaps Cynthia would at last break through to the Father and mend what went wrong between her and her brother. Perhaps Eros would at last thaw the chill and soften the stiffness. Perhaps someone would finally hear *and* touch her.

We will never know. Mainly we talked, although at ends of sessions we touched hands. What crystallized was a tension between a speaking-listening Other and a tactile Other: intimacy without touch and intimacy through touch. In our work there was a primacy of intimacy without touch.

This meant that we had to bear tantalization and longing. A danger was that Cynthia would leave therapy upon discovering that therapy was only therapy. If she did leave, the question was would she leave bitterly and angrily or with something gained or both? Could we endure (enjoy?) what we felt for each other well enough to let something transforming happen, or would we in some way collapse or escape or give in?

Cynthia used the couch for the greater part of our work. For most of our work I was, in a sense, an invisible and immaterial Other, a silence and a voice. The silence of therapy resonated with her father's stony silence and her mother's self-absorption. For periods, Cynthia fell into a sickly, chilling, or wasteful void. At such moments, she felt she might be lost forever, but she came back. Either she came back on her own, through her own natural rhythm of descent and return, or through my voice touching a psychic nerve. Eros and the void were twins. Never had more nerves been touched than by our passage through these twins on the wings of silence and voice.

Therapy was synchronous with the structure of her religion in at least one important sense. Cynthia had to find a way of trusting what she could not touch. The materials of therapy are thoughts and feelings—immaterial, intangible materials. The therapy relationship necessarily structures these immaterial materials and is structured by them.

Nevertheless, a person tries to go beyond everything she or he can think and feel. She or he tries to go beyond the limits of concrete, immediate relationships mediated by bodies. In therapy, "beyond" cannot be "instead of" or "in place of." The strength of therapy is its ability to hold a person to an impasse point—a limit, a distortion, a deficit, a destructive pattern—and encompass it with something more. One goes through the heart of something wrong and finds there is more to oneself than one imagined.

Both therapist and patient must find ways of going through what is wrong with the therapy relationship itself. Cynthia's father's stiff chill and mother's self-absorption became part of the silence of creative work and struggle. The silence of my fear in the face of my feelings became a barrier to be surmounted. Longings are obstacles and gateways.

Self and Other: Ben

A Life of Shame and Idolization

Ben grew up in a world rife with emotional turbulence and scorn. His mother's undisciplined emotionality set the basic tone of the household. She was the one with him most and, one way or another, Ben had to navigate the currents of her chaotic emotionality. This was not a peaceful or withdrawn family. Everyone had their say and was in the fray. This was not a dead family but its very aliveness was menacing. There was no place to be alone or quiet. Ben spent very few quiet moments in his entire life. Quietude was alien and terrifying. Things had to be noisy, and Ben spent much of his adult life keeping them noisy.

Not that his mother was malicious or ill willed or an evil person in the usual sense of the word. She did not beat or neglect Ben. She loved him dearly and "spoiled" him. She catered to him at the same time that she tantalized him. She did not see anyone as truly separate from herself. Her scorn for others, especially outsiders, indicated that she expected others to give her more, to give her everything. Ben grew up demanding more from others than any human being could give. It was humiliating to be human. Ben's pride rose above humiliation but underneath, like his mother, Ben's soul thrived on an atmosphere of humiliation. A double sense of specialness-humiliation bonded family members.

It was natural for Ben to draw closer to people by humiliating them and magnanimously transcending the sense of humiliation. He touched the depths of shame shamelessly. His parents were shameless about shaming others, each other, and their children. They did not give hostile shaming a second thought, but took it as natural.

At times, Ben's father threatened to be physically violent. These moments terrified Ben, who was deathly afraid that his father would carry out his threats to kill him. Here shame and humiliation gave way to straightforward annihilation. It was as if the threat of violence was the ultimate shaming act. Murder would be the logical extension of the writhing death Ben repeatedly suffered in acts of humiliation. Murder was the final heightening and conclusion of shaming activity. Murder would finish what escaped shame. Each ego would triumph over every other ego by successive acts of mortification until obliteration won out.

In one sense, the aim of shaming activity was the ego's triumph over self and other by annihilation. However, the ego seemed to need self and other to stay alive and available for further torture. Obliteration was a mistake, a time for rest, an intermittent surcease until the next wave of tormenting acts could build up. Ben depicted his mother as a "wild animal" who was totally ashamed of herself and totally scornful, inept and spoiling, energetic and unkempt, constantly humiliated and yet indefatigable. He was determined to get away from this mess, but the mess followed him as part of his own makeup.

Ben's father repeatedly humiliated his mother and was himself humiliated. Life shamed him. He was a failure in his own eyes. He could not rise above his circumstances. Instead of being happy that he could make a living and have a healthy family, his eyes were fixed on the fish that got away, the scheme that failed. His life was not good enough and whatever he possessed was a sign of degradation.

His wife and children, like any of his possessions, were not good enough. They were part of a degraded life, signs of failure. Thus nothing Ben did was good enough. His father laughed at Ben, if he took any interest at all. He demanded strict obedience, but lacked any consistent ruling plan or principle. His rule, like his wife's, was one of mood and temperament. Most of the time he did not take much of an interest in what Ben was doing, so that Ben escaped any rule at all. Ego and mood and caprice was everything for everyone. Ben learned to tread his way through seas of shifting feelings. His home prepared him for his life's work.

COMING THROUGH THE WHIRLWIND

A tendency that poisoned him also gave him strength. His mother's idolization of Ben made him feel special, godlike, magnanimous. He could demand anything and she would try to fulfill it. She was his slave. In this regard, Ben's first wife said that she wished she was his toilet paper: she wished to be as close to him as his shit was; she wished he'd wipe his ass with her. Ben slept well through his first marriage. His insomnia began when his human roll of toilet paper left him. He wished to go deeper into the asshole of his psyche. He needed to explore himself. She preferred to remain outside, on the surface, a smile.

Ben's mother's idolization of him became part of his blood. It heightened his sense of vitality. He thrived on idolization, just as he thrived on humiliation. Idolization-humiliation went together. Idolization triumphed over and pushed past humiliation. The idolized self nourished itself on the blood of humiliation like a vampire. It flew above everyday concerns and laughed at mundane worries. Common people, like his father, were ground to pieces by ordinary life. Life destroyed his father but it would not destroy him. The idolized self had an advantage. It would not stoop low enough to be destroyed by life. Life would serve him like a slavish, loving mother. He would find ways to make sure that life fit into the template his mother laid down for him. He would not, like his father, let life judge him. He would move along pockets of admiration, as surefooted as a boy stepping across the stones of a brook.

The Quiet Other

Ben's second marriage was to a woman, Lucy, who was not all surface smiles. She had depressive depths. She thought more slowly and her feelings underwent longer gestation periods. She was capable of excitement but was not wild about noise. She needed time to listen to herself, to let herself grow. In this regard, she was closer to pregnancy as a model for psychic growth. She took time to do things.

For a long time, Ben took it upon himself to save her from herself. He would bring her out. She would blossom with him. He would be her savior. He would force her to communicate, to be more alive, to be more manic. If he could not stand his first wife's superficiality, he could not bear his second wife's formless depression. Yet these women were not inverted images of one another. In a way, Lucy did blossom through her marriage. Her roots went deep. She struggled with problems that did not yield easily. She made contact with life's deeper rhythms. Ben had to grow to keep up with her turtle's pace. Her movements were slow but real.

Much that was superficial in Ben's life began to crack. He could not fly above life with Lucy. She was rooted in earth processes. Often it seemed she had too many roots, not enough branches. She tried to make her branches fit her roots. At times, it seemed she was buried below the surface. She worried whether she would ever emerge. Would her life merely be incubation?

Ben could not stand Lucy's slow-motion rhythm. Was she merely standing still? Dare he (or she) trust in her long-term movement? Her slowness created a vacuum which his panicky rage tried to fill. Could he truly make a place inside himself for her, a quiet place?

A Male Lucy

To some extent, Ben saw me as a male Lucy, an intellectual Lucy, whom he tried to put down. I was quieter than he and took my time. Yet I shared flashes with Ben. Ideas came to me and often I spoke my mind. I could not be sure whether I was right or wrong, but I communicated the essential lines of my convictions and reflections. Ben had to pass through me to be himself. He had to navigate my psycho-cognitive style, my moods and temperament, my risks and holding back. I did not fit his ideal of a superconfident, smooth, successful man, no more than Lucy did.

I was slow like Lucy but my mind was quicker on the draw. I could point out to Ben positions in which he was stuck. If he could see my weakness, I saw his rigidities. His criticisms did not stop my seeing. He could not bully my mind away, no more than he could bully away Lucy's slow, stubborn will and awareness. Lucy and I were stones around his neck, concrete in which his feet were embedded. We did not simply mold ourselves to him, as his first wife apparently did. We maintained our differences in obvious ways. Yet we retained a plasticity and pliability. We molded ourselves to him, as one does with another person naturally, in attempts to reach out and draw closer through vision and understanding and love. Because we could say what bothered us and work on it, we did not have to break away.

Lucy and I slowed Ben down. We did not treat life as he was used to. Glitter did not fascinate us. Lucy did not like someone because he or she was famous, or handsome, or smart. Her liking gravitated to a meld of intelligence and good-heartedness. She knew Ben was a good soul and valued his insights and caring more than his house or position. She saw through selfishness and egocentric hostility. She loved Ben's struggle with Truth: it made more truth possible in her life. She loved Ben's essence, even as she balked at or resisted warped areas. She fought Ben for what was best in him.

Ben's love-hate of truth was mirrored by mine. Therapy involves growth through truth, which is mysterious. Two flawed beings, deficient in many ways, interact in the hope of becoming fuller, stronger, more soundly founded. Both beings are beset by error and the demons they created. Experience and communication are structured by limitations and guidelines and plagued by distortions. It may be impossible to communicate truthfully, since self-deception and self-justification run so deeply. It has often been observed that we scarcely can be sure of anything except vanity. Yet we pray truth wins out and try to let it enter our lives effectively. We enter truth and truth enters us. We are pervaded and uplifted by it. We are renewed by our capacity for truth, in spite of our incapacity. This is what Ben had been longing to hear and have validated, in spite of the cynical ego's dread of losing glory or being overthrown.

Something in Ben gravitated to the truth about his life, no matter what the cost, and this was a matter of faith. Underneath it all is the faith that we are basically good and that goodness will come through. This was Lucy's challenge: to release the basic goodness depressed by her sense of deficiency, to release Ben's essential goodness ensorcelled by his ego.[2]

---

[2]For a relevant discussion of processes of "ensorcellment," see J. Grotstein's "Forgery of the Soul: Psychogenesis of Evil" (1984). See also, W. J. Lowe's discussion of theoretical paradigms dealing with problems relating to innocence and evil, "Innocence and Experience: A Theological Exploration" (1984).

To Ben's surprise and chagrin, he realized how neglectful he had been of core areas of his being. He was stunned by realizing how thoroughly deprived he was intellectually, culturally, and physically. He did not exercise or take good care of his body. Nor did he take good care of his mind. He was satisfied with mental and physical junk food.

In therapy, he began to listen to the small voice within that informed him of his self-neglect. He had always wanted to play more tennis and take walks and eat better food. Why hadn't he? He was vaguely irritated by his failure to study and learn and write more. Yet he avoided such challenges. He also ignored religious promptings, like the impulse to pray. His attitude toward so much that might enrich and uplift him was dismissive. He wanted things to come easily: life should be a summer vacation. He felt better after a workout, physical or mental or spiritual, but television was easier. He was not used to the tension of something building over time: his body, a project, a relationship.

Lucy's values nourished Ben's soul and also maddened him. Why wasn't she more interested in getting ahead and shining? Didn't she want glory? Was she merely modest and shy? Yet she made contact with people, not the same people Ben might have sought. Ben's colleagues liked and respected Lucy. She was warm, perceptive, alive. She had a glow that was real. People could trust her to be herself, even if she was confused about who she was or what she wanted to do. She built a life and helped Ben build life.

Lucy valued the little things of daily life and paid close attention to them. She also reached out for more. Creative work was important to her. Ben tended to play down the importance or goodness of "little things." He measured life on a grander, more materialistic scale. He did not treasure all the goodness he was given and sometimes enjoyed. Nor could he sustain the buildup of creative work for long.

I was a mixture, inasmuch as I loved "small moments" ("the best things in life are free"), yet was involved in creative struggle. I wanted to live decently but, like Lucy, did not want to be consumed by materialism. Lucy and I firmly believed in a transmaterialistic foundation and aim of our beings, and it was this that, ultimately, cemented Ben to us.

Ben and Lucy's marriage would have failed without therapy.

A statement like this places an awesome responsibility on therapy. How dare a therapist decide whether a marriage will succeed or fail? Who has such wisdom or rights? In fact, one does not "decide": one works with negative attitudes of individuals and learns from what happens. There is no doubt that Ben's hostile egocentricity combined with Lucy's depressive tendencies and need for distance would have exploded the marriage. Had they stayed together under such conditions, their lives would have been miserable. Both had broken marriages in the past and would have gone through another broken marriage, if necessary. What makes therapy beautiful when it works is that two good souls who wanted to live well together were given the chance to do so. But this could happen only insofar as each accepted the challenge of each other's and one's own personality.

Lucy and Ben were difficult people whose personalities were troublesome to themselves. Neither was a simple, happy-go-lucky person. Ben glossed over many of his difficulties with manic flights, a sense of glory, a dedication to his trade and the good, material things of life. But he was not at peace with himself. He was easily wounded and enraged. A sense of deprivation scarred him and drove him on. Lucy suffered in a more inward way and was more verbal about a lack of self-worth and lack of confidence. Each was torn apart by tendencies in themselves they could barely locate. Their relationship rubbed their noses in what was wrong with each other and became a kind of training ground for facing themselves.

It would be hard to imagine someone more suited to help Ben face himself than Lucy. Her problems infuriated him, touched his weak points. Yet she loved what was good in him and he knew that. To keep her (and to find himself) he had to reach beyond his sense of deprivation, wounded sensitivity, and egocentric rage. He was forced to rework the materials that echoed and fit his mother's and father's personalities. Egocentricity, in one or another form, was the rule of interchange among Ben's family members. To get along with Lucy, Ben's ego would have to make room for something more, for a searching, human being, for better elements in himself.

It was up to therapy to ratify the message of growth that was hidden in Lucy's resistance to the worst in Ben and in her steadfast love of the Ben he would come to know—the Ben he had been waiting to know.

Catastrophe and Faith

To negotiate therapy one must face catastrophe. The sense of catastrophe has many roots and strands. There are physical catastrophes, storms, droughts, geological upheavals, fires. There are wars, social cataclysms, economic reversals, and criminal actions. There is death. Life is lived with a background awareness of many dangers and with awareness that there will come a time when all these dangers may be as empty as the time before one was born.

There are, too, catastrophes created by human imagination. What if we do not simply die? What if we live forever? What if how we live affects what happens to us after death? What will become of us if we are judged? Primitive fear of danger linked to the will to survive is transferred to an ethical plane. We become sensitive to the ways we survive, to the quality or moral tone of our lives, to issues of integrity. We become tyrannized by the will to be good. Moral growth becomes as or more important than survival.

There are worse tyrannies than growth in goodness. In one form or another, we are driven to enslave one another. We are driven to ascend, to get ahead, to get on top. We supplant or support the stars above us. Division of labor may be based on caste or otherwise ritualized, while also allowing for the play of talent, ambition, and desire. Social and economic catastrophes are, to some extent, contingent on the play of personalities. Some feel it catastrophic, not if they are enslaved, but if they are not powerful or successful enough, if they can not stamp their sense of self on the stage of history.

Therapy mixes successful people, who feel something is missing or fear self-destructive actions will topple them, with many more who feel blocked or misrouted or misshapen, who cannot follow through in what they undertake, or who cannot even make a real beginning. Whatever the relative level of success or failure in various areas, most people in therapy feel or discover that something is wrong about the way they are living. Something in

COMING THROUGH THE WHIRLWIND

their bones does not feel "right," something in the depths of their being feels "off." And whatever this "offness" or "wrongness" is, no matter how subtle, it is catastrophic. It poisons life, it spoils, it accuses, it nags.

In some people, this voice is crazy. It may tell one to kill. A person may feel dishonest not listening to this voice and actually kill people or himself. In such a case, the voice is frozen. It has rigidified and become monolithic. If it could thaw out, it would turn into many voices, each with stories to tell. If it could spin itself out, it might tell many stories of soul murder. It would recount the ways the person was killed by people or forces, the ways it wanted to kill. It might tell the story of how a sensitive, open, and flowing baby became a killer trying to set things right.

Catastrophe compounds catastrophe. Once the psyche sets off in a wrong direction, it dreads the process of resetting itself. Often it monitors itself and tries to reset itself, but its running commentary and attempts make things worse or mark time, like a gerbil on a treadmill. To reset oneself is painful. One has more or less adapted to oneself. One's adaptations themselves may cause pain, but they offer some illusion of control or safety. To undergo corrective change seems impossible or horrible. One dreads giving up everything and starting over. One's attitudes, inclinations, and habits have become routinized, stylized—one's patterns of self-hood flow in one's psychic veins like blood and are subject to analogous diseases (e.g., hardening of psychic arteries, psychic leukemia). In psychotherapy, cure may seem as catastrophic as illness.

Sometimes a person does give up a lot in trying to set things right in therapeutic work. Jobs, relationships, and pastimes may change. What a person thinks important may change or one may find the courage to follow what she always felt was important. One may find oneself traveling in an entirely different direction one barely knew existed.

The most important change may involve a subtle shift in attitude. One develops a sense that inner struggle can be fruitful. One does not merely go around the same old circles with no results. Repetition is not just a sign of being mired in self-destructive patterns but an opportunity, a challenge, a chance to do better.

One appreciates more keenly that repetition is necessary and built into life. We eat and sleep and wake up repeatedly. We repeat sexual preferences and our favorite prayers. Repetition gives us a chance to learn, to dig more deeply. It provides a frame of reference to transcend, a home base for exploration.

We become sensitive to variations that bubble up through our sameness, that give the sameness a new cast. The sameness of our lives takes on a different glow with an attitude capable of allowing life to build on itself. Our discoveries have a more enduring impact. They open real pathways. We ride upon intimations like surfboards, uplifted through the tumult. We begin to practice what we preach and preach what we can practice.

. We pray we are not given more than we can bear. We dread a catastrophe that would break us, one from which there is no recovery. We see that this can happen. Our streets are stained with catastrophes with no way out. We know how cruel life can be. We are all walking wounds. Perhaps we secretly worry that something has gone wrong with us which is irreparable. We hush up our fear that there is something wrong, that our characters and personalities are in some ways catastrophic, that we traumatize, as we enrich, those closest to us. We share our catastrophic and caring selves with each other.

We pray we are not given too little, that we do not give in to our numbness. We harden and build cold shells around brutalized areas. Will we succumb to our shells? Some dread there is nothing within the shells, except more shells. As one digs beneath the rubble, one finds more rubble. There seems to be no end to shatter. One already has gone through too much. One prefers to hide, like a sick animal. Perhaps if one rests and licks wounds for enough lifetimes, one will dare try again. Many lifetimes may have to pass before vitality returns.

In therapy, our sense of catastrophe may be exacerbated or adumbrated but it must be traversed. Psychoanalysts, especially, have catalogued many sorts of psychic catastrophes that appear in the course of therapeutic work: separation-intrusion anxiety, annihilation anxiety, castration anxiety, paranoid-schizoid and depressive anxieties, nameless dread, falling without end, loss of psychophysical integrity, dread of truth and dread of breaking addiction to self-poisoning processes, and more. Winnicott (1974) writes of various psychoticlike agonies that inundate the psyche before it develops the resources to handle them. One may spend one's life trying to catch up to states one could not begin to work with well enough.

Our long period of infantile immaturity gives rise to a sense of deficit that can be exacerbated as development proceeds. The gap between perception and motor coordination is one that never leaves us. Our ability to see is ahead of our ability to do. Many play down the sense of deficiency and concentrate on what they are able to achieve. Others cannot transcend intimations of deficiency and pick at sore spots. A one-sided focus on either strength or weakness can devastate entire communities.

In therapy, one builds the ability to see with many eyes at once, while giving one's main developmental arc expression. One becomes sensitive to nuances of psychic catastrophes in moment-to-moment terms and develops various languages for expressing, investigating, and transcending them. It has been observed that brain-damaged people may experience "catastrophic anxiety" when faced with a situation they cannot handle. They are helped to absorb their helplessness and concentrate on workable areas. Perhaps, in time, brain functioning will expand or develop compensations. Meanwhile the individual learns to circumnavigate what he cannot do and pay attention to what he can do.

In therapy, a person learns to attend to what is possible, with respect for areas of deficit that permeate psychophysical life. This involves more than becoming a good psychic engineer. It ultimately involves a faith that subtends both strength and weakness, ability and deficit.

There is more to therapy than building skills to manipulate psychic materials. Much depends on one's attitude of approach to psychic events, one's relationship to various aspects of self and the selves of others, one's relationship to human capacities. An attitude may run through and organize many worlds of experience: conscious-unconscious, physical-transcendental. What is most relevant is not the content that appears or the dimension that it appears in, but the quality of its appearance and the quality of our relationship to its appearance.

In old-fashioned language, what is involved is discrimination of spirits and the ability to struggle fruitfully with the various spirits through which one approaches life as a whole and in specific situations. A crucial ingredient in the ongoing war of spirits or attitudes of approach is the quality of faith that subtends and supports the capacity to experience.

Faith in what? God? Human capacities? Neither faith in God nor human capacities has protected human beings from one another. Brutality has marked both. Faith in simple goodness perhaps, faith that life is basically good, that experience is worth having. If formal religions practiced what they preached and incarnated a belief in simple goodness, what bloodshed and social injury might have been avoided. All too often, in the name of holiness and prudence, political, economic, and military machinations have been justified; after all, religions must survive in a power-oriented world and, if they are to do any good, must fight not to be eradicated by hostile institutions and tendencies. Meanwhile, secular individualism (and now also communism) has been an ecological disaster.

Psychotherapy is a nest for simple goodness, or rather, it can or should be, and sometimes it is. This is in spite of its various "isms" — psychic or spiritual materialism, narcissism, erotism, and so on. In psychotherapy, one person tries to help, to do good for another. Above all, this is the behavior that is modeled, simple goodness between one human being and another. One wishes another well and tries to prepare or repair him for his journey. It is simple goodness on a level of profound intimacy, a wishing well that cuts below ideologies, including one's own.

Of course, this simple goodness is filtered through a highly sophisticated cognitive apparatus. Freud advocated that the analyst be educated in many areas of cultural life. Everything one is and learns plays a possible role in shaping interventions. One is limited only by one's variable limits. Often enough one relies on Providence, but not without exercising one's own powers. Who gets more from therapy: therapist or patient? Many sessions are characterized by miracles. Stillborn lives begin to move. Hopelessness and self-hate begin to occupy less room. A heart opens. An interest blossoms. Simple goodness has a chance in the battleground of self, first, and in one's larger life as one begins to grow into it.

Perhaps the catastrophe of catastrophes is the shock and breakdown of simple goodness, the doubt that is cast upon its validity or reality. Can a sense of basic goodness withstand the stream of disillusionments that are part of daily living? Disillusionment is necessary if one is to develop awareness of limitations, if one is to set boundaries on vanity. Megalomania must be chastened. But there is a difference between disillusionment that feeds development and disillusionment that crushes, although the line between them may be very fine.

Is love of basic goodness an illusion which must be crushed if one is to be free? Is clinging to hope parasitic? If one annihilates everything in the personality, including love of goodness, will a greater sense of the Good come through no-thingness? In higher religions, we are called to nullify ourselves in God, in Goodness itself.

We resurface after disillusionment. The question is how? To what degree do we contract, become bitter or cynical, self-pitying, chronically rageful and hard or cloying? To what extent does disillusionment free us, permit us to cover more territory, to use ourselves more fully? With what moral and personal quality do we survive our catastrophes and blessings? The ways we survive may be as catastrophic as the horrors we faced or failed to face, since we seal ourselves into our styles of survival.

Winnicott (1969) depicts a moment of total annihilation, a moment of absolute destruction of illusions.[3] Self and other resurface and experience life anew, totally fresh, alive in the joy of coming through all possible destructiveness, alive in the basic goodness of life and personality. The possibility of give and take, of making use of one another for growth purposes, carries us forward. Channels open. Real meeting and living is possible. We come through our sensitivity more honestly. We do not have to be dwarfs or tyrants because of our ability to wound and be wounded.

---

[3]Also, see Eigen, "The Area of Faith in Winnicott, Lacan and Bion" (1981a); *The Psychotic Core* (1986), Chapters 4, 5, and 8; and The Electrified Tightrope (1991d).

Catastrophe and Faith: Cynthia

Cynthia's dream of eating dead Indians (pp. 72–77, 187–190) stimulated exploration of various fears and dreads which, at times, approached catastrophic proportions, but the dream itself did not feel catastrophic. The dream affect was inviting and corrective. Its tone was matter of fact, solicitous, even pleasant. Disgust, pity, and anxiety played an important role in Cynthia's discussion of the dream, but did not dominate or perhaps even characterize the dream itself.

Cynthia's executive ego or persona was bewildered by the mythiclike imagery and drew back in obsessive vacillation, both in the dream and in waking life. The dream led to a wealth of associations relating to deadness, pity, inhibition, and paralysis. It brought Cynthia face to face with major personality blocks and allowed her to taste the possibility of catastrophic anxiety in a relatively benign way. It presented results of cataclysm (deadness, obsessive confusion, inhibition of oral activity) but not cataclysm itself.

The dream also pointed to a new catastrophe Cynthia faced: her entrance into therapy, which she dreaded. She would be stuffed with the dead words and ideas and intentions of the analyst. Rather than eat a dead analysis she would rather not eat at all or rehash pockets of deadness she was used to. Nevertheless, the inviting tone of the dream encouraged me to support Cynthia's initiation into therapy. The dream's atmosphere was intriguing and evoked curiosity. It proposed a ritual of transformation which incorporated deadness in a new way.[4]

It took several years of therapeutic work for Cynthia to be able to face catastrophic states more overtly. The dream in which her father was taken hostage on a college campus came close to depicting a bloodbath (pp. 82–83 ; 190). In the larger world, her father seemed weaker than on the farm. The dream depicted his helplessness and Cynthia's protectiveness, to which she did not

---

[4]For a wonderful discussion of corpse imagery in transformation processes, see H. Zimmer, *The King and the Corpse* (1948).

give in. She left him to his fate and went her own way, although she wondered if a higher authority might help.

Cynthia often felt out of her element, like her father in the dream. She longed for a protective force to save her from life's bloody battles, but also resisted this temptation. The dream nearly depicted how bloody life could be. One strong man after another tried to win the day. She did not stand a chance on the battlefield and would do best away from the fray.

The therapy room was away from the struggle in the raw, a place of insulation. Yet she feared her helplessness as she sank into herself and discovered the bloody battle within. She was the place where all forces crossed. Her father could not save her from what had to be faced and she could not save him. Her megalo-manic benevolence was thwarted when it came to putting the torn pieces of herself together. Nothing she did worked well enough, at least not to her satisfaction. When emotional and behavioral storms struck, the best she could do was to ride them out and hope she survived the worst.

The dream in which Cynthia rolled her boyfriend's (Wes's) car into a ditch filled with water (pp. 84–85) was similar to the cam-pus dream in that Cynthia felt helpless and out of control. Once again she escaped disaster. She climbed to safety as the water rose. The car was lost, but she was saved. She injured the other or, more precisely abandoned the other like a shell. She stepped out of the injured other. In both dreams, she transcended a help-less element. She left a helpless element to its fate as she moved on. She plunged into and transcended her sense of helplessness.

Her dream of eating metal waste (pp. 86–88) depicted an attempt to control catastrophe. She swallowed her hardness and the hardness of others, but did not digest it. Indigestible material weighed her down. There was hard waste in her psychic belly that she could do nothing with. Alien metal composed her core and shell (the car above). Destructive reactions gathered around the hardness that she, at great expense, tried to make her own. The accumulated metallic waste she swallowed not only was indi-gestible, it spoiled digestion processes in general. Here was a catastrophic process she barely sensed and could not easily undo. Her attempt to master catastrophe was as catastrophic as the catastrophe itself.

In her dream of an old, ill uncle dying from falling down and hitting his head (pp. 89–90, 191), catastrophic loss of control was beneficial. A cancerous element died and Cynthia became the executor. Old sick head activity died and Cynthia filled the gap. This illustrates a more general psychological principle: insofar as diseased elements of personality die, there is more room for us. We can occupy more of our personality and grow into our capacities.

A turning point was reached in which Cynthia perceived the catastrophic aspect of psychic growth. Death is part of the language of growth. Cynthia escaped death in the college campus and auto flood dreams, but the threat of death was built into these dreams. To the uninitiated, nightmares are bad experiences to be avoided. To the cognoscenti, they are opportunities to rework bits and pieces of personal catastrophe, the catastrophe we call our personalities.

Bion (1962, p. 8) points to the issue involved when he notes that we do not have nightmares because we have stomachaches, but we have stomachaches if we cannot form nightmares. Cynthia's nightmare-forming activity reached the point where she could link growth with dying. Through repetitive work in therapy, she learned to come through dream death. She expected good things to happen to her if she died properly.

The birdman dream (pp. 90–92, 191–192) would have been a nightmare had it come earlier, but after Cynthia's unconscious learning from the old man dying dream, it was invigorating. There is a structural analogy between Cynthia's position in the birdman dream, and her father's position in the campus bloodbath dream. Her father was pinned in the grasp of a strong man, and she was swept up in the birdman's propulsive force. The birdman, like the gladiators in the college campus dream, exerted a certain mysterious fascination. He was a numinous figure thrown up by the psychic depths. Instead of vacillating or withdrawing, Cynthia was a partner, *his* partner. He thrusted and she encircled him. His power did not harm her. She experimented with it, took it into account, learned to work with and against it, and, ultimately, made it her own.

Her identification with the birdman's phallic power was no mere identification with the aggressor. Through him, she experienced her own naked baby activity, the baby's insistence, demandingness, determination, and freshness. In the dream, her

COMING THROUGH THE WHIRLWIND

primal activity broke out of its shell. It had been bottled up in her and her parents' personalities. What in the past would have turned into a catastrophe, became a taste of freedom. Cynthia experienced herself in a new way.

The fact that Cynthia was working better with potentially catastrophic elements of growth processes did not mean that catastrophe would vanish. Her dreams often skirted catastrophe and sometimes overtly represented multiple catastrophes. For example, Cynthia's dream of a toothless hag (pp. 92–95) was potentially menacing but it provoked an awareness of paranoid defenses and a longing to give herself and others more room. Through the old hag, she was able to experience more thoroughly a kind of creative hollowness, a more positive sense of aloneness. Absolute helplessness was converted to an appreciation of the space within and between people.

Nevertheless, to lose teeth also means to die. In her next dreams (pp. 95–97), Cynthia's father died and she and her mother were doomed. The two were hiding from projectiles, bloody bodies all around. The massacre finally had come. Through the massacre, Cynthia experienced a rage that obliterated everything that held her back. She wiped out all limitations, including herself. This was an outcome she long feared and gravitated toward: total annihilation. If only she might stamp out everything fully enough, she might be able to start over.

For the moment, life was filtered through the image of war and infinite helplessness. She and her parents were at the mercy of anonymous forces that bombarded them. Life was cruel and ruthless and individuals were powerless victims of massive trauma. Cynthia, too, was being annihilated by therapy, assault after assault, trauma after trauma. My personality stung her and left her adrift. Her own psyche needed to produce wave after wave of what could not be faced or worked with or handled well. Her dreams rubbed her nose in deficits and she was overwhelmed by inability and weakness. It was good to give in to images and states she most dreaded. Through bloody images, she recovered the purity of rage and washed herself clean with blood.

If therapy goes well, one does not have to kill others or be killed in a physical sense. One is too busy discovering ways the self kills and is killed from moment to moment and over a lifetime. In therapy, the raw fact of self-feeling comes alive. Intense drama runs through day-to-day existence. One learns to think symbolically, to represent one's state in workable ways. But the state of self is more than a symbolic event. It is human reality *par excellence*, perhaps *the* most basic fact. What one does to/with oneself and others (and vice versa) is the battlefield of battlefields, the true contest and reward.

A New Plasticity

By the time therapy ended, Cynthia was beginning to be "therapy-wise" or better psychically oiled. Her dreams showed a loosening of rigid distinctions. In one dream (p. 98), a woman used her breast on Cynthia like a penis and it felt good. In another (p. 98), men amputated Cynthia's leg inch by inch and her whole family was doomed. A few nights later (p. 98), Cynthia stabbed a male aggressor with a saw. The next night (p. 98), she tilled soil using something like a third leg with a proud sense of achievement. The phallic element changed forms and functions. Cynthia was not tied to a rigid position, whether victim or victor. She went through Eros and murder to fecundity.

In Freudian terms, Cynthia's psychic productions began to be saturated with a rich array of polymorphous perverse positions, the emphasis here on "polymorphous." Bisexual and heterosexual images oscillated in surprising ways. Similarly, images of annihilation and generativity underwent many form changes. It is not unusual for associations and imagery to loosen in therapy. One ordinarily understands this as part of the transitional rite of passage. One's thinking may become more "wild" in therapy and settle into new molds of sanity afterward.

On a deeper level, what emerges is an appreciation for the basic rhythm of falling apart–coming together, which takes many forms. The personality can bear to hold itself together only so long. It must change forms like the body changes positions. Rest oscillates with work, relaxation with tension, although things are rarely so simple. Identifications with various aspects of life, self, and other change. It is unnatural to try to be one way.

We are afraid of our multiplicity. We feel we ought not be both cowardly and brave, male and female, dead and alive, close and distant, omnivorous and steadfast, and so on. For Cynthia, therapy became a place to let down, to let ideas, feelings, and ideas of self–other meld and reshuffle in very specific ways.

The kaleidoscopic reshuffling of personality (Chapter 2) in therapy heightens rather than diminishes sensitivity to details. Although there are families of forms, each form tells a story a little different from all others. Each makes a specific contribution to the generation of self. It is impossible to pay attention to each form the psyche produces and give every form its due. We can spend only so much time listening and talking to ourselves. We very inadequately become partners with our deeper processes.

We select directions to take and pray our selections are right enough. This is complicated by the fact that any time we spend on any of our productions usually turns out to be valuable. We find that, at times, we take paths that are parallel and, at other times, paths that crisscross in complex ways. We ultimately must let our psyche do most of the work but it is important for us to do something.

We delve into samples of possible productions and let most of our images go. Nevertheless, we taste or smell many images we let go, like wetting a finger to see which way the wind is blowing. We consciously and unconsciously scan to see how the ship of self is doing, to check on the quality and goodness of our direction. We also test the quality of our scanning, i.e., scan our scanning, and are never quite sure what we are up against or what we may miss.

Cynthia benefitted enormously from letting these problems wound her. She began therapy ahead of the game by knowing that death of self was important for living. She understood the centrality of crucifixion for aliveness. Yet religion did not help her with many of the specifics of the deaths and rebirths she needed to work on. She could barely guess the kinds of reshuffling human personality was capable of undergoing. She substituted sexual looseness for the psychic plasticity she experienced in her samples of therapy.

It was a tribute to her approach to religious experience that she did not quickly run away from the polymorphous sexual-aggressive aspects of psychic work, nor from linking some of her blocks with early family history. Psychic work gave more backbone to religious experience. It was not enough to gloss over herself in ecstasy-agony or a striving for benevolence. Grueling, detailed work was necessary. Crucifixion was a more subtle and pervasive process than she had envisioned, especially crucifixion of self on specific personality deficits, deformations, rigidities, misdirections. Cynthia learned to make better use of the samples she took of herself.

Cynthia's increased plasticity was pictured in her last dream in therapy (pp. 98–100). She shopped in a big barn for housewares in a going-out-of-business sale. Therapy was about to go out of business. We do all our shopping in a store that is going out of business, since we are all going to die. Housewares refer to the psychic interior, our internal environment, contents and atmosphere, the inner homes we create for ourselves and each other. Cynthia had a say as to what her psychic home would be like. She participated in a process of selection and entered the psychic depths (the barn) to see what was available for use.

She was afraid of losing her autonomy. Her cat clawed her. Exploration required restrictions and discriminations. Animal and child aspects of the self were perceived as fundamental, i.e., in the basement. Her cat was placed temporarily in a cage in the basement, ostensibly for its own protection. Lack of restrictions on her cat-self in real life had led to rigid self-destructive patterns. In the dream, Cynthia transcended her cat. Her cat would not be allowed to deflect her overall movement. It would be free again but perhaps would understand that it was part of a larger whole. Or, if the cat remained fearful-tyrannical, Cynthia would at least have a say in its contribution.

More specifically, Cynthia put the cat in the basement, not merely because it clawed (dominated) her, but because she feared another cat would make it sick. She was afraid of illness by contagion. She understood that madness was contagious and that she was especially susceptible through her cat. Her promiscuity (fear of "pussy" sickness) masked and expressed madness, a madness that could be absorbed by the barn. A larger psychic container (the barn) emerged, which allowed for a good selection of growth possibilities. The possibility of fuller give and take might enable a better use of madness.

Catastrophe and Faith: Ben

Rage and grandiosity fed Ben's sense of aliveness. He found situations that nurtured his grandiosity and enabled him to be rageful in the service of psychological truth. Object loss (divorce, his therapist's death) precipitated panic and fragmentation. Ben tried to reconstitute himself around a new woman and new therapist, so that his old ways of triumphing over self and life would work once more. However, the discovery of panicky fragility and the demands of his new girlfriend and therapy catapulted him into entirely new experiential dimensions. He could not return to his old ways of holding himself together without destroying the new life that might grow.

Ben's dream life was impoverished. It was populated by seductive, aggressive women, criminals, and famous people. His dreams read like tabloids or TV shows obsessed with sex, aggression, and fame. They depicted disasters, tantalization, a tendency to injure and be injured, and the wish for glory. The drama was repetitious: would his ego rise to fame and glory or be shot down by criminal elements or drown in erotic entanglements?

Ben began to see the ways killer aspects of his personality made it impossible for experience to develop fully (pp. 114–115). The killer cut things short and kept things going around the same circles. Ben's personality took quite a pounding from itself. For the first time, Ben began to be afraid of himself and feel despair about getting better. A killer cemented his personality and masked a basic incapacity to process experience in subtle and variegated ways.

Ben's love of excitement did not produce growth. His killer stirred up excitement in order to tone life down. Excitement stopped a deeper order from emerging. His killers used chaotic excitement to blot out awareness of deficiencies. Only after Ben glimpsed his helplessness in the face of his inner predicament did truly nourishing elements begin to emerge. Ben began to focus on the problematic nature of his own personality and, in time, human personality in general.

After simply and clearly expressing his wish that his father be proud of him and his fear that he might not get out of enemy territory (his personality), Ben produced an image of a good-willed and nourishing woman (p. 116). This was the first of a line of good-willed, nourishing images that set Ben free rather than ruled him by excitement, rage, and terror. For the first time, Ben also produced an image of his mother as nourishing and support-ive. The love at the core of her personality was set free from the whirlwind of spiteful excitement and bitter frustration. By discov-ering within himself a dimension deeper than seductive manipu-lation, Ben could begin to let his love of truth have a base other than rage. A growth process was set in motion which aimed at a basic reordering of self.

Ben was able to marry Lucy and experience his longing to be a father. At this point he experienced his psychic predicament more starkly. Ben dreamed of heads floating in space and woke in a panic (p. 118). He found himself in a world of cut-off bodies and heads. It was difficult to tell whether he was more afraid of dying or going on in a fragmented state. His fear subsided as he adjusted to perceiving his predicament, a body without a head, a head without a body. Awareness of fragmentation and nothing-ness was part of what he obliterated with rage. Rage made him feel right and whole and cut off the problem of putting the pieces together. To simply see the truth about himself and stay with it was a new experience. It ushered in the possibility of honest admission and confession.

A little girl baby emerged through Ben's fragmentation, depression, and dread of depersonalization (pp. 123–124). She symbolized faith and life in the midst of horror and impossibility. Like the nourishing, good-willed woman earlier, she was matter of fact, neither more nor less than herself. She represented a way of being at one with oneself, an aliveness more natural and less rigid than rageful tantalization. Between Ben's awareness of fragmentation and the little girl baby's natural aliveness, Ben dreamed of being in a synagogue, his first bit of religious symbol-ism. At last, he touched a reverence and awe deeper than rageful excitement.

When Ben became more serious about becoming a father, he became impotent (pp. 123–130). The dreams of this period contin-ued work through female images and the sense of disaster: his mother died, my head hung slackly as a result of a car accident, a pretty woman reached for his balls (pp. 123–125). Ben feared his supports would die (his internal mother, myself), as had his previous marriage and therapist. Out of disaster came a spontaneous, life-affirming moment: a fine woman liked Ben's balls. His mother's death and my slack head cleared the way for spontaneity. A loss of control led to a deeper order. Balls, not simply penis, were valued: generativity was possible.

In a further dream, Ben's mother was upset with him for trying to talk her out of her feelings when someone died (pp. 127–128). This dream mother was not like his real-life mother. Ben's dream mother was more open and honest. She fought Ben's manic defense for the right to be in contact with deeper feelings. She wanted her open heart, her softness. Such an image suggests growth in feeling and living. Ben was terrified at the prospect of fatherhood. His soft penis dramatized his fear but also represented a softening process that he needed to internalize.

Twenty years earlier, Ben entered therapy for help with impotence. He solved his impotence by throwing himself into a manic life-style. His relative success and pleasures worked until the beginning of middle age. At the mid-point of his life, disasters struck. What worked at twenty failed at forty. Ben had to reorient himself and become more of the man he wanted to be, not merely in superficial ways, but in terms of deeper values. He began to live more in accord with the deeper truths he talked about. He could no longer use his penis any way he wished. The heart-penis-generativity connection was growing.

Psychic Zig-Zag

Ben's dreams achieved a peak moment when Ben learned that the amniocentesis was normal (pp. 131–132). He dreamed of his baby boy-to-be dancing the dance of life. There was a church and choir, a lovely and affectionate woman who validated him, a multicolored fish turning into a bird, a beatific experience. In such a dream, the essential joy of life is distilled. Afterward, work begins anew.

Ben's dreams tried to work out new relationships between male and female currents (pp. 133–137). Good male and female images continued to evolve but a balance of power was difficult to achieve. One or the other might dominate at a given moment, but his dreams expressed the radical importance of both.

Ben's dream father entered the scene and became increasingly important. He resembled his real-life father but behaved more like a guide. With this new inner father, Ben was able to face deeper levels of disaster. In one apparently catastrophic image, Ben's penis dropped off (p. 135). His father spoke highly of Ben's mother and reconnected Ben's penis to an opening below his belly button. Ben felt more solid as a result of this re-working. He was more firmly connected to male and female elements in a very physical way. Catastrophic loss led to new openings, new connections, a reshaping of self.

Ben's new and tentative body ego solidity did not hold up when his baby boy, Ron, became a toddler. Ron was strong willed, affectionate, demanding, sensitive, and rebellious. Ben was thoroughly shaken by the sense of impotence Ron could induce and had to battle with rage and helplessness and his fear that Ron was taking a wrong turn. He dreamed of an amorphous, marshmallowy guy and that his father was an abusive alcoholic (pp. 138–139). His helpless rage seemed insoluble and promoted a sense of fragmentation. Ben felt glued to the sickest aspects of his personality.

For a time, Ben went downhill. He felt critical of his wife and others. Nothing pleased him. He dreamed of heavy drinkers and of taking his son to visit a psychotic woman patient (pp. 140–141). He felt hysterical a lot of the time. His son's willfulness scared him. In addition to making him helpless, it portrayed his own tyrannical bent. It intensified his sense of helplessness in the face of his own personality problems. He would have to let go and find new ways to exercise authority. Further growth of flexibility and insight was needed.

Ben's association of the child self with drunkenness and psychosis was crucial. The young child can be incontinent emotionally and physically. The child may lose emotional control when he cannot get what he wants with body and will. Images of drunken men, a psychotic woman, and demanding child depicted stormy, uncontrollable emotionality. Ben's psychotic patient tended to be hysterical, caring, helpful, yet would do almost anything to get her way. Ben had to convert hysterical emotionality to flexibility and absolute demandingness to firmness. Superficial controls

COMING THROUGH THE WHIRLWIND

and adaptations had to be surpassed in favor of a deeper search. Ben felt more alone than ever when he realized that his wish for fusional control did not work with a two-year-old.

The issue became a little clearer when Ben clearly expressed his wish to be my favorite patient and his publisher's favorite author. He wanted to be the star god child. His son was a competing god child, a center of his mother's and father's universe. Ben's own ego was in danger of being displaced by his love for his son. His son supported and jolted Ben's narcissism. The idea of being a father was more tolerable than the reality. Body ego fragmentation was connected with the shock to his narcissism and the displacement of god ego by deeper requirements. Ben's sickness seemed magnified precisely when the stakes were higher, when a decentering and reshuffling of personality was at hand.

Dream images stimulated reflection on the complexity of Ben's dilemma. In an important scene, white almond nuts were in the toilet bowl on which Ben sat (p. 147). He vacillated between flushing and saving them. What was more important than a decision was seeing how thoroughly madness and nourishment were intertwined. Ben tried to shit away his balls but their nourishing nature could not be lost. He associated creativeness with shit, madness, and nourishment. Creativity is not clean. One is no toilet bowl god above his products. Ben was fascinated with the white almonds and did not know what to do with them. He feared creativeness because of its link with the strange, the uncontrollable, the mad, and the dirty. He idealized creativeness because of its link with generativity, nourishment, inspiration, and the sublime. Idealization stopped him as much as fear or, rather, fear and idealization fed each other.

The image of a bug in a pearl (pp. 148–151) involved similar associations. It set madness in the center of a valuable jewel. In this dream, the spoiled gem was returned to its seller, a woman caught up in an ideology of superficial independence. Earlier in his life, Ben admired this woman and lived like her. Now he was enmeshed in family life and feared his bugginess would injure his child. His love for his boy made him want to be a better father. He could not get away with foisting off a bug as a pearl. His madness pained him more than ever. If he was going to be true to himself and his family, he had to open to new levels of interactiveness. He could no longer substitute the bugged pearl for the real item.

The bugged pearl is a vision of the flawed self. One wants to get the bug out of the pearl, to affirm the self as a flawless jewel. We feel the soul is basically good and pure and want to undo the spoiling. In therapy, Ben entered the pearl to wrestle with the bug. One bug after another met him. He found a kind of navel in which he and I melded and fought, therapy bugs, therapy pearls. He became one with me and repudiated his oneness with me and tasted his native self (p. 152). We fought until we became inter-mingling pools of blood (p. 155–157).

Body parts became fluid representations of personality func-tions which reworked themselves. Phallic-anal-vaginal elements blended in new combinations (pp. 155–157, 163–165). The self stretched and strengthened as it tried out new permutations of intrusive-receptive tendencies on mental and body ego planes. Ben saw his ego as god and saw beyond his ego god. He lost his legs to mother and tried to get his legs back (pp. 165–168). No matter how much Ben worked on himself, flaws, limitations, and difficulties remained. The catastrophes of his upbringing and times were etched in his character and disposition. He sensed a purity or wholeness beyond them, but, in one or another form, they remained the materials with which he worked. There seemed to be no end to bugs and pearls, to therapeutic move-ment, to living possibilities.

What Does Therapy Offer?

One can point to other times and places and find many ingre-dients of the therapeutic relationship. Dreams have played an important role in history. Relationships have played important roles in healing. Confession is a kind of talking cure and magnet-ism a kind of charismatic cure. The use of animal and body sym-bology appears in philosophy, religion, folklore, and literature. Everyday relationships may be supportive and challenging in more ways than therapy relationships. Yet, for better or worse, the way of speaking and being in psychotherapy is not quite like anything the human race has seen before.

We are very much in the process of finding out what psychotherapy offers. Psychoanalysis has made possible new kinds of relationships. Before psychoanalysis, two people did not sit in a room and talk with such specificity about upbringing and about body parts and functions as symbols of psychic capacities. They did not so consciously use the relationship between them as a way of observing and experiencing their capacity for relationship in general. Psychoanalysis has given rise to so many different forms of psychotherapy. Every human capacity has its say in one or another kind of therapy.

There are dangers. People who voyage through therapy can become therapy addicts or specialists. Therapy becomes their lives. They cannot speak to people who do not share similar kinds of experience and language. Indeed, therapists who use different kinds of therapy language have a hard time talking to each other. Therapists and patients may become insufferably analytic and boorish. Not infrequently, patients become therapists themselves and, like vampires, reproduce. Therapy may conspire to reinforce an infantile and inadequate existence.

However, my experience is that therapy usually raises the level of a person's life. It helps fill out and reset oneself. One talks about things one did not know one could talk about and discovers new ways of relating to self and other. One learns, person-to-person in the therapy relationship, how personalities impact on each other and how raw impacts are transformed into reactions, images, and influences. One observes traps form and open and how one's psychic equipment fights past, succumbs to, or works with itself. Therapist and patient move through, with, alongside, and against each other and come to see what they are doing, creating contexts for further seeing and being. Their relationship exists as a proving ground, a probe, a medium for growing the capacities needed for what they hope to do together.

Dependency plays an important role in therapy and life. People are often afraid of dependency and rightly so. Enslavement is a danger. But simple defensiveness against dependency is no answer in the long run. A mother may stop payment for an adult child because of fear that her son is getting too dependent on therapy. Her son may never have worked in his life, be crippled, fragmented, unable to sustain himself—yet she fears his dependency in therapy! Another mother, too busy to care for her child, fires a maid because she fears her child has begun forming too close a relationship to the woman. There is dread of intense, dependent relationships with a paid professional, even if nothing better is offered in daily living.

Of the two patients in this book, Cynthia's therapy was the shorter. It took her longer to get into therapy than Ben and she stayed less time. It may be that the erotic longings she aroused in me precipitated the brevity, possibly an enactment of the abrupt break with her brother following her father's discovery of them in the barn. I doubt that it was so simple, since she had a pattern of enacting erotic dramas that worked against her. In therapy, we sustained erotic longings without acting them out as part of a larger work process. It could as easily be said that she left because we did not act them out but this also would be an oversimplification.

For many years, Cynthia's sincere belief that she should and could work things out on a spiritual plane precluded entry into therapy. Therapy was viewed as an enemy of spirituality. It took many years for her to admit that she was caught in psychological patterns that worked against spiritual life as well as against her own everyday existence. Whatever she built she undid. It took time before this cycle felt more like a trap than freedom.

The relatively few years Cynthia spent in therapy might be viewed as part of her pattern to dip in and out, to do and undo. However, to enter therapy at all was an enormous step and to stay a few years was a momentous undertaking. She told and retold her story until she could link up surface happenings with deeper currents. She worked over many details of her life and, for the first time, made vital and effective use of dreams. This alone enabled her to create links between different levels of being. She saw how the spiritual and psychological could correct, challenge, and stimulate each other in ways previously unimaginable.

It is not surprising that Cynthia's foray into the world of psychotherapy did not last longer. If nothing else, it was a relatively successful introduction into processes she could use again. She discovered that therapy was not as destructive as she feared. She survived it and made significant gains. She gained more of herself. She did not have to shut out her psychological self because of her spiritual commitment. She entered more deeply into Being by passing through therapy.

Perhaps a few years was all she could take or needed. She left when she got a job that better fit her values and in which she could make use of herself more fully. She felt more of a sense of direction. She was not chewing up and spitting out her life, but doing something that made sense. Possibly she would marry and have a family, too, but that remained to be seen.

Would all this have happened without therapy? It did not occur before she finally threw in the towel and sought help. My belief is that Cynthia could not have done it alone. Spiritual counseling was not enough. She needed to experience what was wrong with her and realign herself with deeper, objective, psychic currents.

Ben was in therapy more than three times as long as Cynthia. Why was it necessary for him to stay so much longer? Did he benefit from his stay? Would Cynthia have benefitted if she stayed longer? Why does one person stay twenty years, another three, or six?

Ben tasted and explored many more aspects of madness than Cynthia. He faced a megalomania that runs through human life more openly and thoroughly and persistently. Was he more mad, megalomanic, dependent to begin with? How is it possible to make such judgments?

Part of the "answer" has to do with disposition, "bent," vocation, interest, and talent. Ben was addicted to the search for psychological truth. He believed in psychotherapy and made his living at it. For him, psychotherapy was not a last resort, an oddity, or shameful. It was a noble striving, a human privilege, a celebration and exploration of (inter)subjective being. Ben did not have to apologize for psychotherapy. It provided him with a vehicle for experiencing guts, heart, and brains in ways that led to more life. Psychotherapy was more than a peripheral adjunct: it was *his* way. He was more sensitive to it, more in love with it, more dedicated to purifying this human instrument and making it better—first of all, by making himself better.

Perhaps more than any other single factor, my own lifelong love affair with psychotherapy acted as a confirming model, a gift of permission. It was all right for Ben to be the kind of person he was, the kind of person he needed to become. One was not a sissy or second-best for loving the human psyche. We psyche lovers have a right to exist, a place in the scheme of things, a significant purpose. Intellectual and economic history has not

made us superfluous, although we are not in the "mainstream."
We tinkerers in the basement may prove even more important in
times ahead, especially to those who get tired of material pleasures and economic and technological switch-pulling.

It is impossible to reduce the processes and results of therapy
to a few basic profiles. Nevertheless, taken together, the two
patients focused on here honed distinct "gems" which refracted
psychic light into moving, useful, and healing colors. For Cynthia, the valorization of the psychological dimension allowed her
to relax her guard, work with more of herself, and concretize her
values and strivings in real efforts. Religion and law left out crucial aspects of herself. She feared she would betray her trust in
God by making use of psychotherapy, but the opposite happened. At last, healing became possible and she could begin to
build with the varied strands of her being.

Ben, the psychotherapist, faced what he talked about: the
madness of the self. Through therapy, he became more of the
therapist and man he was meant to be. He experienced and
learned about the psyche first hand. Perhaps most importantly,
he tasted the biggest struggle of all: the need and difficulty of
constituting a psyche capable of tolerating and working with
itself. As he did so, his life changed profoundly. His work filled
out and became more meaningful, he had inklings of a deeper
spiritual life, he established a loving family and good home, and
he reached out to his community.

Materialism and Integrity

A religious lawyer and a narcissistic psychotherapist—both
deeply committed to the business of living, both needing help.
Would their colleagues have any idea of the depth and breadth of
their struggles? Of the worlds that beat within them? We all share
the human psyche. We are all human subjects. We share the
psychological, the tension-bliss of impalpable awareness, the
struggle between good and evil, the struggle with various forms
of madness, and the need to build a psyche capable of tolerating,
working with, and going beyond itself.

COMING THROUGH THE WHIRLWIND

Both of these patients learned to listen to their lives. They allowed their lives to have an impact on them, and they learned new ways of processing this impact. Both had to work with one or another form of materialism.

Cynthia battled erotic materialism. For years, she used her body to discharge life's tensions in such a way that she discharged her life as well. She needed to learn not to run from her body, but not to exploit it either.

As she helped herself more, she began to help others, particularly people she felt could not help themselves. Cynthia linked up helping herself with helping others as a lawyer and, for the moment, found peace in this coming together of inner and outer possibilities. She looked for ways that struggle would be fruitful.

Although she helped others, Cynthia did not leave herself out. With her recognition of the importance of psychological life, working productively with herself became a "must." She could not turn back from her discovery of psychological reality, but she needed to integrate it with something more.

Cynthia found the prevalence of greedy materialism distasteful and worked in its interstices—with its casualties. She knew how close she had come to being a casualty herself, how close her life had come to eating itself up. The very vastness of possibilities overwhelmed her. Life's palette and canvas seemed limitless. She did not know how to draw upon her resources in ways that might work. She did not know which sorts of experience to rely on, nor how to bring herself together in ways that fit her varied pulls. Therapy was a kind of difficult cocoon which enabled Cynthia to develop new sorts of relationships to the dimensions that constituted her life.

Ben's adult life was beset by an unconscious contradiction. He cherished an ideology of psychological growth, premised on the pursuit of psychological truth. At the same time, he tried to make psychological truth fit his narcissistic-materialistic worldview. He twisted truth to support his need to be triumphant. His ego gloried in materialistic success.

A number of factors conspired to make this contradiction insupportable. His wife, who elevated his narcissism, left him. Economic inflation made his overextended style of living untenable. He approached middle age with the realization that the most important things in life eluded him. He remained childless. He was in danger of destroying a budding relationship. He did not know how to be nurtured or to nurture without ripping himself or others apart. Most importantly, he was in danger of failing to do justice to the best that was in him, to his creative self, to his longing for truthful and fruitful living.

He was torn between the apparently irreconcilable demands of psychological truth and materialistic success. He needed to grow a psyche capable of supporting both. This meant more than being able to tolerate the tension between integrity and survival. Ben would have no peace unless his psyche was organized around a primacy of truth. Only then would materialistic achievements have substance.

Ben was forced to come to grips with the shakiness of egoistic and materialistic glory. He wished things were otherwise. He wished things were easier. He had to face a heritage of resentment and bitterness about the nature of things. But, like Isaac in Genesis, he dug wells through layers of narcissistic-materialistic strivings.

One cannot wish shakiness away. But in Ben's life, the shakiness of things made visible a depth of experience that otherwise might have remained closed. Shakiness jolted Ben out of complacent self-deception and brought him face to face with the realization of how impossibly difficult it was to become a human being.

One's Basic Attitude of Approach

The heroic voyagers in psychotherapy who were the central subjects of this book, demonstrated that perhaps the essential business of therapy involves a growth or shift in attitude. Perhaps what changed most in each of these persons was the way they approached themselves, their own psyches, and the psychic life of others. An attitude of respect for psychic reordering processes evolved.

This is no facile achievement. One has to learn to get underneath one's caricatures, one's stories. The extent and complexity of psychic life is awesome. One may experience helplessness in the face of the immensity of intersubjectivity. One has to accustom oneself to working with samples of all that could be worked with, with signals wrested from a changing horizon. The way one works with any small infinity one finds is more important than trying to possess a great quantity of infinities.

One of the most important results of the therapy samples described in this book was that each person, in his or her way, tasted, studied, and became partners with basic processes that give order and fluidity to psychic life. They tasted first hand how shifting nuances of self–other relations impact on the quality and direction of personal movement. They grew in awareness of the momentous contributions mental and physical experiential dimensions make to building self.

They grew in realization of the task human beings face in the battle for both integrity and survival, for integrity and glory: how to participate in the growth of a psyche capable of supporting the shifting, multiple dimensions of existence, and how to support the acts that it plays a role in mediating.

The kind of therapy presented here was not always clear. Clarity was not its first aim. Its first aim was to evoke a sense of processes involved when psychic movement proceeds from ground up, as well as from top down. Attitudes run through psyche at all levels. If one's attitude of approach does not change through and through, it risks not changing at all. Growth is uneven. One does better in some areas than others. Nevertheless, the biblical call for a change of heart, of basic attitude, is a passionate call to all one's mind and heart and soul and might. In psychotherapy, we try to grow the capacity to participate as fully as possible in that change.

REFERENCES

Atwood, G. E., and Stolorow, R. D. 1984. *Structures of Subjectivity*. Hillsdale, N.J.: Analytic Press.

Balint, M. 1968. *The Basic Fault*. London: Tavistock.

Bion, W. R. 1962. *Learning from Experience*. Northvale, N.J.: Jason Aronson, 1983.

_____. 1970. *Attention and Interpretation*. Northvale, N.J.: Jason Aronson, 1993.

_____. 1977. Personal conversation, New York.

Bollas, C. 1987. *The Shadow of the Object: Psychoanalysis of the Unthought Known*. New York: Columbia University Press.

Ehrenzweig, A. 1971. *The Hidden Order of Art*. Berkeley, Calif.: University of California Press.

Eigen, M. 1973. Abstinence and the schizoid ego. *International Journal of Psycho-Analysis* 54. Also in *The Electrified Tightrope* (1991d).

_____. 1977. On working with "unwanted" patients. *International Journal of Psycho-Analysis* 58. Also in *The Electrified Tightrope* (1991d).

_____. 1980a. On the significance of the face. *Psychoanalytic Review* 67. Also in *The Electrified Tightrope* (1991d).

_____. 1980b. Instinctual fantasy and ideal images. *Contemporary Psychoanalysis* 16. Also in *The Electrified Tightrope* (1991d).

_____. 1981a. The area of faith in Winnicott, Lacan and Bion. *International Journal of Psycho-Analysis* 62. Also in *The Electrified Tightrope* (1991d).

_____. 1983a. A note on the structure of Freud's theory of creativity. *Psychoanalytic Review* 70. Also in *The Electrified Tightrope* (1991d).

_____. 1983b. Dual union or undifferentiation? A critique of Marion Milner's sense of psychic creativeness. *International Review of Psycho-Analysis* 10. Also in *The Electrified Tightrope* (1991d).

_____. 1984. On demonized aspects of the self. In *Evil: Self and Culture*, M. C. Nelson and M. Eigen, eds. New York: Human Sciences Press. Also in *The Electrified Tightrope* (1991d).

_____. 1985. Towards Bion's starting point: between catastrophe and faith. *International Journal of Psycho-Analysis* 66. Also in *The Electrified Tightrope* (1991d).

_____. 1986. *The Psychotic Core*. Northvale, N.J.: Jason Aronson.

_____. 1989. Aspects of omniscience. In *The Facilitating Environment*, M. G. Fromm and B. L. Smith, eds. New York: International Universities Press. Also in *The Electrified Tightrope* (1991d).

_____. 1991a. Winnicott's area of freedom: the uncompromiseable. In *Liminality and Transitional Phenomena*, N. Schwartz-Salant and M. Stein, eds. Wilmette, Ill.: Chiron Publications.

_____. 1991b. On Bion's no-thing. *New Ideas in Psychology* 9 (forthcoming).

_____. 1991c. The immoral conscience. In *The Self-Righteous Patient*. Binghamton, N.Y.: Haworth Press.

_____. 1991d. *The Electrified Tightrope: Selected Papers*. London: Free Associations Press.

Elkin, H. 1972. On selfhood and the development of ego structures in infancy. *Psychoanalytic Review* 59.

Emery, E. 1991. The countertransference dream. Paper read at the National Psychological Association for Psychoanalysis, New York City, April 10, 1991.

Federn, P. 1953. *Ego Psychology and the Psychoses*. London: Maresfield Press.

Field, J. (pseudonym of M. Milner). 1934. *A Life of One's Own*. London: Chatto and Windus, reprinted, Penguin, 1952.

_____. 1937. *An Experiment in Leisure*. London: Chatto and Windus.

Freud, S. 1905. Jokes and their relation to the unconscious. *Standard Edition of the Complete Psychological Works of Sigmund Freud*, vol. 8. London: Hogarth Press, 1973.

_____. 1918. From the history of an infantile neurosis. In *Standard Edition of the Complete Psychological Works of Sigmund Freud*, vol. 17. London: Hogarth Press, 1971.

_____. 1920. Beyond the pleasure principle. *Standard Edition of the Complete Psychological Works of Sigmund Freud*, vol. 18. London: Hogarth Press, 1971.

_____. 1927. The future of an illusion. *Standard Edition of the Complete Psychological Works of Sigmund Freud*, vol. 21. London: Hogarth Press, 1973.

_____. 1940. An outline of psycho-analysis. *Standard Edition of the Complete Psychological Works of Sigmund Freud*, vol. 23. London: Hogarth Press, 1971.

Green, A. 1975. The analyst, symbolization and absence in the analytic setting (on changes in analytic practice and analytic experience). *International Journal of Psycho-Analysis* 56.

_____. 1976. Conceptions of affect. *International Journal of Psycho-Analysis* 58.

Grotstein, J. 1979. Who is the dreamer who dreams the dream and who is the dreamer who understands it? *Contemporary Psychoanalysis* 15.

———. 1981. *Splitting and Projective Identification*. Northvale, N.J.: Jason Aronson.

———. 1982. Newer perspectives in object relations theory. *Contemporary Psychoanalysis* 18.

———. 1984. Forgery of the soul: psychogenesis of evil. In *Evil: Self and Culture*, M. C. Nelson and M. Eigen, eds. New York: Human Sciences Press.

Jacobson, E. 1964. *The Self and Object World*. New York: International Universities Press.

Jung, C. G. 1954. On the nature of the psyche. In *Collected Works* 8:159–234. Princeton, N.J.: Princeton University Press, 1969.

———. 1955. *Mysterium Coniunctionis. Collected Works*, vol. 14. Princeton, N.J.: Princeton University Press, 1963.

———. 1958. The transcendent function. In *Collected Works* 8:67–91. Princeton, N.J.: Princeton University Press, 1969.

Kaplan, A., trans. 1979. *The Bahir*. York Beach, Maine: Samuel Weiser.

Kohut, H. 1971. *The Analysis of the Self*. New York: International Universities Press.

Kurtz, S. 1989. *The Art of Unknowing*. Northvale, N.J.: Jason Aronson.

Lacan, J. 1977. *Ecrits*. A. Sheridan, trans. New York: Norton.

———. 1978. *The Four Fundamental Concepts of Psycho-Analysis*. A. Sheridan, trans. Jacques-Alain Miller, ed. New York: Norton.

Leavy, S. A. 1980. *The Psychoanalytic Dialogue*. New Haven, Conn.: Yale University Press.

———. 1988. *In the Image of God*. New Haven, Conn.: Yale University Press.

Lifschitz, M. In press. *Without Memory, Understanding and Desire*. New York: Irvington Press.

Lowe, W. J. 1984. Innocence and experience: a theological exploration. In *Evil: Self and Culture*, M. C. Nelson and M. Eigen, eds. New York: Human Sciences Press.

Mahoney, P. J. 1987. *Freud as a Writer*. New Haven, Conn.: Yale University Press.

Masson, J. M. ed. 1985. *The Complete Letters of Sigmund Freud to Wilhelm Fliess 1887–1904*. Cambridge, Mass.: Harvard University Press.

Matte-Blanco, I. 1975. *The Unconscious as Infinite Sets*. London: Duckworth.

———. 1988. *Thinking, Feeling, and Being*. London: Routledge.

Milner, M. 1956. The sense in nonsense (Freud and Blake's *Job*). In *The Suppressed Madness of Sane Men*. London: Tavistock, 1987.

———. 1957. *On Not Being Able to Paint*. New York: International Universities Press, 1973.

———. 1987. *The Suppressed Madness of Sane Men*. London: Tavistock.

Noy, P. 1968. The development of musical ability. *The Psychoanalytic*

Study of the Child, vol. 68. New York: International Universities Press.

Ogden, T. H. 1989. *The Primitive Edge of Experience*. Northvale, N.J.: Jason Aronson.

Phillips, A. 1988. *Winnicott*. Cambridge, Mass.: Harvard University Press.

Robbins, A. 1989. *The Psychoaesthetic Experience: An Approach to Depth Oriented Treatment*. New York: Human Sciences Press.

Rosenfeld, H. 1987. *Impasse and Interpretation*. London: Tavistock.

Rycroft, C. 1968. *Imagination and Reality*. New York: International Universities Press.

Schwartz-Salant, N. 1982. *Narcissism and Character Transformation*. Toronto: Inner City Books.

_____. 1989. *The Borderline Personality: Vision and Healing*. Wilmette, Ill.: Chiron Publications.

Scholem, G. 1969. *On the Kabbalah and Its Symbolism*. New York: Shocken Books.

Steinsaltz, A. 1988. *The Long Shorter Way: Discourses on Chasidic Thought*. Northvale, N.J.: Jason Aronson.

Stolorow, R. D., and Lachman, F. M. 1980. *The Psychoanalysis of Developmental Arrest*. New York: International Universities Press.

Suzuki, D. T. 1970. *The Field of Zen*. New York: Harper and Row.

Ulman, R. B., and Brothers, D. 1988. *The Shattered Self*. Hillsdale, N.J.: Analytic Press.

Winnicott, D. W. 1953. Transitional objects and transitional phenomena. In *Playing and Reality*. New York: Basic Books, 1971.

_____. 1958. *D. W. Winnicott Collected Papers: Through Paediatrics to Psycho-Analysis*. New York: Basic Books, reissued as *Through Paediatrics to Psycho-Analysis*, 1975.

_____. 1965. *The Maturational Processes and the Facilitating Environment*. New York: International Universities Press.

_____. 1969. The use of an object and relating through identifications. *International Journal of Psycho-Analysis* 50:711–716. Also in *Playing and Reality* (New York: Basic Books, 1971).

_____. 1971. *Playing and Reality*. New York: Basic Books.

_____. 1974. Fear of breakdown. *International Review of Psycho-Analysis* 1.

Zimmer, H. 1948. *The King and the Corpse*. J. Campbell, ed. New York: Pantheon Books.

INDEX

Aaron's rod, 201–202
Addiction, 138, 199, 219
Affects, xiii, 89
Aggression, 109, 157, 230
Alchemical images, 36
Alcoholism, 199
Amniocentesis, 131, 232
Anality, 163–166
Analytic office, 41
Annihilation, 109, 114, 166, 211,
    222, 226–227
    anxiety, 219
Archetypes, 36
Artist, 36–37
Art therapy, 38
Attitude, 2, 5, 7–8, 11–13, 24, 26–28,
    33, 39–40, 53–54, 197, 200–201,
    215–216, 218–221, 241–242,
    affective, xi–xiv
Atwood, G. E., 43

Baby, see Infant
Balint, M., 38
Ben, xv–xvii, 4–7, 44–45, 47–49, 52,
    178–179, 182, 185–186, 193–202,
    210–217, 230–235, 237–240
Bible, the, 37, 61, 178, 181–182, 201
Bion, W. R., 10, 20–21, 24, 27–29,
    33–34, 40, 42, 225
Birth, xvii, 94, 178, 196, 198, 204
Blake, William, 33, 40
Body, xiv, xvii–xviii, 13–14, 22, 38,
    77, 83, 185–189, 192, 194, 196–200,
    202, 215, 233, 240

and mind, 186–187, 199–200,
    202
    imagery, 94, 163
    symbology, 235
Body self, xiv–xvii
Bollas, C., 41
Breakdown, 13, 19

Cain, 181
Castration, 165
    anxiety, 219
Cat, as symbol, 229
Catastrophe, xiii, xvi–xvii, 20, 30,
    40, 53–54, 83, 88–90, 95, 104,
    178–179, 182, 192, 204, 217–226,
    233, 235
"Catastrophe therapy," 100
Common sense, 50
Communication, 184, 207–208, 214
Communism, 221
Compassion, 193
Confession, 235
Consciousness, xvii, 12, 20, 22, 25,
    26–27, 30–31, 33–34, 37, 198, 200,
    220
    personal, 21
Container, 82–85, 138, 184
Control
    ideology of, 180
    illusion of, 218
    loss of, 232
Corpse imagery, 223
Creativity, xii, xvi–xvii, 9–10, 17, 19,
    23–24, 26, 30, 33–35, 166, 181–182,
    202, 210, 215, 234, 241